HO
CHI
MINH

A POLITICAL BIOGRAPHY

HO
CHI
MINH

A Political Biography

Jean Lacouture

Translated from the French by Peter Wiles
Translation edited by Jane Clark Seitz

VINTAGE BOOKS
A Division of Random House • New York

CONTENTS

HO
CHI
MINH

A POLITICAL BIOGRAPHY

1

THE PEASANT

It is now almost half a century that Ho Chi Minh has been fighting, secretly and valiantly, as guerrilla leader and as President. Almost half a century during which, at the heart of the Third International and for the cause of the Leninist revolution and the Vietnamese nation, he has carried on a battle which is without precedent because of the diversity of tactics and situations, the versatility of the game, the risks run, the sacrifices made, the fantastic superiority of the arms pitted against him by his adversaries—this small man, with a face the color of tea, a beard the color of rice, a piercing look beneath a forehead crowned by a somewhat absurd lock of hair, and with a rather ridiculous silhouette in a jacket of brown cloth. This is a man so fragile that he seems to survive only by the sheer force of his imagination in the midst of a battle fought by a people as frail, as frugal and as stoic as he.

Lenin's fight ended early in 1924, Trotsky's in 1940, Dimitrov's in 1948; Mao did not really emerge until 1927, Tito until 1942. Ho Chi Minh, who was so strongly influenced by the French Revolution, has been a militant socialist since the Russian Revolution. He has been a member of the French Communist Party, the Russian Communist Party, and probably of the Chinese Communist Party; he was the founder of the Indochinese Communist Party, then of the Viet Minh, then of the Lao Dong. He at one time shared the misery of the proletariat of Africa and America. He has known, with iron shackles on his feet, the prisons of Yunnan.

Condemned to death by the colonial courts, Ho escaped deportation and the guillotine ten times, and wore the robe of bonzes and the uniform of the Chinese Eighth Army. When he seized power, a power which was of necessity accompanied by bloody repressions, he confronted, one after the other, two Western empires. What other revolutionary of these times would have defied the existing powers with such obstinate perseverance?

Ho Chi Minh is not Lenin or Mao. If genius has marked the surprising Vietnamese revolution, it is to be found rather in its military leader, Vo Nguyen Giap. But if Ho Chi Minh (once known as Cung, and Nguyen Tat Thanh, and Ba, alias Nguyen Ai Quoc, alias Vuong, alias Chin, alias Line, alias Tran*) did not invent a doctrine, he was and remains today an incomparable man of action—others bitterly but justifiably call him an agitator. He is the man who remains awake when everyone else sleeps.

* For the sake of clarity, the name Ho Chi Minh will be used throughout the book.

This ingenious empiricist, this prodigious maker of history brought his nation back to life, built a state, conducted two wars which were essentially wars of the oppressed. His fight against the French brought the liquidation of a great colonial empire. The one he is fighting against the United States shows the limits of technical power when it confronts the courage and determination of men.

Of all men alive today, Ho is perhaps the one who has best shown the power of will, armed with an inexorable ability to wield power and rooted in national aspirations.

To the north of old Annam,* not far from the lush delta of Thanh Hoa, lies a region famous for its dense population, the poverty of its inhabitants and the intractable nature of its sons. This is the region of Nghe Tinh, composed of two provinces—Nghe An and Ha Tinh—and bordered by the Gulf of Tonkin. Its capital was once Vinh; but Vinh, already battered by French artillery between 1947 and 1954, has been completely demolished in the raids carried out by the United States Air Force since February 1965.

Above this plain soar gray birds, wild geese with enormous wing spans. Their melancholy cries drift in from the sea, full of nostalgia, vague fear and the insatiable desire for change. The sea's presence is felt everywhere; but strangely Nghe Tinh seems to turn its back on the great gulf. Its people are not sailors but peasants with salt-worn hands.

The area is like a mirror, with glimmering beaches and sea-green fields, a long pearl-colored mirror reflecting the first foothills of the Annamese cordillera. This spongy

* Translator's note: Vietnam under French rule was divided into three sections—Cochin China at the southern tip, with Saigon as its capital; Annam extending up the coast north of Cochin China with its capital at Hué; and at the very north, Tonkin with Hanoi as its capital. What the French called Indochina consisted of these three areas, plus Laos and Cambodia. The 1954 Geneva accords divided Vietnam into North and South at the seventeenth parallel.

land is a hinge between laboring Tonkin and aristocratic Annam, between mountain and sea, the north and the south and, in earlier centuries, between the mandarin scholars and the mandarins of the court.

"Land of green waters and blue mountains," says a popular song. But the soil is arid, and in the summer a torrid wind blows from Laos, cracking the earth and scorching the plants. Typhoons are common and the rains torrential. Nothing is more beautiful, nothing harsher than this climate. It is obvious that landscape does not determine the character of its inhabitants; to suggest that Ho would have become a middle-of-the-road conservative had he been born on the gay, sunlit island of Bentré would be absurd. Yet it must be said that the challenge posed by the land of Ho's birth is strong indeed.

"It is the land of the wooden fish," say Vietnamese of the other provinces. Not long ago in Nghe Tinh, when a man set out on a journey he would put a small wooden fish in his pocket. He was so poor, like so many others of his region, that all he could afford to order in the little village eating-house was a bowl of rice and a bowl of *nuoc-mam,* the national condiment. In order not to appear too poor, he would slyly slip the fish into the *nuoc-mam* and thus give the impression of a man dining in earnest. Moreover, the little fish soaked up some of the pickle juice and was pleasant to lick later while trudging along the road.

It was Nghe Tinh which in earlier centuries produced the winners of all the scholastic and literary prizes in Hué. In an area so densely populated that some families have to live on the proceeds of a paddy measuring one-eighth of an acre, what could a clever child do but study in the hope of becoming a scribe or a schoolteacher or even, one day, a *doc phu* or *tong doc,* for district and provincial governorships were not always won through corruption, intrigue or royal favor—sometimes these appointments were made on the strength of intellectual accomplishment.

From Nghe Tinh also had come for many centuries all but a few of the country's revolutionaries. This is hardly surprising, given the density of the population, the high proportion of intellectuals, education and frustration and mental alertness, plus an acquaintance with wide horizons. All these helped to make Nghe Tinh the home of insurrections, a school for revolutionaries. Indeed, it was an unwritten law at the court of Hué that mandarins from this region should never be given posts in the central government; they were regarded as born troublemakers.

This unproductive soil breeds men of inspiration, the kind who either make history or write it. One such was Mai Hac De, who, as leader of the peasant revolt in the eighth century, drove out the Chinese overlords and proclaimed himself emperor. Another was Nguyen Du, author of the outstanding masterpiece of Vietnamese literature the *Kim Van Kieu*.

No other part of Vietnam has been so deeply marked by the country's long history. It was from here that, early in the fifteenth century, King Le Loi launched his war of liberation against the Chinese occupants. From the Ru Thanh, a steep slope overlooking the plain, one can still see traces of a Chinese citadel dating back to that time— a landmark of great historical interest, for Le Loi was possibly the earliest exponent of the strategic use of mountain paths. By employing these, he successfully outflanked the Chinese garrisons in the plain, and some observers believe his strategy may have been a model for the resistance methods used from 1946 to 1954 against the French and for the present war against the Americans. Only a few miles from the house where Ho was born stands a temple dedicated to the memory of one of the guerrilla-king's companions. Here then are just a few examples of the power of this land and its integral part in Vietnamese history.

Reminders of the past are to be found in even the most minor aspects of everyday life. Those long years of cam-

paigning against the northern invader saw the introduction
of the type of barrow which still goes squeaking and clatter-
ing along the roads, with the burden distributed evenly on
either side of a stout central wheel made of wood; all over
Vietnam, these vehicles are known as "Nghe An barrows."
Again, in Nghe Tinh, up until the beginning of this century, male villagers wore brown canvas skirts, in defiance
of imperial edicts. The central government finally stamped
out this custom on grounds of indecency. Even the women
were legally required to wear trousers. Thus in Nghe Tinh,
there were strains and stresses at all levels.

The establishment of the colonial regime confirmed
the region's role as a permanent cradle of revolution.
In 1885 the French General de Courcy tried to force the
young king Ham Nghi to ratify the treaty establishing
Annam as a French protectorate. Instead, the young king
chose to flee. An uprising followed, in response to appeals
by the nationalist mandarins; it was known as the Scholars'
Revolt. Its main breeding ground and last bastion was
precisely Nghe Tinh, and its leader, Phan Dinh Phung, was
a native of the province, as were nearly all the men who
subsequently roused Vietnam against France's colonial authority, from the pamphleteer Phan Boi Chau and the reformist Phan Chu Trinh to Tran Phu and Le Hong Phong,
the first two general secretaries of the Indochinese Communist Party. And in addition to these there was a certain
Nguyen Tat Thanh, who was later to adopt many other
names, achieving fame among his own people as Nguyen
Ai Quoc and attracting worldwide attention as Ho Chi
Minh.

Everything known about Ho's life prior to 1941 is frag-
mentary, controversial and approximate. Certain phases of
his career are well documented, and his friends have always
been willing to reminisce about him. But there are too many

gaps and shadows to make the story intelligible. For a long time it was doubted whether Ho Chi Minh really was Nguyen Ai Quoc, founder of the Indochinese Communist Party, the revolutionary whose legend had fired the imagination of young nationalists for twenty years and whose name appeared so often in the files of the French security police in Hanoi.

But it is impossible to doubt that the statesman and the revolutionary exile are one and the same man. So many witnesses—especially those French Socialist and Communist leaders who knew the young revolutionary Nguyen Ai Quoc at the Tours Congress or the Marseilles Congress— were sure that the man named Ho Chi Minh, head of the Vietnamese government who came to negotiate in France in 1946, was the same man who had been their youthful comrade.

Among other proofs, there is the technical one submitted by one of the best Indochinese specialists of the French *Sûreté*. In August 1945, during the inauguration of Ho Chi Minh, this Frenchman closely examined Ho's ears. "His ears?" I asked. "Next to fingerprints, the best way to identify people is by their ears. . . . Impossible to mistake them. They were definitely the ears of Nguyen Ai Quoc, whom we had so often scrutinized in photos."

If any such doubts persisted as late as 1960, they were finally dispelled by an official pamphlet published at that time by the Hanoi government. Its opening words were as follows: January 1919 . . . Ho Chi Minh, then residing in France and known under the name Nguyen Ai Quoc, sends a petition to the Versailles Conference.*

But other doubts continue to hang over his early life. One thing we can be sure of is the general mood of the country at the time of his birth. One word sums it up:

* *Les Grandes Dates du parti de la classe ouvrière du Vietnam* (Great Dates of the Vietnamese Workers' Party), Hanoi, 1960.

bitterness. For a long time his energies were to be spent in struggling against France. Why? The reason is simple. The French colonial system in Indochina at the end of the nineteenth century was not good. Not that it merely practiced destructive and mindless oppression—teams of administrators, formed at about that time, began to reduce the abuses of mandarin rule; civil engineers built roads and bridges; a few magistrates administered real justice; schools were opened and efforts made to combat disease.

Such advances might have been beneficial in Gabon or Senegal, where there was no substantial opposition to the French, but in Annam and Tonkin most of the elite and many of the ordinary people viewed France's colonial presence as a cruel foreign occupation violating their national integrity and undermining a civilization of which they were proud. From the Scholars' Revolt in 1885 to Fai Fo's rebellion in 1908 and the uprising in 1916 instigated by Duy Tan, Vietnamese nationalism was seldom quiescent. Its most original expression was the mass of secret societies such as the Phuc Quoc, whose leaders lived abroad but whose followers were forever devising acts of revenge against the French, especially in the areas of Hué and Vinh.

At the time Ho Chi Minh was born, in 1890, the colonial regime was still in its violent initial phase, far removed from the sort of stability it was to achieve at the start of the twentieth century and in the years following World War I. France was certainly not viewed as an apostle of a new civilization, except by a very small number of intellectuals. Rather, she was felt to be a predator who had followed China's lead in the ceaseless attempt to remold Vietnam's personality and destroy the existing secular harmony between soil, man and king.

Hence the movement toward rebellion and revolution was rife at all levels of Vietnamese society, especially in the inflammable region of Nghe Tinh. After Phan Dinh Phung's Scholars' Revolt (the Van Than, or promonarchist movement), Phan Boi Chau launched his Trip to the East (Dong Du) movement which supported the pretender Cuong De, who had fled to Japan. In Tonkin, Hoang Hoa Tham (known in France as De Tham) was engaged in guerrilla warfare against the French forces, while the Tonkin Organization for Patriotic Teaching (Dong Kinh Nghia Thuc) sought to preserve the nation's culture from contamination by the French. And Phan Chu Trinh was conducting a reformist campaign which made due allowance for France's cultural and technical contributions, but which afterward lent active support to Ho when he was under sentence of death and later faced deportation.

The Vietnam of the late nineteenth century was alive with resentment and with the spirit of revenge. Traditional society was shaken, threatened and cheated, while the bourgeoisie which would create the pattern of colonial rule had not yet been born. Ho's country might be conquered, but it was neither benumbed by defeat nor resigned to its alienated status.

Because of this general mood, all aspects of French rule seemed objectionable—the massive conscription of northern coolies, to provide labor for the plantations and estates of Cochin China; the spread of the sale of alcohol; the informal toleration of the consumption of opium; the efforts to raise troops for service in Metropolitan France; the propensity of military and civil servants to take advantage of the young ladies of Hué or Can Tho.

France's reputation suffered badly in its everyday encounters with the Vietnamese people. She was seen as a nation of tax collectors, customs men, recruiting sergeants, policemen. And grimly dominating this general poor impression was the name of Poulo Condore, that small penal settlement in the South China Sea where militant nationalists or those designated as such by some avaricious informer or ruthless official went to suffer and die. Is it surprising that a proud man born in this climate would have chosen to fight for the emancipation of his country from a France whose regime made it detestable?

There is very little concrete information about the birth, family and childhood of Ho Chi Minh; one has to rely on the recollections of various companions and political foes. One such foe is Paul Arnoux, who spent twenty years trying to subdue Ho's activities. He was originally in charge of keeping official watch on Annamese immigrants in Paris; he then created the Indochinese *Sûreté* (security police) before becoming commissioner of police under Admiral Decoux. Arnoux, now in his eighties, has a very clear memory of the milieu which shaped Ho Chi Minh. He described it to me:

> When I first went to Annam in 1907 the older scholars in Hué spoke of a man of great learning who was a mandarin in Ha Tinh Province. He was reputed to know as many Chinese characters as any man in Vietnam, where there were many who had this skill. His name was Nguyen Sinh Huy.
>
> A few months later this man was dismissed from office. In some police reports he was accused of alcoholism, in others of embezzlement. Rather minor failings, they were widespread in the administration and smilingly overlooked so long as the offenders were politically tame. In fact, Nguyen Sinh Huy was really fired for his nationalist sympathies and because he was one of those Annamese who refused to learn French, in order not to "ruin" his own language—a weak excuse for a scholar of his caliber. One of his sons was called Nguyen Tat Thanh: this was the future Nguyen Ai Quoc, the future Ho Chi Minh. Thus, Ho's life began in an atmosphere of anger, bitterness, of hatred toward France. . . .

Furthermore, the father's attitude to the colonial power dated back to an earlier time than his dismissal. Nguyen Sinh Huy is reputed to have taken part in the Scholars' Revolt of 1885 and to have encouraged those about him to

admire Phan Boi Chau, whose anti-French pamphlets—
notably the famous *Lettre écrite d'outre-mer avec du sang*
(Letter from Abroad Written in Blood)—had enjoyed a
limited circulation since the turn of the century, fanning
the flames of nationalism in Tonkin and Annam.

Nguyen Tat Thanh was born in Kim Lien, a small village
in the Nan Dan district, on May 19, 1890—such, at least, is
the official date observed in Hanoi today. The Song Lam
valley, where Kim Lien lies, is a mass of paddies interspersed
with other small fields of mulberries, maize and sugar cane,
surrounded by tall bamboos. In this town, the birthplace
of the leader—a long straw hut of the usual peasant type—
has been preserved.

An evocative, if somewhat laudatory account of those
years is given by Hoai Thanh and Thanh Tinh in *Souvenirs
sur Ho Chi Minh* (Recollections of Ho Chi Minh).* This
book is the primary source used here, though it must be
noted that these authors refer to Ho's father as Nguyen
Sinh Sac, rather than as Nguyen Sinh Huy, which is the
name attributed to him by everyone else.

But in any case there is no dispute about the patronymic
name Nguyen Sinh. And the earliest of Ho's many names
appears to have been Nguyen Sinh Cung, which he kept
until about the age of ten, when his father, following a
common tradition, chose a new one for him. It is this second
name, Nguyen Tat Thanh, which is used by the official
historians in Hanoi.

Nguyen Sinh Huy (or Sac) was no ordinary man, and his
qualities in many ways foreshadowed those of his remarkable son. The son of a peasant and a "woman of second
status," he tended buffaloes and worked on a farm before
marrying his employer's daughter. Her dowry consisted of a
tiny paddy and the straw hut, where their first three children, including Ho, were born. Nguyen Sinh Huy passed

* Foreign Languages Publishing House, Hanoi, 1962.

the exam in Chinese literature, earning the title of Pho Bang (a minor doctoral degree). He taught in Hué, and then in Thanh Hoa, and was finally appointed secretary at the ceremonials office of the imperial palace in Hué in 1905, shortly after the death of his wife and youngest child.

But he loathed the nature of his work. "Being a mandarin," he used to remark, "is the ultimate form of slavery." Afterward he became deputy prefect at Binh Khe, but showed such contempt for the duties involved that he was dismissed by the French authorities. From then on, he lived the life of a wanderer. While his son roved about the world in the vanguard of revolution, old Nguyen Sinh Huy roamed from Saigon to Phnom Penh and even Angkor, eking out a living by setting bones, telling stories and working as a scribe. He wandered for over twenty years, poor and respected—a free man.

In 1925, a certain Le Manh Trinh met the old man in Saigon—"a thin, sunburned figure in his sixties, with prominent cheekbones, a sparse goatee and an everlasting black silk suit, a man radiating strength and energy. He spent much of his time with the young, and we had fallen into the habit of calling him 'Uncle'*. . . ." He died in a pagoda in western Cochin China around 1930.

His children worked hard and, under the influence of an uncle who supported the De Tham (a Vietnamese nationalist group engaged in guerrilla warfare against the French) even more staunchly than their father did, they had become ardent nationalists. Ho's elder sister, Thanh, practiced Oriental medicine. She became manager of the noncommissioned officers' mess in Vinh and began stealing arms and ammunition for the guerrillas. "Other women bring forth children, you bring forth rifles," said the provincial mandarin who sent her to prison, where she remained for several years. She never married. In 1945 she

* We shall see later the full significance of this word.

was struck by the resemblance between photographs of the
new head of state and her younger brother. She put a brace
of ducks and twenty eggs in a basket and set out for Hanoi.
Ho received her with open arms. Afterward she went back
to her village, where she died in 1954.

Ho's brother, Khiem, who was also a militant nationalist,
gained his reputation from a letter he once wrote to Albert
Sarraut, who was then governor general, protesting against
the abject poverty which the people of Nghe An had to
endure. But his temperamental nature, apparently soured
by drink, made it impossible for him to engage in any sustained activity beyond teaching Quoc Ngu (the romanized
transcription of Vietnamese which has become the national
language). When he died in 1950, the villagers received the
following telegram from President Ho:

> The onus of public affairs* has not allowed me to look
> after him during his illness or to attend his funeral today.
> I humbly apologize for this failure in brotherly devotion
> and beg you to forgive a son who has had to put affairs of
> state before family feelings.   Chi Minh.

Ho's childhood followed the same pattern as many
another spent in the Vietnamese countryside. He passed
his time in the straw hut which was his home, the ponds
where he loved to fish, and took occasional visits with his
father to Hué. He was only ten when his mother died; he
still wore his hair gathered in two small knots, like all
children in that part of Vietnam. It was then that his father
gave him the name Nguyen Tat Thanh. He was a student
in a period when the atmosphere was blacker than ever.
The colonial administration had introduced forced labor
for the purpose of building the road between Hué and
Vinh, coolies were deserting, and several came to hide in
his home.

---

* The war against France was then raging, and Ho was fighting underground in Tonkin.

The rebellions were failing, one after another: Phan Dinh Phung had been defeated; the De Tham had been forced to give up the battle; Phan Boi Chau had failed in his attempt in 1901 to seize the citadel of Nghe An. Meanwhile the great pamphleteer Phan Boi Chau had made friends with Nguyen Sinh Huy and his children. He wanted them to go with him to Japan, where he was planning the restoration of an ardently nationalist dynasty. But old Huy urged his sons to study French, not because he had any intention of bowing to the will of the foreign power but because he felt the country's future interests would be served by a broadening of their culture. However, the lessons of the intractable Phan Boi Chau were not lost on young Ho. He never forgot the nationalist leader's advice: Those who wish to liberate the country will have to form a strong party.

At fifteen he started going to Quoc Hoc Secondary School, where both Vietnamese and French were taught, and whose headmaster had at one time served in the Foreign Legion. While there, he was involved in the insurrectional movements of 1908. After four troubled, disappointing years of study, the young man headed south to Phan Tiet, a small port town renowned for the manufacture of *nuoc-mam*, the national condiment mentioned earlier. Here, in a small school financed by one of the *nuoc-mam* factories, Ho taught Quoc Ngu and French from January to September 1911. One day he vanished.

He had set out for Saigon, where he immediately enrolled in the vocational school near the old market. He put his name down for a course in marine navigation; however, Ho was already thinking of leaving—for China, where the Revolution of 1911 had just broken out, or for France, where the militant Phan Chu Trinh was working. Two months after enrolling, he found a way to leave on a French steamboat.

2

THE EMIGRANT

Like the Irish and the Sicilians and the southern Greeks, the men of Nghe An Province were quite willing to leave their country and start a new life abroad. They were, as we have seen, driven by want. In Ho's case, economic necessity was allied to two other things: his inability to adjust to life under colonial rule, and the urge to meet the challenge of unfamiliar cultures. In the last days of 1911 he joined the crew of the *Latouche-Tréville,* a liner in service on the Haiphong-Marseilles run, as mess boy. He now gave his name as Ba; he was twenty-one years old, and his mood was a predictable blend of bitterness and optimism.

Working on a ship whose passengers were vacationing colonials cannot have softened his already formed judgment

of the French. He spent two years at sea, going ashore at all
the principal ports of Africa and the Mediterranean; Oran,
Dakar, Diégo-Suarez, Port Saïd, Alexandria, where he observed conditions closely akin to those in Vietnam, and his
findings were to constitute the factual basis of his first book,
Le Procès de la colonisation française, an indictment of
France's whole colonial record. In Marseilles he had the experience of being addressed as *Monsieur* for the first time
in his life. In a previous biography, Wilfred Burchett insists
that these early encounters with France were enough to
persuade Ho that the people of Metropolitan France were
very different from the overseas colonials—a view now permanently incorporated in the apologetics of the party.*

It was in Le Havre, on the eve of World War I, that the
young Vietnamese broke off his career as a seaman. After a
voyage to Boston and New York, for a while he worked as a
gardener at Sainte-Adresse. Then he went to London instead of going to Paris—perhaps he was still loath to accept
the hospitality of a nation which unlawfully ruled his own
country.

Although the frail young scholar from Kim Lien had
already been toughened by experience, he must have felt
oppressed by the gloom, grime and sheer vastness of London. He eked out a living by washing dishes and shoveling
snow. It is said that he subsequently worked under the
celebrated Escoffier in the kitchens of the old Carlton Hotel.
The truth of this is unimportant, though experience of
cooking as a fine art may have softened somewhat his harsh
view of France. What *is* important is his decision to join a
clandestine organization of Oriental expatriates, the Lao
Dong Hoi Nagai (Overseas Workers). He took an intense
interest in the Irish uprising, mingled with Fabians, read
books on politics—he learned the meaning of the word
revolution.

* Wilfred Burchett, *North of the Seventeenth Parallel,* Delhi, People's
Publishing House, 1956.

But soon his qualms about living in France were over-ridden by a sense of urgency; he realized that nothing he did in London could have much influence on his country's future. And in spite of the war, in spite of the fact that the Annamese were subject to the draft, he made his way to Paris in the darkest days of 1917—a few weeks before the Bolsheviks seized control of the Winter Palace in Petrograd and Lenin set up the dictatorship of the proletariat.

The France Ho discovered at the end of 1917 seemed altogether different from the France—oppressor of his country—that he knew in the East. Here was a nation at war, menaced on all sides and swept by powerful revolutionary currents. Its proud, suffering people seemed in many ways like his own.

So, he thought, France was not exclusively a nation of policemen and customs officials. There were also the masses —the vast working class—warm, sentimental, poor. He, like the hundred thousand or so Annamese soldiers and workers whom the war had brought to France, was comforted in these alien and bewildering surroundings by the sympathy of their French counterparts. Though indignant at the mass deportation of Annamese, he acknowledged that it was helping to establish a genuine bond of friendship between them and the French.

Even before fully realizing his position as a young Annamese patriot, he was struck by the similarity between the lot of the exploited inhabitant of a colony and that of the European worker—and it was to this parallel, as we shall see, that he was to devote one of his earliest articles. No one could have felt more naturally drawn to organized labor and the parties of the left. Had he stayed at home, he might never have progressed beyond an extremist form of nationalism, without ideological perspective and concerned exclusively with evicting the foreign invader—a form of nationalism perhaps even tinged with racism, as in the case of the Phuc Quoc movement.

Living immersed for a while in a hierarchical, industrialized society broadened his outlook and gave a political
slant to his thought. Contact with the French Left was soon
to turn an angry patriot into a modern revolutionary. The
colonial system had made him a stranger in his own country; the French in France were to make him a fellow citizen.

Ho's experiences in Paris during the next five years were
of the kind that make a man feel both exasperated with and
profoundly attached to a country. He endured extreme
poverty, shared in the hardships of others, lived on uneasy
terms with the police, was involved in political clashes, and
slowly discovered a civilization which derived an added
insidious charm from its visible signs of decadence. As the
European conflict drew to a close and gave way to never-
ending negotiations, Ho served out his apprenticeship in
life, politics and revolution.

Young Nguyen Tat Thanh had already changed his name
once. For two years he had been Ba, the boy on the
Latouche-Tréville, but it would be absurd to go on using
a servant's nickname. In choosing a new name it was as
well to adopt one with an impressive ring, he decided to
call himself Nguyen Ai Quoc. Nguyen is the most common
patronymic in Annam, but at the same time it was the
family name of the imperial dynasty; *ai* is a prefix denoting
affection; *Quoc* means country. So now he was Nguyen the
patriot, and it was under this name that he was to be known
to the police, to the readers of countless tracts, to the Comintern, and in popular legend in Vietnam.

He and his friend Phan Van Truong lived in shabby
lodgings in the rue Marcadet, and then at 6 rue des Gobelins; later he shared rooms at 9 impasse Compoint with
several of his compatriots. He mostly did photographic
work. In an edition of *La Vie Ouvrière* there is a classified
advertisement that says "If you would like a lifelike me-
mento of your family, have your photos retouched at
Nguyen Ai Quoc's. A lovely portrait in a lovely frame for

45 francs." The intricacies of Chinese calligraphy may have given him deft fingers, but he met with little commercial success and was often unemployed.

Still, this very lack of employment gave him plenty of time to meet and talk with the politically minded, to feel his way toward socialism, to read and eventually to write. He gathered around him a number of other Annamese revolutionaries: Phan Chu Trinh, Phan Van Truong, Nguyen The Truyen. He made his first political contacts in a small bookshop on the quai de Jemmapes, run by a militant worker named Hasfeld and said to be frequented by Leon Trotsky. He was at first friendly with prominent revolutionary trade unionists, such as Monatte and Bourderon, and with pacifists like Marcelle Capy. Paul Vaillant-Couturier encouraged him to write for *L'Humanité* and accepted several pieces under the general heading "Reminiscences of an Exile," as well as a playlet entitled *Le Dragon de Bambou* (The Bamboo Dragon); and from Karl Marx's grandson, Jean Longuet, came an invitation to contribute to *Le Populaire*. It was at this time that he became the first Annamese member of the *Jeunesses socialistes,* the Young Socialist movement.

In a hostile piece called *Le Mystérieux Ho Chi Minh,* published in 1953 by the B.E.I.P.I. (an anti-Communist bulletin), Ho Van Tao, who knew the young revolutionary at that time writes:

. . . a wraithlike figure always armed with a book—who read Zola, France, Shakespeare, Dickens, Hugo and Romain Rolland. He became friends with an old anarcho-syndicalist militant, Jules Raveau, who had recently returned from Switzerland, where he had been working with Lenin and Zinoviev. An admirer of Sorel and Ernest Coeurderoy, intimately associated with the Bolshevik group, he was for Ho an unfailing source of information, guidance and anecdotes. He was for a long time an adviser to the young Annamese, who as a result became a regular visitor to the tiny editorial

office of *La Vie Ouvrière,* in the district of Belleville, where
there was a powerful revolutionary tradition. Tales of the
men and women of the Commune who were slaughtered by
M. Thiers' soldiers and now lay in the Père Lachaise ceme-
tery merged in the young man's mind, with memories of the
uprisings staged by his own countrymen.

Ho Van Tao refers to the portrait of Ho which Jacques
Sternel drew at this same period and which was afterward
published in *La Révolution prolétarienne:*

> He was still just an obscure photographer who had diffi-
> culty making a living. . . . A small frail young man with a
> gaunt face and an expression of great gentleness, aglow with
> the flame which so often burns in the eyes of people who are
> exalted by an idea. . . . He was highly emotional. . . . For
> reasons which are not clear, some of his friends in those days
> used to call him "little M. Ferdinand."

As a member of the Young Socialists and a contributor to
three left-wing papers, he was soon approached by a member of the *apparachik* of the Third International—one of
the Vouiovitch brothers. And this meeting with a wholly
remarkable figure, now unaccountably forgotten, cannot
have failed to affect certain decisions which he made soon
afterward.

One evening in 1919 the young Japanese writer Kyo
Komatsu was attending a rally in the Salle Wagram, organized on behalf of Sacco and Vanzetti, when one of his
neighbors tapped him on the shoulder. It was an Oriental
—a thin young man with a drawn face and burning eyes.
"Are you Chinese or Annamese?" the stranger demanded
flatly. "Japanese," said Komatsu, and he introduced himself. After listening to a speaker with the dark, drooping
mustache of a woodlander (it was Marcel Cachin, later a
leader of the French Communist Party), they went to the
nearest café, where Nguyen Ai Quoc embarked on a heated

account of his country's woes. They met again, several times, and wandered about Paris together, discussing the future of Asia

A few months later Paul Arnoux, the police official entrusted with the supervision of Annamese nationals residing in the French capital, paid a visit to the Salle des Horticulteurs where Félicien Challaye, a teacher who had been preaching the cause of Indochinese emancipation ever since his return from a trip to the Far East was to talk. Standing by the door was a slight young man with an enormous forehead and abrupt gestures who was handing out leaflets denouncing colonialism in the most violent terms. Arnoux had heard of Nguyen Ai Quoc before. When one of his spies told him the young man's name, he asked if a meeting could be arranged. It was, the first of several meetings held in a small café near the Opéra over the years 1919 and 1920.

There is no telling what Ho thought of Arnoux. But Arnoux, at least, speaks with a certain affection and respect for this fiery young man who spoke so poignantly of his village, his family, his country, and of the injustice his father, Nguyen Sinh Huy, had suffered. "How could I ever forgive France for perpetrating such crimes?" he would demand with blazing eyes.

Arnoux called on Albert Sarraut, Minister for Colonial Affairs, and told him that he ought to meet Ho. The minister was skeptical; he insisted that there was no such person as Nguyen Ai Quoc, that the name was merely a pseudonym employed by Phan Chu Trinh. But in the end Ho was accorded an interview by the minister's principal undersecretary. The interview established his identity, if nothing else, and it also provided the police with the opportunity to take and file their first photograph of him. It shows him with a small hat perched on top of his head, looking delicate and unsure of himself, a bit lost, a bit battered, like Chaplin at his most affecting.

Already his political activities were more aggressive and better directed; he was no longer content with hotheaded conversations in cafés, or with meetings held under police surveillance, or with those rowdy debates when he talked of the abuses of the colonial administration. When the Versailles Peace Conférence started work, Ho and his friend Phan Van Truong—aided by the remarkable Phan Chu Trinh—drew up an eight-point program for their country's emancipation and forwarded it to the conference secretariat in Januray 1919. Today this plan, inspired by President Wilson's Fourteen Points, sounds extremely moderate. It asked for permanent representation in the French parliament; freedom of the press; freedom to hold meetings and form associations; amnesty and release of political prisoners; government by law instead of government by decree; equality of legal rights between French and Annamese.

Such demands were too restrained to win publicity for the small group of Indochinese émigrés. When Ho tried to argue their case with Wilson himself at Versailles he was unceremoniously shown the door; so many other minorities, Arabs, Kurds, Armenians, were clamoring for international help. Ho had to comfort himself with the enthusiastic welcome extended by Vietnamese industrial workers when, immediately after this setback, he set out on a tour of the provinces. He had already acquired a considerable hold over his compatriots working in France. Any young Vietnamese newly arrived in Paris in the early 1920's was bound to get his bearings from this shabby but fiery figure who wandered from one industrial slum to another, sleeping in garrets; who welcomed friends at all hours of the night to the first-floor room at 3 rue du Marché-des-Patriarches where he worked on his articles and rested when he could. There was a spellbinding quality about his whole manner and appearance. "Your studies can wait—come and work with us," he would say to his young compatriots at the students' quarters in the rue du Sommerard. His tone, though very mild, was irresistible.

One of these students, Bui Lam, has set down his somewhat idealistic impressions of the period in *Souvenirs sur Ho Chi Minh* (Recollections of Ho Chi Minh) quoted earlier.

At Versailles, where the imperialists were sharing the colonial cake, a Vietnamese called Nguyen Ai Quoc had made an unheralded demand for self-determination in Vietnam.* To us, it was like a flash of lightning, the first thunderclap of spring. . . . Here was a Vietnamese insisting that his people be accorded their rights We took our hats off to him. No two Vietnamese residing in France could meet, after this, without mentioning the name of Nguyen Ai Quoc. . . .

After Bui Lam had read the articles which his hero had contributed to various reviews, he decided to go and see him.

I made my way to 6 rue des Gobelins and knocked at the door, with pounding heart. What sort of welcome would I get from him? Standing before me was a man of thirty or thirty-two, lean, graceful, light-complexioned, an engaging figure in his shiny dark suit; he looked at me with his large, amazingly bright eyes.

Ho plied him with questions about Vietnam, dwelt on the unshakable ties existing between the proletariat in France and the proletariat in the colonies, and then hurried him off to an art gallery where, as Bui Lam records with naïve admiration, "he knew everybody, and where a good many French people came up to him and shook hands. . . ."

Ho indeed had a lot of friends—not only French, but African and West Indian as well. One night in 1920 a young

---

* A considerable overstatement, of course.

man called at the home of Marcel Babut, a militant Socialist
who had contributed to *La Patrie annamite* in Hanoi, and
who had intervened on behalf of his friend Phan Chu
Trinh when the latter was under sentence of death for
publishing an article in that magazine demanding freedom
for Vietnam. Tears were streaming from the young man's
eyes. "Is it you, M. Babut?" he asked. And before Babut
had a chance to reply, the visitor threw wide his arms and
hugged him, sobbing. This was typical of Ho at the time.

Between 1920 and 1923 his political activity in France
took three main forms. He played a full part in the Socialist
Congress at Tours and joined the Communist group headed
by Cachin and Frossard; he published his violent pamphlet
Le Procès de la colonisation française; he set up the Intercolonial Union, becoming founder, editor and distributor
of its organ, *Le Paria* (The Outcast).

Marcel Cachin later wrote:

> It's impossible to forget the presence at the [Tours] Congress
> of an Indochinese delegate then living in France. Forcefully
> denouncing the shameful exploitation of his twenty million
> fellow countrymen at the hands of French imperialism, he
> called on the Socialists to lend support to the downtrodden,
> hampered, butchered, poisoned native population. Who was
> this delegate from the Far East? None other than Ho Chi
> Minh.*

On December 28, 1920, *L'Humanité* published a memo-
rable photograph taken at the Tours Congress and subsequently reproduced in several magazines and two or three
books. It depicts Ho, or Nguyen Ai Quoc, a beardless, wild-
haired figure in a stiff white collar and baggy dark suit,
probably hired for the occasion. Next to him is Paul Vail-

---

* *Les Grandes Dates du parti de la classe ouvrière du Vietnam* (Great
Dates of the Vietnamese Worker's Party), Hanoi, 1960.

lant-Couturier, gazing with friendly eye at this odd man
out among the burly mustachioed Socialist militants. Paul-
Boncour, who was present at these sessions, afterward wrote
(with a certain apprehensiveness, as though troubled by a
memory of the Yellow Peril) of this "young Indochinese
issuing incitements to rebellion." Ho must have felt isolated
and rather lost; he later admitted that he had difficulty in
keeping up with the brilliant verbal jousting between Léon
Blum and Paul Vaillant-Couturier, Sembat and Clara
Zetkin.*

What Ho said at Tours is still on record. In the report of
the procedings given in *L'Humanité* he was named as
Nguyen Ai Quai; in the official transcript (pp. 131–133) he
appears simply as "the delegate from Indochina." He made
his speech on December 26, 1920, in the old Salle du
Manège, following the delegates from various French de-
partments.

Chairman: Comrade Indochinese Delegate, you have the
floor.

Indochinese Delegate [*Nguyen Ai Quoc*]: Today, instead
of contributing, together with you, to world revolution, I
come here with deep sadness to speak as a member of the
Socialist Party, against the imperialists who have committed abhorrent crimes on my native land. You all have known
that French imperialism entered Indochina half a century
ago. In its selfish interests, it conquered our country with
bayonets. Since then we have not only been oppressed and
exploited shamelessly, but also tortured and poisoned piti-
lessly. Plainly speaking, we have been poisoned with opium,
alcohol, etc. I cannot, in some minutes, reveal all the atrocities that the predatory capitalists have inflicted on Indochina. Prisons outnumber schools and are always over-

* Vaillant-Couturier was an important leader of the French Communist
Party. Sembat was a Socialist leader, and Clara Zetkin an active French
Communist intellectual.

crowded with detainees. Any natives having socialist ideas are arrested and sometimes murdered without trial. Such is the so-called justice in Indochina. In that country, the Vietnamese are discriminated against, they do not enjoy safety like Europeans or those having European citizenship. We have neither freedom of press nor freedom of speech. Even freedom of assembly and freedom of association do not exist. We have no right to live in other countries or to go abroad as tourists. We are forced to live in utter ignorance and obscurity because we have no right to study. In Indochina the colonialists find all ways and means to force us to smoke opium and drink alcohol to poison and beset us. Thousands of Vietnamese have been led to a slow death or massacred to protect other people's interests.

Comrades, such is the treatment inflicted upon more than 20 million Vietnamese, that is more than half the population of France. And they are said to be under French protection! The Socialist Party must act practically to support the oppressed natives.

Jean Longuet: I have spoken in favor of the natives.

Indochinese Delegate: Right from the beginning of my speech I have already asked everyone to keep absolute silence. The party must make propaganda for socialism in all colonial countries. We have realized that the Socialist Party's joining the Third International means that it has practically promised that from now on it will correctly assess the importance of the colonial question. We are very glad to learn that a Standing Delegation has been appointed to study the North Africa question, and, in the near future, we will be very glad if the Party sends one of its members to Indochina to study on the spot the questions relating to this country, and the activities which should be carried out there.

(A right-wing delegate had a contradictory opinion.)

Indochinese Delegate: Silence! You for the Parliament!

Chairman: Now all delegates must keep silence! Including those not standing for the Parliament!

Indochinese Delegate: On behalf of the whole of mankind, on behalf of all the Socialist Party's members, both left and right wings, we call upon you! Comrades, save us!

Chairman: Through the applause of approval, the Indo-chinese Delegate can realize that the whole of the Socialist Party sides with you to oppose the crimes committed by the bourgeois class.*

Jean Longuet again recalled the steps which he had taken in Parliament on behalf of the oppressed. To this, Vaillant-Couturier retorted; "Parliament is not the only place where one must fight on behalf of the oppressed nations."

A fascinating skirmish, this, touching on some of the major bones of contention which then existed in the Socialist camp and served to divide Andler, Rosa Luxemburg, Lenin and Stalin. The reference to Enver Pasha reveals the mistrust felt among the broad sectors of revolutionary opinion for anything resembling support of "reactionary" forms of nationalism at the expense of mother countries with a substantial working class. To Vaillant-Couturier, though not to Jean Longuet, the problem no longer presented itself in terms of justice for native populations (though this was how Ho had presented the question) but of nations to be set free. These same disputes were to recur later.

Thus Ho did not hesitate long in deciding which International was the right one for him. Affinities of temperament and his own acute sensitivity might have prompted him to join such opponents of violence as Jean Longuet or Paul Faure. But he had already forged too many links with the other camp, received too many promises, made too many plans—Moscow was the starting point of the great revolution which would sweep away the machinery of exploitation; Cachin and Frossard were the men he would follow—and above all Vaillant-Couturier, whose emotionalism and eloquence had cast a spell over him.

* Bernard B. Fall (ed.), *Ho Chi Minh on Revolution: Selected Writings, 1920–66* (New York: Praeger, 1967), pp. 3–4.

The best possible account of the reasons which led to his choice was given by Ho himself in an article published forty years later, on the occasion of his seventieth birthday; entitled "The Path Which Led Me to Leninism," it appeared in the July, 1960, issue of *L'Echo du Vietnam*.

After World War I, I made my living in Paris, now as a retoucher at a photographer's, now as a painter of "Chinese antiquities" (made in France!). I would distribute leaflets denouncing the crimes committed by the French colonialists in Vietnam.

At that time, I supported the October Revolution only instinctively, not yet grasping all its historic importance. I loved and admired Lenin because he was a great patriot who liberated his compatriots; until then, I had read none of his books.

The reason for my joining the French Socialist Party was that these "ladies and gentlemen"—as I called my comrades at that moment—had shown their sympathy toward me, toward the struggle of the oppressed peoples. But I understood neither what was a party, a trade-union, nor what was Socialism or Communism.

Heated discussions were then taking place in the branches of the Socialist Party, about the question whether the Socialist Party should remain in the Second International, should a Second-and-a-half International be founded, or should the Socialist Party join Lenin's Third International? I attended the meetings regularly, twice or thrice a week, and attentively listened to the discussions. First, I could not understand thoroughly. Why were the discussions so heated? Either with the Second, Second-and- a-half, or Third International, the revolution could be waged. What was the use of arguing then? As for the First International, what had become of it?

What I wanted most to know—and this precisely was not debated in the meetings—was: Which International sides with the peoples of colonial countries?

I raised this question—the most important in my opinion
—in a meeting. Some comrades answered: It is the Third,
not the Second International. And a comrade gave me Lenin's "Thesis on the National and Colonial Questions," published by *L'Humanité,* to read.

There were political terms difficult to understand in this
thesis. But by dint of reading it again and again, finally I
could grasp the main part of it. What emotion, enthusiasm,
clear-sightedness, and confidence it instilled in me! I was
overjoyed. Though sitting alone in my room, I shouted aloud
as if addressing large crowds: "Dear martyrs, compatriots!
This is what we need, this is the path to our liberation!"

After then, I had entire confidence in Lenin, in the Third
International.

Formerly, during the meetings of the Party branch, I only
listened to the discussion; I had a vague belief that all were
logical, and could not differentiate as to who was right and
who was wrong. But from then on, I also plunged into the
debates and discussed with fervor. Though I was still lacking French words to express all my thoughts, I smashed the
allegations attacking Lenin and the Third International
with no less vigor. My only argument was: "If you do not
condemn colonialism, if you do not side with the colonial
people, what kind of revolution are you waging?"

Not only did I take part in the meetings of my own Party
branch, but I also went to other Party branches to lay down
"my position." Now I must tell again that Comrades Marcel
Cachin, Vaillant-Couturier, Monmousseau and many others
helped me to broaden my knowledge. Finally, at the Tours
Congress, I voted with them for our joining the Third International.

At first, patriotism, not yet Communism, led me to have
confidence in Lenin, in the Third International. Step by
step, along the struggle, by studying Marxism-Leninism
parallel with participation in practical activities, I gradually came upon the fact that only Socialism and Communism can liberate the oppressed nations and the working
people throughout the world from slavery.

There is a legend, in our country as well as in China, on the miraculous "Book of the Wise." When facing great difficulties, one opens it and finds a way out. Leninism is not only a miraculous "book of the wise," a compass for us Vietnamese revolutionaries and people: it is also the radiant sun illuminating our path to final victory, to Socialism and Communism.*

* Fall, *op. cit.*, pp. 5–6.

3

THE
MILITANT

Ho enrolled in the ninth cell of the French Communist Party, which had the reputation of being the intellectuals' cell. Among its chief militants were the lively journalist Georges Pioch (later on the staff of *L'Oeuvre*) and Boris Souvarine, the most brilliant Marxist theoretician then in Paris. It was in their company that he attended the party congress in Marseilles in December 1921. At that time *L'Humanité* published a sketch by H. P. Gassier, depicting Ho with a long face, hollow cheeks and a tumbling lock of hair.

In Paris he was a regular visitor to the town hall of the third arrondissement, near the Carreau du Temple, which was a kind of staff college for the party. It was run by an old

militant named Radi, who had two sons, Voltaire and Re-
nan. Both made friends with Ho—especially the former,
Voltaire, who was extremely active in the Communist youth
movement. It was the amiable and urbane Georges Pioch,
however, who by example persuaded Ho that he ought to
acquire skill in conversation and public speaking. With this
end in view he started attending meetings at the Club du
Faubourg, recently founded by Léo Poldès. He joined in
the debates, sounding awkward at first, trying not to stam-
mer, trying not to lisp, as he supplied his audience with
strongly worded evidence of colonialist exploitation.

He made no attempt to spare the feelings of the French
working class or even his fellow Communists. In the edition
of *L'Humanité* dated May 25, 1922, he wrote:

> The French party has taken on a particularly delicate task;
> its colonial policy . . . must contend with the indifference of
> the proletariat at home toward the plight of the proletariat
> in the colonies . . . [and] with the prejudices of the French
> worker, to whom the native is an inferior being, quite with-
> out importance, while to the native, the French of whatever
> class are wicked exploiters. . . .

But he was naturally harsher on the Vietnamese overlords and "collaborators." In 1922 when Emperor Khai
Dinh of Annam paid a visit to Marseilles, where a colonial
exhibition was being held, Ho marked the occasion by
publishing a playlet, *Le Dragon de bambou* (The Bamboo
Dragon), ridiculing the customs of the imperial court in
Hué; furthermore, he addressed an open letter to the
sovereign in which he wrote, among other things:

> Apart from the racehorses at Longchamp and the pretty
> Frenchwomen at the Opéra, what else has Your Majesty
> deigned to see in the course of your educational visit to this
> poetic land of France?

The French people are enamored of justice, freedom and work. Has Your Majesty deigned to realize this? Has Your Majesty received any inkling of the spirit of brotherhood and the deep, noble love of peace which animate the people of France, a people who have won their freedom through revolution, shattering the despotic yoke of emperors and kings so that they might become rulers of their own destiny?

What has Your Majesty managed to perceive beyond the dutiful flattery of the official speeches and of the hireling press? Has your august attention ever once been drawn to the existence and achievements of Pasteur, Voltaire, Victor Hugo and Anatole France?

Soon afterward, determined to nourish his new revolutionary faith with lessons drawn from his detested past, he wrote *Le Procès de la colonisation française.** This little book, only about a hundred pages long, was published by the Librairie du Travail on the quai de Jemmapes. The title on the cover was printed in three languages—Arabic, Chinese and French. Vietnam was given the most space because the author had more experience with the abuses of colonialism there, but he tried scrupulously to cite other examples of colonial abuses from Dahomey, Madagascar and the West Indies.

The book was not a nationalist protest which cited the case of a single oppressed country, but an indictment of an international system which the author felt should be opposed on an equally international scale. He ends the penultimate chapter with a manifesto for the Intercolonial Union, concluding with Karl Marx's famous "Workers of the world, unite. . . ."

Ho had chosen his line—though it was by no means inflexible, as we shall see. But he was not yet in command of his talent. The work is so clumsy, and often so mediocre in tone,

* Reprinted by Foreign Languages Publishing House, Hanoi, 1962.

that there are grounds for wondering whether the author of
the preface, Nguyen The Truyen, Ho's friend and collabo-
rator, may not have written the entire book. *Le Procès de
la colonisation française* is a shapeless series of anecdotes and
rapid social sketches illustrating with a certain vividness the
particular abuses and general horror of the colonial regime;
the banal choice of material and poor presentation seem
unworthy of Ho Chi Minh.

The reader can judge for himself. Denouncing the practice of sending the dirty blacks and dirty Annamese to the
battlefields, he writes:

> [They] left their skins in the poetic desert of the Balkans,
> wondering whether the motherland intended to enter the
> harem of the Turk as first wife; otherwise, why should they
> have been sent to get killed in these countries? Yet others,
> on the banks of the Marne or in the mud of Champagne,
> heroically allowed themselves to be massacred to water the
> laurels of the chiefs with their blood and to sculpture the
> marshals' batons with their bones.*

The antiquated style of *L'Humanité* was religiously observed. Living abroad had not, it seemed, benefited Ho's
command of language, but the remarkable thing about this
botched, though sometimes moving, book is the global conception of the problem of the oppressed, the constant effort
not to isolate the colonial question from many other problems. The same attitude was evident in edition after edition
of *Le Paria,* the journal to which Ho devoted two years of
his life and which had previously printed a number of
articles reproduced in *Le Procès de la colonisation française.*

Le Paria appeared from April 1922 until April 1926. In
all, there were thirty-eight issues. It came out monthly at
first, then bimonthly; eventually it was published at longer

* Bernard B. Fall (ed.), *Ho Chi Minh on Revolution: Selected Writings,
1920–66* (New York: Praeger, 1967), p. 68.

and less regular intervals, especially after Ho's departure for Moscow late in 1923. It cost twenty-five centimes, and scarcely an edition appeared without a printed appeal for new subscribers and a list of donors: "Duport, tannery worker, five francs; Miloudi, Kabyle, one franc. . . ." The managing editor was named as a certain Stephany, and the original address given as 16 rue Jacques-Callot. But *Le Paria* moved, and its principal home became 3 rue du Marché-des-Patriarches. At first the heading carried the words "Tribune of the Colonial Peoples." But after January 1924 it read, more significantly, "Tribune of the Colonial Proletariat."

It consisted of a single sheet, correctly printed and made up, and by way of illustration there were either one or two photographs or else a few line drawings. Most of the drawings were very poor, especially those by Ho himself in clumsily executed sketches of bone-thin coolies hauling bloated colons in strange vehicles with elliptical wheels. Some editions carried Arabic and Chinese translations of the main headline: another example of Ho's wish to present the colonial rebellion in global terms. But the publication's attacks were directed almost exclusively against French colonialism, ignoring other instances of overseas oppression.

Few well-known names other than Ho's appeared in *Le Paria*—even his pieces were signed Nguyen Ai Quac, instead of Nguyen Ai Quoc. But it did occasionally publish articles by the Syrian leader Rachid Rida, or by Marcel Cachin (on the Riff War). Also it featured items on Algeria, signed variously, "Hadj Bicot," "Ali Baba" and "Al Djezairi"; these may have been the work of Hadj Ali Abdel Kader, founder of the Algerian Communist Party, though not—as has sometimes been suggested—of Messali Hadj. The Algerian contributor expressed himself in a peremptory, indeed violent, manner; but it was not independence he was demanding, but merely a single electoral roll. Then a keen advocate of integration, he wrote: "The

Crémieux Decree* must be extended to the entire native population. . . ."

Ho worked intensely on his articles for *Le Paria*, and his contributions make very interesting reading today. As previously remarked, *Le Procès de la colonisation française* includes a number of articles originally printed in *Le Paria* —the most vehement, but not the best. Issue Number 2, for instance, contains a very curious satirical piece under the heading "Zoology." Composed in the manner of Buffon, and incorporating quotations from Darwin, it describes a strange animal endowed with a measure of "imitative intelligence." What really distinguishes the animal, however, is its *fascinabilité* which Ho defines as follows: "If you take the largest and strongest member of the herd and fasten a bright substance to its neck, a gold coin or a cross, it becomes completely docile. . . . This weird and wonderful animal goes by the name of *colonis indigeniae,* but depending on its habitat it is referred to as Annamese, Madagascan, Algerian, Indian. . . ." And the author observes in a postscript: "In the near future we shall be introducing you to a closely related species, the proletarian." The whole piece is brought off with the style and verve of a skilled polemicist.

And so is the "Open Letter to Albert Sarraut, Minister of Colonial Affairs." Sarraut had recently set up a special department (to which belonged Arnoux, mentioned in the previous chapter) for keeping watch on the Annamese émigrés. Thanking the minister for his concern, Ho wrote in the August 1922, issue of *Le Paria:*

> At the time when Parliament is trying to save money and cut down administrative personnel, when there is a large budget deficit, when agriculture and industry lack labor, when attempts are being made to levy taxes on workers'

* The Crémieux Decree (1848), under the Second Republic, granted French citizenship to all Algerian Jews.

wages, and at a time when repopulation demands the use of all productive energies, it would seem to us antipatriotic at such a time to accept personal favors which necessarily cause loss of the powers of the citizens condemned—as *aides-de-camp*—to idleness and the spending of money that the proletariat has sweated hard for.

In consequence, while remaining obliged to you, we respectfully decline this distinction, flattering to us but too expensive for the country.

If Your Excellency insists on knowing what we do every day, nothing is easier: We shall publish every morning a bulletin of our movements, and Your Excellency will have but the trouble of reading.

Besides, our timetable is quite simple and almost unchanging.

Morning: from 8 to 12 at the workshop.

Afternoon: in newspaper offices (leftist, of course) or at the library.

Evening: at home or attending educational talks.

Sundays and holidays: visiting museums or other places of interest.

There you are!

Hoping that this convenient and rational method will give satisfaction to Your Excellency, we beg to remain. . . .*

NGUYEN AI QUOC

Ho's articles were seldom so light in tone. His charges against the French colonial administration were usually backed up by figures rather than metaphors, by distressing reports rather than vengeful laughter. In general he was not fastidious in his choice of ammunition and did not bother with subtle shades of meaning: no colonial official could be anything but a sadistic blackguard, no French professional soldier anything but a loathsome butcher. All the same, one would prefer to think it was not Ho who

* Fall, *op. cit.*, pp. 16–17.

worded the brief unsigned article concerning Marshal Lyautey's departure from Rabat which began: "The disreputable old fogey is leaving Morocco so that he can nurse his 'syph' in France."

Somewhat unexpectedly, Issue Number 9, dated December 1922, contained an article previously published in *La Dépêche coloniale*. Headlined " A Yellow Bolshevik," it branded Ho as a "careerist without personality or mandate." It was immediately followed by an ardent defense of Ho, signed by his friend Nguyen The Truyen: "He was living happily among his own people. At a tender age he saw the French behead one of his compatriots. Indignation drove him away. . . ." And as proof of the attachment which the people of Vietnam had felt toward Ho throughout his long exile, Truyen reported the passionate concern with which young and old had asked him time and again on a recent visit to Annam: "Does such a man really exist? Is he not the fruit of our own imagination? Can he be a man of flesh and blood?"

No one could accuse *Le Paria* of masking its true colors: the people who ran the paper were quite open about their political allegiance and the kind of future they desired. When Lenin died, every available inch was filled with reverential praise of the October revolutionist; and when the Krestintern (Peasant International) held its congress in November 1923, *Le Paria* treated the event as though it were the annual meeting of a parent company. There was hardly a number which did not laud some Soviet achievement or some Communist victory, whether it was the development of the collective farm system or the opening of the University of the Peoples of the East in Moscow. Finally, during the 1924 election campaign *Le Paria* lent wholehearted support to "the only party to put up a native [non-European] in Paris. . . ." This was the Communist Party.

Articles signed by Ho continued to appear as late as Issue

Number 30, published in December 1924; but there are
strong grounds for supposing that he had already gone to
Moscow and that his contributions were mailed from the
Soviet capital at least since the beginning of 1925. The last
article to appear under his name in *Le Paria* was entitled
"Hands Off China." This was the first time he had written
about China and Anglo-Saxon colonialism, and it is not
surprising that, viewed from Moscow, this particular country and this particular threat should seem of paramount interest to a dedicated revolutionary.

Side by side with *Le Paria,* Ho had been trying for several
months to bring out a review in Vietnamese called *Vietnam
Hon* (Soul of Vietnam). He was supported in the attempt by
Bui Lam, whose account of an early meeting with Ho
appears in Chapter 2. But the venture seems to have died
an early death.

So in late 1923 Ho's first "French cycle" came to an end.
Apart from two or three short visits he did not see Paris
again until 1946, when he returned as head of the first Vietnamese government. Some writers, however, have suggested
that he went back to France again in 1925, after his first
trip to Moscow. According to Bernard Fall,* he offered
the Communist press a series of articles at this time which,
possibly written in Moscow, bore the signature Nguyen O
Phap (meaning Nguyen the Anti-French); allegedly it was
this detail which resulted in their being turned down by
Jacques Doriot, the man then responsible for overseas
affairs in the French Communist Party.

Be that as it may, Ho had spent six crucial years in France
from the early winter of 1917 until the end of 1923. He had
seen a war won and a peace all but lost. He had felt a new

* Bernard Fall, *Le Viêt Minh* (Paris: Armand Colin), p. 27.

revolutionary spirit take hold of Paris with the coming of
cubism and surrealism and, in politics, the emergence of
the Radical Coalition within the Horizon-Blue Chamber.*
At long last there had been signs that the Establishment
might be capable of understanding a colonial issue: it was in
1921, in fact, that Maurice Barrès, Paul de Cassagnac and
several of their right-wing colleagues had signed a petition
calling for a review of the system of government which had
been imposed on Tunisia.

Prior to his arduous years of Leninist training and
revolutionary activity in Moscow, Canton and Hong Kong,
Ho served his apprenticeship in life and friendship and
politics in defeated but proud and vibrant Paris, a city
thirsting for fresh truths and new reasons for living. The
experience was to remain with him forever. This intractable
Asian Communist has always retained a secret memory,
linking himself with the self who was once a French Socialist, was called Comrade by Longuet and Vaillant-Couturier,
who read Proudhon and Michelet to his young compatriots
in a tiny room in the rue du Marché-des-Patriarches.

As has been said before, the exact dates of his departure
from Paris and arrival in Moscow are still enigmas, strange
though this may seem in the case of one of the outstanding
figures of world Communism. The best guide in the matter
is Ruth Fischer, who was then the German Communist
Party's representative at the Comintern and who was a genuine friend of Ho's. This is amply borne out by her remarks
to me a few months before her death, and by the chapter
about Ho in her book *Von Lenin zum Mao*.† According to

* The Horizon-Blue Chamber was elected the day after the end of
World War I. It was very nationalistic (the blue horizon is the color of the
French soldier's uniform).

† Düsseldorf: Diederichs, 1956. (Ruth Fischer died in Paris in March
1961.)

her written account, it was in 1922 that he left Paris for
Moscow, where, she says, he attended the Fourth Congress
of the Communist International, playing an extremely
active part in the establishment of the southeast Asian
department.

But if Ho did go to Moscow in 1922, he cannot have
remained there long. An official pamphlet published in
Hanoi states that he left Paris in June 1923. The brief
biography by Truong Chinh (of which more later) expresses
the same view held by Wilfred Burchett: that Ho arrived in
Moscow a few days after the death of Lenin—in other
words, in January 1924. Burchett quotes from the touching
letters which Ho left behind for his friends on *Le Paria*—
Algerians, West Indians, Madagascans, Senegalese—bidding
them "to educate the masses in order to lead them to independence." In any case, on January 27, 1924, *Pravda*
published an article by Ho on the death of Lenin. "Lenin is
dead," he wrote, "What are we going to do? That is the
question the oppressed masses in the colonies are anxiously
asking themselves. . . ."

Kyo Komatsu has given an account of a conversation
which he and Ho had in Paris in November 1923. "Come to
Moscow with me," said the Vietnamese, "At last I'm to
become acquainted with the birthplace of the Revolution."
The Japanese said he would rather devote himself to art and
literature, and Paris suited him better for that purpose.
"What kind of art can you practice in this rotten society?"
retorted Ho. "We will make the revolution, and then you
can write for the free men in a classless society!"

But Ho made the journey alone. It seems certain that he
lived in the Soviet Union throughout 1924, taking a course
at the University of the Peoples of the East and writing
several articles for *Pravda,* as well as two pamphlets—*China
and Chinese Youth* and *The Black Race*. He established a
remarkable position for himself in Comintern circles. Ruth
Fischer told me:

When he first arrived, he seemed very inconsequential. He had neither the dash nor the presence of that other Asian revolutionary, the Indian leader Roy. But he immediately won the respect and even the affection of us all.

Amid these seasoned revolutionaries and rigid intellectuals, he struck a delightful note of goodness and simplicity. He seemed to stand for mere common decency—though he was cleverer than he let on—and it was his well-earned good name which saved him from getting caught up in internal conflicts. Also, he was temperamentally far more inclined strongly toward action than toward doctrinal debates. He was always an empiricist within the movement. But none of this detracted from his colleagues' regard for him, and his prestige was considerable. He played a very big part in things, bigger than some of the better-known Asian leaders of the time—Mao did not come to the fore till later.

Although fate had robbed him of the chance to meet Lenin, he was able to associate freely with some of the dead leader's closest companions: Bukharin, Radek, Zinoviev and —even more significantly—Stalin, who as former People's Commissar of Nationalities, had made a particularly close study of the various colonial systems. He also met the leading foreign delegates of the Comintern—Dimitrov (who became one of his mentors) Kuusinen and Thaelmann. Finally he came into contact with the principal Asian revolutionaries, Li Li-San from China and J. H. Roy, the only person to pass an unfavorable verdict on Ho, or at least on his intellectual powers.

The highlight of Ho's first stay in Moscow was his participation in the Fifth Congress of the Communist International, held between June 17 and July 8, 1924. His two contributions to the debates, as recorded in the transcript (published in 1925 by the State Publishing House in Moscow) are of exceptional interest. The International of 1924 was not the spineless affair which Internationals became toward the end of the Stalin era. The discussions were full of life. Ho was able to convey his ideas with a startling and exciting freedom of tone. True, he was merely following Lenin's and Stalin's lead in criticizing his party for "doing nothing whatever in the colonial sphere." But his attacks were remarkably vigorous, and nationalist fervor shone through the surface ideology. He said, "We shall establish facts that are beyond imagining and that tempt one to believe that our party is systematically ignoring all matters relating to the colonies." And he went on to list the endless series of blunders perpetrated by *L'Humanité:* neglecting to publicize the policy decisions taken by the Peasant International; praising the exploits of the Senegalese boxer Siki,* but making no mention of the proletariat in Dakar; acclaiming the aviator Pelletier d'Oisy, who had recently set up a new flying time between Paris and Saigon, but showing little concern for the Indochinese peasant, and so on and so forth. . . .†

In a second speech bristling with facts and figures, Ho denounced the systematic dispossession of peasants, from Cochin China to Kabylia in North Africa and made much of the links existing between colonialist exploitation and the Catholic missions. But the most curious aspect of Ho's remarks is the extent to which they foreshadow Maoist thought by laying such emphasis on the peasantry per se as a revolutionary factor:

> The revolt of the colonial peasants is imminent. They have already risen in several colonies, but each time their rebellions have been drowned in blood. If they now seem resigned, that is solely for lack of organization and leadership. It is the duty of the Communist International to work toward their union. . . .

* Victor over Georges Carpentier.
† These observations led to a sharp reassessment of the colonial line pursued by the French Communist Party.

It must be remembered that although he was of rural origin, he had spent the past dozen years or so in an environment that was urbanized, industrialized, and proletarian. And in those days it was highly unusual and significant that a member of the French Communist Party should dwell on problems relating to the peasantry and colonial oppression.

As a man who had addressed the Fifth Congress of the Communist International, Ho was a well-known and influential revolutionary by the end of this first Russian chapter in his extraordinary career. The next period, the Chinese, was to last almost twenty years. It contains some of the most amazing episodes in a life story which at times reads like a tale from the *Arabian Nights*. But for all the picaresque adventures and sudden reversals of fortune, the main theme is always clear: national emancipation via international revolution. Thus, even his most obscure debates with the Kuomintang, with the "war lords" in the north, and with the tiny bands of Vietnamese nationalists in exile, have to be seen in the light of his anxiety to destroy the colonial system in Indochina.

It was in December 1924 or January 1925 that Ho journeyed from Moscow to Canton; he was sent by the leaders of the International to assist Borodin, the Comintern's envoy to the revolutionary government. The exact nature of his duties was ill defined: he may have been either Borodin's secretary or translator. But his previous status in Moscow leads one to suppose that he had in fact been attached to Borodin as what we would now call an "expert" in Asian politics. At all events, he was discreet in his work. Although André Malraux is most certainly an astute novelist and penetrating observer, he did not consider Ho worthy of mention in his book *Les Conquérants* (The Conquerors), in which Borodin is one of the central figures. Obviously,

Malraux retained only a very faint memory of the Vietnamese revolutionary at Borodin's side.*

In fact, Ho would seem to have given more attention to Indochinese politics than to the Chinese revolution during his stay in Canton, where Vietnamese nationalism had recently erupted in dramatic fashion: six months earlier a young Vietnamese named Pham Hong Thai, a member of the revolutionary group known as the Tam Tam Xa (Union of Hearts), had thrown a bomb at the car of Merlin, Governor General of Indochina, who was then on a visit to Canton. The attack proved unsuccessful, though it made a deep impression on the Vietnamese people. According to Truong Chinh,† Ho concluded that "assassinating Governors General was not the way to achieve the overthrow of the colonial regime. To secure victory for the revolution, a powerful political party was needed."

Ever since French rule came to Indochina, Canton—like Yunnan Province—had been a revolutionary center for the Vietnamese. The presence in the city of the exiled revolutionary Pham Boi Chau had attracted a sizeable group of young rebels, but they had soon been disappointed by the old nationalist's lack of any coherent doctrine. It was from among them that Ho recruited the first cell in the Vietnamese revolutionary movement (or Annamese movement, as it was then referred to). The creation of this movement was obviously his principal objective, his essential mission, though he never forgot that he was operating within an international framework.

Ho's activities as an "instructor in revolution" took several forms. His first task was to win the Vietnamese exiles over from the predominantly nationalist Tam Tam Xa and

* In a conversation which I had with him in March 1947, Malraux admitted that he could not say for certain whether or not he had met Ho.
† *President Ho Chi Minh, Revered Leader of the Vietnamese People* (Hanoi, 1966), p. 15.

incorporate them in a more obviously progressive organization.

Thus it was that in June 1925 Ho and two Vietnamese revolutionaries, Ho Tung Mau and Le Hong Phong, who had taken refuge in Canton, set up the *Vietnam Thanh Nien Cach Mang Dong Chi Hoi* (Association of Vietnamese Revolutionary Youth), which was destined to achieve fame under the abbreviated name Thanh Nien—which was also the name of the newsletter that Ho published for a period of two years. This band of exiles and its tiny publication were the seeds of the Indochinese Communist Party, the People's Army and the Democratic Republic of Vietnam. *Thanh Nien* did not immediately appear to be a Marxist sheet, and the topics it dealt with were primarily nationalistic. But the authors subtly incorporated some of the basic terms and expressions of Leninist dialectics in the attempt to pave the way for the "second phase" of the revolution.

For Ho knew well enough that the audience he must reach consisted, in the main, of tradition-bound peasants. Therefore he had deliberately divided his campaign into two stages: the first was basically national, appealing to the "most conscientious elements in every class" with a view to establishing a "bourgeois-democratic" regime; the second led to socialism only after a transformation of economic and social conditions that might take several decades. *Thanh Nien* was the ideal organ for the "first phase," and Ho the ideal man to oversee that phase and the subsequent transition.

But it would have been impossible for the man who had talked so eloquently at the Fifth Congress of the International to restrict himself, in thought and action, to a partnership so cautiously "nationalistic." In 1926 he wrote *Chemin de la révolution* (The Road to Revolution), which gave a more openly Marxist-Leninist complexion to the struggle for Vietnamese independence. He stressed three fundamental ideas:

1. The revolution is a task for the broad working-class and peasant masses, not for a handful of men. Hence the need to organize the masses.

2. The revolution must be directed by a Marxist-Leninist party.

3. The revolutionary movement in every country must be in close touch with the international proletariat. Action must be taken to ensure that the working class and the toiling masses are able to distinguish the Third International from the Second.

He wrote:

One becomes a revolutionary because one is oppressed. The more oppressed one is, the more unshakably resolved one is to carry out the revolution. The bourgeoisie rose against the feudal system, which was oppressing it. Today that same bourgeoisie is tyrannizing over the working class and the peasantry, which thereby become the driving forces behind the revolution.

The workers and peasants constitute the most considerable revolutionary force in society because they are the most oppressed and the most numerous. Being without property, they have nothing to lose but their chains, and they have everything to gain. So they constitute the most resolute forces, the basic constituents of revolution. As for the students, traders and small employers, they too are oppressed by capitalism, but far less so than the workers and peasants. They are merely their allies in the revolution.*

At the same time, Ho was intent on converting the small band that had already gathered about him into a hard core of activists. He gave lectures on Marxism and urged his companions Ho Tung Mau and Le Hong Son to enroll in the Chinese Communist Party and thus guarantee future contact with it. He sent a third colleague, Le Hong Phong,

* *The Selected Works of Ho Chi Minh* (Hanoi: Foreign Languages Publishing House, 1961), p. 53.

to be trained at the Moscow Military Academy so that he might afterward organize the shock troops of the Vietnamese revolution. Other young activists were sent to the Whampoa Military Academy where, under the direction of Borodin (who had two assistants: a politician named Chou En-lai and a soldier named Chiang Kai-shek), Russian specialists were training the Chinese army. And he was already dispatching several of his new agents to Indochina with orders to set up the first active cells in the country. One of the men entrusted with this suicide mission was destined to go far in the movement: he was the son of a mandarin at the court of Hué, and his name was Pham Van Dong.

Finally, in an attempt to widen the scope of his activities, he tried to set up a League of the Oppressed Peoples in association with the Indian leader Roy and a number of Korean nationalists. The idea came to naught. He did, however, establish contact with the Pan-Pacific Workers' Union and attended its first congress in 1927.

What sort of man was Ho, or Nguyen Ai Quoc, in his Canton days? The account published in 1962 by Nguyen Luong Bang,* who in time became one of the leaders of the Vietnamese revolution, tells of a certain Vuong—"thin but healthy-looking, extremely bright-eyed, dressed in the manner of Sun Yat-sen, with an engagingly gentle way of speaking. . . . Vuong, who appeared to be some kind of ringleader, was recruiting volunteers to spread the word throughout the country. Bang offered his services. Vuong asked whether he had thought it over carefully and then told him how cautious he must be: The colonialists will be on your tail. Keep away from your friends' houses. Don't hesitate to pose as a degenerate if it will help put the police off the scent. . . ."

Five years later, Nguyen Luong Bang was arrested in Shanghai. After working him over, the police showed him a

* One of the contributors to the volume *Souvenirs sur Ho Chi Minh* (Recollections of Ho Chi Minh), published in Hanoi.

photograph—Vuong's. "Your chief, Nguyen Ai Quoc, has been caught in Hong Kong." they said. "You might as well come clean." This was how Bang learned that the revered national leader was this same Vuong who had made a revolutionary of him.

But in the meantime "Vuong" had been leading an eventful life. In the spring of 1927 Chiang Kai-shek, who was Borodin's pupil, Chou En-lai's colleague, and Sun Yat-sen's heir—the same Chiang Kai-shek who had helped train so many Vietnamese revolutionaries in Whampoa—showed his true colors and crushed the Canton Commune in a matter of months. This inevitably led to a break with the Soviet Union, the disbanding of the unions and the slaughter of the Communist militants. The Thanh Nien and Ho's revolutionary school were swept away in the general turmoil. But Ho and his lieutenants had foreseen the danger and fled—some to Hankow, others to Shanghai and thence to Hong Kong, where the Thanh Nien held its congress in May 1929. He did not attend, however; he had left China some time earlier, at the end of 1927.

By spring 1928 he was back in Moscow. After a series of talks with the heads of the Comintern he traveled to Brussels, where with Mme. Sun Yat-sen, Nehru and Hatta* he took part in the Congress against Imperialist War. Following a brief visit to France in 1928, he stayed for a while in Berlin, Switzerland and Italy.

The following autumn he sailed for Siam (now Thailand) with a triple objective: to set up party cells among the substantial Vietnamese colony there; to foment trouble at the expense of the administration in nearby Indochina; and to reorganize the Comintern's network in Southeast Asia.

In November 1928 there was talk of a certain "Old Chin" in the northeastern provinces of Siam. He was rumored to

* *Mohammed Hatta was Sukarno's closest associate in the Indonesian nationalist movement and was prime minister of the Republic of Indonesia from 1948 to 1950.*—Ed.

have come from China. But the Vietnamese in Siam saw quickly that he was one of their own people. In Udon Thani, and subsequently in Sakon Nakhon, he founded a newspaper called *Thanh-Ai* (Friendship), opened a school where both Thai and Vietnamese were taught, and set up a forest cooperative. The villagers worshiped the Lord High Genie Tran—the departed spirit of Tran Hung Dao, the legendary sovereign who had defeated the Mongols. So Old Chin composed a song of praise to the "guardian spirit of the mountains and waters of Vietnam"—the requirements of the nationalist phase were leading him on to strange ground. However, for Nguyen Ai Quoc, or Vuong, or Chin, anything that exalted anything strictly characteristic of his native country paved the way for the revolution.

Clad in the robes of a Buddhist monk, he afterward lived for a while in Bangkok, studying and preaching and at the same time setting up cells within the pagodas, training the young bonzes in a comprehensive social philosophy which embraced everything except the foreign invader and his hirelings. Traces of the networks he then established and of the watchwords he imparted came to light years later, in 1945, in south and southeastern Cochin China—and perhaps in the period from 1963 to 1966, when the Buddhists rose against the authorities in Saigon. After all, Buddhism is rooted in attachment to the fatherland, the land of one's ancestors. It attaches importance to the real, the immediate, the given, the experienced. It sets the perfect stage for a skilled Marxist like Ho.

4

THE
UNIFIER

But the time for dual tactics was nearly over. Inside Vietnam, there was popular unrest, echoing agitation abroad. For the working class, though still small in number, was beginning to emerge as a political force; already there were centers of fairly dense population in the industrial zones. In 1928 the mining industries employed 30,000 workers (including 25,000 in the coal fields of Tonkin), 3,500 in the cotton mill at Nam Dinh and 2,000 in the Franco-Annamese Weaving Company—to say nothing of the 3,000 or more who worked at home. A pamphlet published in Hanoi in 1962 observes: "This demographic concentration gave the proletariat the requisite strength and conditions for the revolution. And in fact, after waging an increasingly bitter struggle against the French employers, it felt the need of a Communist party to direct it."

A series of strikes in 1928 showed how discontented these industrial workers were, and how well organized. In February there was a strike at the Indochinese Brewery and Icehouse in Saigon; in March at the petroleum refinery in Haiphong; in April at the rubber plantation in Tay Ninh (in Cochin China); in May at the cement factory in Haiphong; in October among the rickshaw-men in Hanoi; in November at the Nam Dinh spinning works. And in 1929 came strikes by the railwaymen of Vinh and at the aviation works in Hanoi.

It seemed possible that the Vietnamese revolution was about to take on a Marxist-Leninist complexion and acquire its own Communist party. Arguments for and against such a development were already raging within the various cells of the Thanh Nien in China, Siam and, above all, Vietnam itself. Today it is almost impossible to tell whether Ho was in favor of going over to the strictly Leninist phase. The Vietnamese revolutionary movement still took its lead from the Thanh Nien, which was of his own careful devising and which some Marxist historians* describe as "proto-Communist." Was it wise to exceed the self-imposed limits of this formula, and so risk losing all support which was purely nationalist in origin?

In fact, even before the birth of the Thanh Nien (for which it was to provide a nucleus), Ho had set up a Communist organization called the Brigade of Communist Youth (Thanh Nien Cong San Doan). This "Iron Guard" was made up of nine members, including Ho Tung Mau, Le Hong Son and Le Hong Phong. As for the newsletter *Thanh Nien*, it ran to eighty-eight issues between June 1925 and April 1927; after Issue Number 60, it had taken

* Jean Chesneaux, for instance.

the line that the formation of a Marxist-Leninist party was an absolute necessity.

The creation of the Indochinese Communist Party seems to have been a result either of the leader's being deliberately by-passed or, at the very least, of an outbreak of rivalry during his absence among various factions within the Thanh Nien and other "proto-Communist" groups, such as the Tan Viet.

The best guide to the extraordinary complications surrounding the birth of the Indochinese Communist Party (and indeed the whole period from the May 1929 congress of the Thanh Nien to the foundation of the Communist Party proper) is contained in the history book published by Hanoi University and edited by the former Communist leader in Cochin China, Tran Van Giau.

This account confirms that Ho was still in Siam in the early months of 1929. His closest subordinate, Ho Tung Mau, had been jailed by the Kuomintang. So it was Lam Duc Thu who took the initiative. Meeting (May 1–9) in Hong Kong, the Thanh Nien congress heard the delegation from Tonkin propose the immediate establishment of a Communist party. Most of the other delegates regarded the measure as premature. Three of the four delegates from Tonkin thereupon left the proceedings and returned to Vietnam. In the end, the conference was sufficiently impressed by their initiative to adopt a motion calling for the establishment of an openly Marxist-Leninist organization, and a letter was sent to the Comintern, seeking its approval. To all intents and purposes, the Thanh Nien had ceased to exist: the dissident Tonkin delegation may have been a minority, but its defection had jarred the others into realizing that the organization was no longer an effective instrument.

Back in Hanoi, the Tonkinese had already established their first party cell at 5 boulevard Doudart de Lagrée (now known as the rue Ham-Long). It was made up of seven members, who on June 17, 1929 proclaimed the birth of the Indochinese Communist Party (Dong Duong Cong San Dang). Its area of activity was to be Tonkin (Bac Bo) and north Annam.

The Thanh Nien delegates from Cochin China and south Annam followed suit in October 1929 by setting up the Communist Party of Annam (Annam Cong San Dang). Not to be outdone, Thanh Nien's rival group, the Tan Viet Cach Mang Dang (Revolutionary Party of the New Vietnam) promptly created a third Communist organization, the League of Indochinese Communists.

This fragmentation of the Vietnamese revolutionary potential was largely due to Ho's long absence—according to Nguyen Luong Bang,* whom we quoted earlier, the leader may have returned to China in 1929. But if he did, it was only for a few weeks.

He was back in Siam by summer of that year. His comrades visited him there, realizing that he was the only person who could reunite the strands. Already he was a key figure in Far Eastern politics. According to French sources of the period, he was then in touch with:

1. The Far Eastern Bureau in Shanghai, the Comintern's coordinating and supervisory agency, apparently set up in 1929 to provide local political groups with the unity of action which the corresponding trade union organizations had attempted to supply, as early as 1926, by organizing the Pan-Pacific Workers' Union;

2. The Secretariat of the Pan-Pacific Union (from 1930 to 1931 this was managed jointly with the Far Eastern Bureau);

3. The Communist organizations in Indonesia, Malaysia and Siam, which were controlled by him between March

* *Souvenirs sur Ho Chi Minh* (Recollections of Ho Chi Minh), Hanoi: Foreign Languages Publishing House, pp. 61, 119.

1930 and June 1931, as head of the Southeast Asia Bureau;

4. The French Communist Party, apparently through the secretariat of the pro-Communist labor union C.G.T.U. (*Confédération Générale du Travail Unitaire*);

5. The Anti-Imperialist League (set up in Berlin in 1925), and its Far Eastern department.

In July 1929 Ho's presence in Siam was disclosed to his senior colleagues in the Thanh Nien by a certain Cao Hoai Nghia, who had chanced to meet him there—this, in spite of the fact that the leader had instructed everyone to keep the news secret. By telling his comrades of Ho's presence in Siam, Cao Hoai Nghia thought he was helping his party; in fact, he saved it. The Thanh Nien leaders immediately sent a courier to Siam, telling Ho of their predicament and asking him to come to Hong Kong to put matters in order.

Meanwhile, the heads of the Comintern were losing patience with the situation. They instructed Tran Phu, a young schoolmaster who was then Vietnam's chief representative in Moscow, and who afterward became first secretary of the united party, to visit Ho and stress how urgent it was that the three groups be brought together.

Ho, however, kept his comrades waiting until January 1930—perhaps he wanted them to measure the full cost of acting precipitously while his back was turned. When he finally went to Hong Kong, he immediately summoned a pair of delegates from each of the two Communist organizations which had split from the Thanh Nien, drew up a new program and forced a union of the splinter groups. This maneuver is believed to have been accomplished (according to most trustworthy sources of the Vietnam party) in the stands of Hong Kong Stadium during a soccer match on February 3, 1930. He instructed the two groups to join the Tan Viet, which had so far held aloof, and the union was effected in Cochin China, not long afterward, by the local leader Ngo Gia Tu.

The new party was organized along overtly Communist lines. Everything was at first provisional, however, for the three groups needed time to merge officially, and the various offices had to be filled by election, in keeping with the rules laid down by the Comintern. The seat of the Central Committee was transferred to Haiphong. From then on, members residing abroad (though this did not apply to Ho himself) were no longer entitled to act in a supervisory role but only as contacts and agents. So now the party was established on the soil of Indochina, in direct contact with the masses, as orthodox principles demanded.

From February 3, 1930, until October of the same year the party bore the name Vietnam Cong San Dang, or Vietnamese Communist Party. In October, Ho summoned the regional delegates to Hong Kong to dispose of various organizational procedures and to change the party's name to Dong Duong Cong San Dong, or Indochinese Communist Party—a title more in keeping with the spirit and regulations of the Comintern because of its more internationalist tone. At this time the seat of the Central Committee was transferred from Haiphong to Saigon.

On February 18, 1930, Ho had ordered the publication of a manifesto summing up the party's aims with these ten points:

1. To overthrow French imperialism, feudalism and the reactionary Vietnamese capitalist class.
2. To make Indochina completely independent.
3. To establish a government composed of workers, peasants and soldiers.
4. To confiscate the banks and other enterprises belonging to the imperialists and put them under the control of the government.
5. To confiscate the whole of the plantations and property belonging to the imperialists and the Vietnamese reactionary capitalist class and distribute them to poor peasants.
6. To implement the eight-hour working day.

7. To abolish public loans and poll tax. To waive unjust taxes hitting the poor people.
8. To bring back all freedoms to the masses.
9. To carry out universal education.
10. To implement equality between man and woman.*

In his biography of Ho, Truong Chinh† prefaces these ten points with a remark which anticipates the slogan used as a definition for the Vietnamese revolution as a whole: "At that time Ho was concerned with carrying out a bourgeois-democratic revolution which had to encompass the agrarian revolution."

Meanwhile the leader was unable to get back into his own country. By this time the *Sûreté* was keeping close watch on his every movement. Louis Arnoux, the man in charge of the operation (the same who had kept an eye on the young émigré in Paris, a decade earlier), tells of the thoroughness with which he followed Ho all over Asia, from Bangkok to Hong Kong, from Hankow to Tashkent and to Singapore: "He knew me well enough to realize that as long as I was alive and had a free hand there was no chance of his returning to Indochina. . . ." But events proved him wrong—in 1941, three years before the Japanese removed Arnoux from office, Ho made contact in upper Tonkin, with a group of comrades who were there on a scouting mission.

Before long he was back in China. In the early winter of 1930, Nguyen Luong Bang‡ received an unexpected billet-doux in Shanghai which said, "Darling, I await you in Tien Thi's billiard room." He hurried to this address and found Ho there. The leader's observations were somewhat different in tone from the "ten points" drawn up in Febru-

* Bernard B. Fall (ed.), *Ho Chi Minh on Revolution: Selected Writings, 1920–66* (New York: Praeger, 1967), p. 129.
† *President Ho Chi Minh, Revered Leader of the Vietnamese People* (Hanoi), p. 98.
‡ *Souvenirs sur Ho Chi Minh,* p. 65.

ary: "The situation doesn't call for sweeping phrases about 'the proletariat.' Our first task must be to overthrow the French colonialists and set the nation free, and for that we must arouse a sense of patriotism in every single person. . . ."

But 1930 was not simply the year in which the Indo-chinese Communist Party came into being; it was also the year of the most violent nationalist uprising in Vietnam since the century began, even bloodier than the insurrections of 1908 and 1915. Three years earlier a young Tonkinese schoolmaster named Nguyen Thai Hoc had formed a new nationalist party, the Vietnam Quoc Dan Dang (soon widely known as the V.N.Q.D.D.), inbuing it with the ideas of the Kuomintang and urging its members to engage in direct action. Early in February 1930 the Yen Bay garrison in Tonkin mutinied as a result of infiltration by members of the V.N.Q.D.D. Several officers and aides were murdered. The mutiny was to have been the signal for a general riot, but none occurred. The Air Force bombed the post and compound and strafed the surrounding villages; several rebel leaders were arrested and subsequently guillotined— a few, however, managed to reach Yunnan Province, China, where Ho encountered them ten years later.

Ill timed and hastily improvised, the incident at Yen Bay merely disclosed the political immaturity of the men behind it. But it made a remarkable impact on the general public and caused deep feeling in France. Above all, it served as a warning to the Communist leaders, who were preparing for their first major ventures inside Indochina.

In April 1930 the Central Committee of the new Communist Party met in Hong Kong to consider the mistakes of the rebels at Yen Bay and to draw up other plans. Ho did not attend, and the chair was taken by Tran Phu, who had arrived from Moscow a short while previously.

It was in the summer of 1930 that the Nghe Tinh soviets sprang up in northern Annam. In the very heart of Ho's arid, overpopulated native province, which he had left twenty years earlier, the peasant masses were rising in protest for the first time; they were well organized and determined to fight against the terrible poverty they suffered that year. On September 12, six thousand peasants formed in columns and staged a tragic hunger march on Vinh. Large estates were divided and people's councils established. These soviets were termed "Xo-Viets" and the nationalist ring of the suffix added considerably to their popularity.

One wonders how much all this was due to the spontaneous wrath of the peasants, and how much to instructions issued from Hong Kong by the young Vietnamese Communist Party, which perhaps wanted to subject its frail, untried unity to the baptism of fire. The affair never degenerated into a crude jacquerie, and the skill with which it was organized shows the professional touch—though people who have had access to the party's restricted files insist that, here again, the men officially in command were pushed aside—if not by-passed—by their own followers.

In *Indochine S.O.S.*, Andrée Viollis has given a heart-rending account of the repression that followed. Nevertheless, the Annamese Communists had achieved a considerable psychological success and given proof of a strength hitherto unsuspected. Far better than the makeshift terrorist methods employed by the nationalists which ended in bloody failure at Yen Bay was the ability of the Nghe Tinh Xo-Viets to mobilize the masses by challenging the legitimacy of the colonial regime, thus causing the peasantry—or a considerable section of it, at least—to realize that the time for submission was past, and the revolution had become a practical possibility.

The achievement was costly, however. Now began the testing period which party historians refer to as the "ebb tide." Several of Ho's lieutenants were arrested on Indo-

chinese soil and sent to the island penal settlement at Poulo
Condore; among them were the future prime minister,
Pham Van Dong, and the future vice-president, Ton Duc
Thang, who had been one of Ho's fellow students in 1911
at Saigon Technical School and fought in Russia at André
Marty's side in the Black Sea Mutiny of the 1905 revolution.
And Tran Phu, the party's secretary general who was (ac-
cording to party historians) so cruelly tortured by the Indo-
chinese police that he died in Cholon hospital in April
1931.

The leader was still in Hong Kong, living under the
name Tong Van So.* The Vinh court sentenced him to
death in his absence, and the French *Sûreté* asked the
British authorities to extradite him. Less in the interests of
humoring them than of quelling subversion in British-
controlled territories in Southeast Asia, the British arrested
Ho on June 6, 1931, after first apprehending two Comintern agents in Singapore and Shanghai—Joseph Ducroux,
the French Communist, and his colleague Noulens, whose
real name was Ruegg and who was probably a Soviet citizen
(both had served as liaison between the I.C.P., Moscow
and the French Communist Party).

Joseph Ducroux has given an account of his meetings
with Ho in Hong Kong just before they were both arrested.
Ducroux arrived there in April 1931 and was almost immediately put in touch with Ho by mutual associates:

> He looked astonishingly thin and lithe. He was clean-
> shaven at the time, apart from a few hairs on his upper lip.
> His face was sharp and seemed almost charred. . . . I've sel-
> dom met a human being who lived so frugally and was so
> disdainful of every comfort. The energy he showed! He was
> taut and vibrant. . . . He had only one thought in his head—

* Truong Chinh, *President Ho Chi Minh, Revered Leader of the Vietnamese People* (Hanoi, 1961), p. 62.

and it has, I think, obsessed him all his life long. His country. Vietnam. I won't say he wasn't a sincere internationalist, a true revolutionary. But to him, Vietnam has always come first. . . .

Moreover it was clear, against the background of Hong Kong, where there was such a medley of Southeast Asian crises and conflicts and where as a Marxist he might have campaigned for a good many causes, that Indochina was the focal point of his every deed and every concern. But he still spoke with considerable authority of the French political scene, about which he kept himself extremely well informed, and of his comrades back in Paris—men like Cachin and Vaillant-Couturier. . . . He devoted little time to doctrinal debates. He was first and foremost a militant, an organizer.

When I left for Saigon he gave me the names, or rather the aliases, of two reliable comrades, "Le Man" and "Ly Que," who, he said, would put me in touch with anyone else I needed. As indeed they did. These two comrades, who clearly regarded Ho as an influential leader (though not as a messiah or generalissimo), made a perfect job of organizing my mission in Indochina, where for a month I journeyed freely, making numerous contacts.

Eventually I was arrested in Singapore, not by the French colonial police but by the British police; evidently they were better organized. Who informed on us, I cannot say. But I'm convinced that Ho, Noulens and I were the victims of a single, extensive swoop on the part of the British authorities. . . . In fact I was sentenced to only eighteen months, for using a false identity—a charge which, I must confess, was not without foundation. . . .*

The question was: Would Ho and Ducroux be handed over to the Indochinese *Sûreté?* The International Red Aid, a Communist legal-defense organization, campaigned for their release. To "avert the extradition of the two revolutionary militants and their recapture by the French

* Interview with the author, November 1966, Paris.

torturers," the international secretariat of the Anti-Imperialist League urged British workers to "compel the Labour government to respect the right of asylum."

In *North of the Seventeenth Parallel,* Wilfred Burchett* describes the extraordinary reversals of fortune in the legal battles which followed. He draws attention to the tireless efforts made on Ho's behalf by a British anti-imperialist lawyer named Frank Loseby and describes how the case was argued before the Privy Council by Sir Stafford Cripps, future Chancellor of the Exchequer, who was then a militant left-winger. It would appear that Ho was transferred to Hong Kong prison hospital because of a rapid worsening of the tuberculosis from which he had suffered for years.

Then there is a gap in the story. The last entry made in the file marked "Nguyen Ai Quoc" at the offices of the Hanoi *Sûreté* reads: ". . . died in Hong Kong prison, 1933. . . ." And indeed the news was authenticated by *L'Humanité* and the Soviet press. In Moscow, the Vietnamese students at the Stalin Institute organized a joint memorial ceremony for Nguyen Ai Quoc and Tran Phu; a representative of the Comintern delivered a funeral oration.†

And when in 1945 a Cao Bang intelligence officer cabled a report to Paris that the Ho Chi Minh whose name kept cropping up along the Chinese border was none other than the renowned Nguyen Ai Quoc, creator of the Indochinese Communist Party, an official in the rue Oudinot immediately wired the following message to Hanoi: "What kind of lunatic is sending us information like that? Everyone knows Nguyen Ai Quoc died in Hong Kong in the early thirties. . . ."

A number of experts who had rejected reports of his death in Hong Kong prison, and had endeavored to pick up the trail, claimed that he was in Bangkok. One of them

---

* Second revised edition, published (1957) in Hanoi by the author.
† *Souvenirs sur Ho Chi Minh*, p. 126.

insisted that Ho could never have reached the city and survived there unless he had first agreed to help the British Intelligence Service. This would provide an interesting explanation for his strange disappearance from Hong Kong prison. . . . But to anyone familiar with Ho's character, the theory sounds implausible. When I put it to M. Arnoux, he at once retorted: "A man like Ho Chi Minh work as a British agent! And in the thirties, too! Why, I didn't dare ask him to work for *me*—not even at the start of his career!"

It was apparently around July 1932 that Frank Loseby and his wife managed to get Ho out of the prison hospital, slip him aboard a boat and hide him in Amoy, where he lay low for six months. According to Nguyen Luong Bang, he resumed his political activities in Shanghai in the early days of 1933:

> Chiang Kai-shek and his clique were hunting the Communists, and Party militants dared not even look at one another in the street. Uncle Ho was wondering how to get in touch with the Chinese Communist Party when, by good fortune, Paul Vaillant-Couturier [member of the Central Committee of the French Communist Party], arrived in Shanghai. Thanks to him, Ho was able to reestablish his links with the Chinese Communist Party. Put aboard a Soviet liner, he landed at Vladivostok, where he caught the train to Moscow. . . .

In 1935 he took part with Le Hong Phong, the I.C.P. delegate to the Seventh Congress of the Communist International, at which the I.C.P.'s membership was formally recognized. Then for a time he studied at the Lenin Institute, where he was known under the name Livov. He taught there too, giving lectures on the history of Vietnam to the students in the Asiatic department. These lectures were written in verse, as a means of "making study easier."

At the 1935 Congress it was Le Hong Phong, not Ho, who was elected to the Central Committee of the International. But shortly afterward Phong returned to Southeast Asia, was arrested, and died in prison. Ho took over his duties. His desire to do so was intensified by the fact that the Seventh Congress had come out in favor of a line which Ho, like Dimitrov, had been advocating for a long time: the creation of popular fronts.

In fact, he was then in almost open conflict with the leadership of the I.C.P. because of its decision to hold the first party congress in Macao in March 1935 while he and Le Hong Phong were away. It is notable that in his biography of President Ho, Truong Chinh devotes only three lines to this event. The pamphlet containing a preface by Pham Van Dong* makes no mention of it at all. . . .

The book *Les Grandes Dates du parti de la classe ouvrière au Vietnam* (*Great Dates of the Vietnamese Workers' Party*) is rather more revealing. It states that the Macao Congress had decided that time and circumstance were strongly in favor of revolution. In particular the conference had decreed: "It must not be forgotten that only armed warfare—the supreme form of class warfare—can lead to the overthrow of the oppressors. In the years between 1930 and 1931 we won considerable successes, despite our setbacks. This proves that the class struggle must be organized and carried on with heroism and resolution."

The semiofficial work quoting this passage appends the comment that the Macao Congress was plainly incapable of "appreciating at their rightful value the changes which had occurred in the country and in the world."

Three months later the International Congress urged a far less extremist general line. This is how Ho summarized the new policy, in a report dated July 1939:

    1. For the time being, the party cannot put forth too high a demand (national independence, parliament, etc.). To do

---

* Truong Chinh, *President Ho Chi Minh*.

so is to enter the Japanese fascists' scheme. It should only claim democratic rights, freedom of organization, freedom of assembly, freedom of press and freedom of speech, general amnesty for all political detainees, and struggle for the legalization of the party.

2. To reach this goal, the party must strive to organize a broad Democratic National Front. This front does not embrace only Indochinese people but also progressive French residing in Indochina, not only toiling people but also the national bourgeoisie.

3. The party must assume a wise, flexible attitude with the bourgeoisie, strive to draw it into the front, win over the elements that can be won over and neutralize those which can be neutralized. We must by all means avoid leaving them outside the front, lest they should fall into the hands of the enemy of the revolution and increase the strength of the reactionaries.

4. There cannot be any alliance with or any concession to the Trotskyite group. We must do everything possible to lay bare their faces as henchmen of the fascists and annihilate them politically.

5. To increase and consolidate its forces, to widen its influence, and to work effectively, the Indochinese Democratic Front must keep close contact with the French Popular Front because the latter also struggles for freedom, democracy, and can give us great help.

6. The party cannot demand that the front recognize its leadership. It must instead show itself as the organ which makes the greatest sacrifices, the most active and loyal organ. It is only through daily struggle and work that the masses of the people acknowledge the correct policies and leading capacity of the party and that it can win the leading position.*

In June 1936, while the first national conference of the I.C.P. was rethinking the party's attitudes (even going so far as to distinguish between the "ultra-imperialists" and

* Fall, *op. cit.*, pp. 130–31.

the "anti-Fascist imperialists," certain steps were taken by Leon Blum's Communist-backed Popular Front government. It sent a commission of inquiry to Vietnam, led by ex-Minister Justin Godart; it granted a political amnesty and ordered the release of several of Ho's colleagues—men such as Pham Van Dong and Tran Van Giau; it accorded the I.C.P. the legal right to function on Indochinese soil. This should have been the time when Ho Chi Minh came into his own. His influence showed clearly enough in the behavior of the Communists, especially in Cochin China between 1935 and 1937. But it must also be said that there were certain attitudes and feelings that were peculiar to that area which comprised southern Vietnam. After all, the electorate of Saigon had placed two Communists on the municipal council in 1935, and three in 1937. As a result, a number of Communist activists worked side by side with the Trotskyites,* even producing a joint campaign organ (*La Lutte*), while in Hanoi in the north the newspaper *La Volonté indochinoise* was published under the editorship of Pham Van Dong. (Southern eccentricity continued to manifest itself since 1960 in relations between Hanoi and the National Liberation Front.)

On May 1, 1938 a joint demonstration in Hanoi by the Socialists and Communists brought tens of thousands of workers together, French and Vietnamese standing side by side.

The party's period of legal activity was short-lived. By the end of 1937, however, it had begun to operate underground again. But for this, the I.C.P. might well have lost its leaders at the time of the 1939 repression. In fact, nearly all of them—Pham Van Dong, Vo Nguyen Giap, Dang Xuan Khu—fled to China on the outbreak of war. All the

---

* An agreement to this effect was signed in 1933. The report published in 1939 (i.e., after this experiment) denounces the idea of collaborating with the Trotskyites, who in the meantime had become "pro-Fascist thugs" (a judgment which is certainly unjust in reference to Vietnam).

same, nearly a thousand arrests (including those of Tran Huy Lieu, Duong Bach Mai and Nguyen Van Tao) were to reduce the party to a state of helplessness for the entire period of Admiral Decoux's administration—indeed until the Japanese coup on March 9, 1945, which overthrew France's authority.

For Ho, the years 1934 through 1938 had been the most peaceful and studious of his life. Although residing in Russia, he had been remote from the quarrels and purges rending the Soviet Communist Party and the International. He had never lost touch with his own I.C.P. which, after the cruel "ebb-tide" of 1931 and 1932 had reemerged as a lawful entity before the new wave of repression in 1939 drove it underground. From Moscow, and likewise from Sochi, where he had been sent to recuperate (for the terrible Russian winter had done nothing to help his tuberculosis), he regularly dispatched articles on doctrine to *Tin Tuc* (The News), the I.C.P.'s official organ in Saigon. These contributions were signed Line—an appealingly mild nom de plume.

By the early summer of 1938 he seemed cured. But on the Asian fronts, things were going badly. The Japanese were winning victory after victory. In Indochina, as in France, the Popular Front experiment was coming to an abrupt end. In August 1938 Ho returned to China, where the Japanese threat had compelled Chiang Kai-shek to re-ally with the Communists. As a result, there was nothing to prevent Ho from journeying to Yenan, except the normal risk of being ambushed. He trudged along like Mother Courage, pushing a cart before him.*

In Yenan he stayed at the so-called Garden of the Apple-trees. But his idyll there was short-lived. The general staff of the Kuomintang asked the Chinese Communist Party for instructors, to teach its troops guerrilla tactics. Con-

* *Souvenirs sur Ho Chi Minh,* p. 74.

sequently he was appointed to the rank of political commissar and attached to the mission headed by General Ying
(who afterward became a field marshal in the People's
Army). Ho found himself indoctrinating Chiang Kai-shek's
troops—just as Chou En-lai had done, ten years earlier, in
Whampoa.

In February 1940 Ho was in southern China,* where he
met some of the senior members of the I.C.P. who had
been driven out by French repression. Among them were
the two men who were to become his staunchest and ablest
deputies: Pham Van Dong, a mandarin's son from Quang
Ngai who had become a revolutionary at twenty and a Communist at twenty-five; and Vo Nguyen Giap, a former
history teacher who had been a model militant before revealing his gifts as a strategist. It was there—in the provinces
of Yunnan and Kwangsi—that in 1940 Ho molded the team
and worked out the strategy that have guided the development of the Vietnamese revolution.

* *Ibid.,* pp. 75–76.

5

THE
PRISONER

After his first adventure in China and his long stay as a scholar-recluse in the Soviet Union and before returning to his own country and founding the Vietminh—at this time, when he was still in China, what was Ho like and what was he doing?

Using the name Tran, he appeared at Hoang Quang Binh's barbershop in the southern town of Tsungshan, looking like "an old local peasant, very gentle, with nothing whatever surprising about him except the liveliness in his eyes."[*] He began a practical course in political philosophy

---

[*] *Souvenirs sur Ho Chi Minh* (Recollections of Ho Chi Minh), Hanoi: Foreign Languages Publishing House, p. 140.

and behaved in the general manner of a secular saint, chopping wood, stopping the barber from beating his wife (Revolutionary ethics, Comrade!) and feeding a little boy; he played a role that was part Buddha and part Lenin-in-Finland.

In Kunming in Yunnan Province, where he was staying in May 1940, Ho was at last united with the two men who were to become his trusted disciples, Dong and Giap. This is how Vu Anh describes one of Ho's meetings with them: "Tran (Ho) and I had hired a sampan so that we could take them for a trip. . . . Uncle said gaily: 'Young Dong hasn't aged much;' Then, turning in Giap's direction: 'He's still as fresh-looking as a girl of twenty. . . .' "*

Of far greater value, however, is the account which Vo Nguyen Giap himself has given of his crucial encounter with "Uncle." Early in May 1940 the general-to-be had managed to slip away from Hanoi and the Thang Long School, where he taught history; he had crossed the Rubicon—he was staking everything on the revolution's success. With Pham Van Dong he set out to meet the mysterious "Vuong," reputed to be the same Nguyen Ai Quoc who fired the imagination of every young Vietnamese revolutionary, the man who had laid demands before the Versailles Peace Conference, the hero of *Le Paria* and of the Tours Congress and of the International. For a long while Giap had gone around with a photograph of Ho in his pocket; and he had read the articles signed "Line," which were published openly in Vietnam from 1936 until 1938.

And now suddenly came the meeting aboard the sampan:

A man of mature years stepped toward us, wearing European clothes and a soft felt hat. Compared with the famous photograph, now twenty years old, he looked livelier, more alert. He had let his beard grow. I found myself confronted

* *Ibid.*, pp. 157–58.

by a man of shining simplicity. This was the first time I
had set eyes on him, yet already we were conscious of deep
bonds of friendship. . . . He spoke with the accent of central
Vietnam.* I would never have believed it possible for him
to retain the local accent after being so long abroad. . . .†

At this time Ho was following developments closely and
keeping a sharp analytical eye on the new situation resulting from the fall of France and the arrival in Indochina of
large contingents of Japanese troops. It was by no means an
unqualified blessing that the French should have been
defeated by the fascists; the aging colonial regime would
be gradually replaced by Japanese overlordship, backed up
by military might. But on the other hand, the destruction of
colonialism marked the fulfillment of a revolutionary aim.
Moreover, the Japanese threat led to a working compromise
between the Vietnamese independence movement and the
Kuomintang, the only Chinese force with which Ho and his
colleagues had any dealings; Mao's Yenan, like Moscow,
was too remote.

It was time to organize a practical strategy combining the
revolutionary daring of the thirties and the Popular Front
tactics decided on at the Moscow congress in 1935. The way
must be paved for a broadly based coalition which would
assume power eventually. The takeover could not be immediate because, as the leader said repeatedly, "the hour
for insurrection [had] not yet struck." The uprisings in
northern Tonkin (September 1940), in western Cochin
China (November 1940), and in his own province of Nghe
An (January 1941) struck him as premature. At the same
time, he saw them as proof that the Vietnamese people were
maturing and girding themselves for action on a larger
scale.

* Giap is a native of Quang Binh Province, adjoining Nghe Tinh.
† *Souvenirs sur Ho Chi Minh*, p. 177.

It was in the winter of 1940 that he organized the first "liberated zone," that of Pac Bo, in the region of Cao Bang. And at the end of January 1941, Nguyen Ai Quoc—who was already being referred to as Uncle Ho (derived from Ho Quang, the name by which he was known in Maoist circles in Yenan)—slipped back into his country after thirty years' absence. He set up his headquarters at Pac Bo, quite close to the Chinese border but inside Vietnam, among the limestone reaches between Cao Bang and Tsin-tsi. He had discovered a large cave set in the mountainside, with a stream running close by; here he lived for over a year, among the stalactites, the tropical creeper, the thickets, the piles of fallen rock. He named the mountain Karl Marx, the stream Lenin. He worked hard, giving tireless instruction to the men around him. In the indigo-colored clothing favored by the highland population, he roamed the area, distributing the small newsletter stenciled by his comrades; it was called Viet Lap (Independent Vietnam).

And it was here that from May 10 to May 19, 1941, Ho convened and presided over the eighth plenum of the Central Committee of the Indochinese Communist Party.* In a hut made of branches, with only a bamboo table for furniture (the delegates sat on blocks of wood), one of the most famous organizations in contemporary history came into being: the Vietminh.

Around its founder were grouped the leading exponents of Vietnamese Marxism: Hoang Quoc Viet, Truong Chinh, Pham Van Dong, Hoang Van Thu, Vu Anh, Phung Chi Kien, Vo Nguyen Giap. Responding to Ho's personal suggestion that patriotism be encouraged as a means of broadening the bases of the movement and successfully carrying out a nationwide insurrection, the Central Com-

---

* Hoang Quoc Viet, *Récits de la résistance vietnamienne* (Accounts of the Vietnamese Resistance), p. 162.

mittee voted in favor of forming a "broad National Front uniting not only the workers, the peasants, the petits bourgeois and the bourgeois, but also a number of patriotic landowners." In the agrarian sphere he persuaded them to adopt, for the time being, the following limited aim: "Confiscation of the estates of traitors so that they may be divided among the poor peasants."

The decision was a crucial moment in the history of the Vietnamese revolution—perhaps the most crucial of all, for it was then that Ho revealed his true character as an active believer in the patriotic revolution. For twenty years his nationalist tendencies had been oppressively curbed by the attitudes of the Third International. In the cave at Pac Bo he had found the courage to confront the problem of nationalism. The man who had been compelled to haul down the banner of the Vietnamese Communist Party and substitute that of the Indochinese party, the man who had been pained by the suppression of all references to the Vietnamese nation now deliberately conferred the name *Cuu Quoc* (National Salvation) on the movement. Henceforth the emphasis would be on Vietnam's history, its flag, its culture—and, necessarily, on the peasantry rather than the proletariat. (Only a few weeks later, the Nazi invasion of Russia was destined to rehabilitate Peter the Great, Alexander Nevski and the Holy Volga. Ho had anticipated Stalin on the road to neonationalism.)

The League for Vietnamese Independence (Vietnam Doc Lap Dong Minh, or Vietminh for short) was set up at this time for the purpose of "uniting all patriots, without distinction of wealth, age, sex, religion or political outlook so that they may work together for the liberation of our people and the salvation of our nation."

Its program defined only the "immediate" objective: "After the overthrow of the Japanese fascists and French imperialists, a revolutionary government of the Demo-

cratic Republic of Vietnam will be set up in the spirit of the
new democracy; its emblem will be the red flag with a
gold star."*

Only this final stipulation reveals the long-term aims of
the men who took the oath in the cave at Pac Bo. But Ho
laid great stress on the nationalist complexion of the struggle ahead, and on the need for all to fight together, in an
address to the people which he composed at the end of the
conference and broadcast on June 6, 1941 from the small
Chinese township of Liaochu—hence the title *Lettre de
l'étranger* (Letter from Abroad), given to this famous text.
The opening words are significant:

> Elders!
> Prominent personalities!
> Intellectuals, peasants, workers, traders, and soldiers!
> Dear compatriots!
>   Since the French were defeated by the Germans, their
> forces have been completely disintegrated. However, with
> regard to our people, they continue to plunder us pitilessly,
> suck all our blood, and carry out a barbarous policy of
> all-out terrorism and massacre. Concerning their foreign
> policy, they bow their heads and kneel down, shamelessly
> cutting our land for Siam; without a single word of pro-
> test, they heartlessly offer our interests to Japan. As a re-
> sult, our people suffer under a double yoke: they serve not
> only as buffaloes and horses to the French invaders but also
> as slaves to the Japanese plunderers.
>   . . . More than 20 million sons and daughters of Lac Hong†
> are resolute to do away with slavery. . . .
>   Now, the opportunity has come for our liberation. France
> itself is unable to dominate our country. As to the Japanese,
> on the one hand they are bogged in China, on the other
> they are hamstrung by the British and American forces and

---

* *Les Grandes Dates du parti de la classe ouvrière au Vietnam* (Great
Dates of the Vietnamese Workers' Party), Hanoi, p. 41.
  † The legendary founder of the Vietnamese nation.

certainly cannot use all their forces to contend with us. If our entire people are united and singleminded, we are certainly able to smash the picked French and Japanese armies.

Compatriots throughout the country! Rise up quickly! Let us follow the heroic example of the Chinese people! Rise up quickly to organize the Association for National Salvation to fight the French and the Japanese.

Elders!

Prominent personalities!

Some hundreds of years ago, when our country was endangered by the Mongolian invasion, our elders under the Tran dynasty rose up indignantly and called on their sons and daughters throughout the country to rise as one in order to kill the enemy. . . . The elders and prominent personalities of our country should follow the example set by our forefathers in the glorious task of national salvation.

Rich people, soldiers, workers, peasants, intellectuals, employees, traders, youth, and women who warmly love your country! At the present time national liberation is the most important problem. Let us unite together! As one in mind and strength we shall overthrow the Japanese and French and their jackals in order to save people from the situation between boiling water and burning heat. . . .

Revolutionary fighters!

The hour has struck! Raise aloft the insurrectionary banner and guide the people throughout the country to overthrow the Japanese and French! The sacred call of the fatherland is resounding in your ears. . . .

Victory to Vietnam's Revolution!

Victory to the world's Revolution!*

Even here, the final sentence shows the revolutionary still lurking beneath the patriot. But how could Ho fail to link preparations for a local uprising with what was now turning into a worldwide conflict? In this same month the Soviet Union was invaded by Hitler's armies. Six months later,

* Bernard B. Fall (ed.), *Ho Chi Minh on Revolution: Selected Writings, 1920–66* (New York: Praeger, 1967), pp. 132–34.

United States forces were attacked at Pearl Harbor. And late in 1941, while Ho labored at Pac Bo—training cadres; translating a history of the Soviet Communist Party and Sun-tse's *Art of War;* writing a series of pamphlets on guerrilla warfare—the early guerrilla bands comanded by Vo Nguyen Giap and the highland leader Chu Van Tan were, on his instructions, being converted into "propaganda units" (at that time regarded as being more useful than military formations) and extending their area of operations southward into the provinces of Tuyen Quang and Thai Nguyen.

In July 1942, Ho decided to make another journey into China. He had two objectives. The first, and more official, was to make contact with Chiang Kai-shek, on behalf of the League for the Independence of Vietnam, and secure his support in the common struggle against Japanese fascism. The second, of course, was to reopen communication with the Chinese Communist Party—and, by extension, with Moscow—for the purpose of explaining the "National Front" strategy, which the Vietnamese Communists had elected to adopt, in keeping with the pronouncements of the last congress of the International.

At the time of his departure, the leader picked a new *nom de guerre:* Ho Chi Minh. As we have seen, he was already known to his Chinese comrades as Ho Quang; to the prefix *Ho* he now added the words *Chi Minh* (Who Enlightens).* He was the torch to an even greater extent than he was the leader. Yet he was careful not to play the seer. Practical as ever, he equipped himself with visiting cards bearing his name and introducing him as a Chinese journalist resident in Vietnam.

But he did not get far. He and his guide were arrested

---

* Probably inspired by Ho Qui Ly, a renowned historical figure, who was a native of Nghe Tinh. It is perhaps worth noting that the ideograph means "light."

as soon as they crossed the frontier. It is hard to say how
quick the Kuomintang was to realize the true value of the
capture. This much is certain: the establishment of the
Vietminh conflicted with the plan then being effected by
Marshal Chang Fa-kwei and his political adviser, Shao
Wen, to establish a Vietnamese party in China which would
owe sole allegiance to the Kuomintang. There could be no
question of allowing another Yenan to ferment on the
southern borders of China.

Ho's comrades learned soon enough of his arrest. Indeed,
the day came when they were informed of his death, which
—like his earlier "death" in Hong Kong eleven years before—was accepted without challenge for months afterward.

Vo Nguyen Giap has related this episode with wit and
feeling.

One day I received a letter from Pham Van Dong . . . in-
forming me that Uncle Ho had just died in the jails of the
Kuomintang. We were almost paralyzed with grief. We
organized a ceremony of commemoration for our revered
leader, and Comrade Dong was given the task of writing
his funeral oration. We opened Uncle's rattan case in search
of mementoes. One of our comrades was dispatched to
China, with orders to locate his grave. . . . A few months
later we received a newspaper mailed from China. On the
wrapper were a few lines of verse in a hand which was well
known to us:

The clouds are setting the peaks aglow,
The peaks are hugging the clouds—
I wander alone, roused to feeling,
Scanning the distant southern sky:
I am thinking of my friends.

We were wild with joy, and no less astonished. We fired
question after question at Comrade Dong, who had brought
the sad news to us. "But," he insisted, "the Chinese governor
told me: *'Su Liu! Su Liu!* (Already dead!)'" "No, no, your

ear confused the tonic accents; what he must have said was
'*Chu Liu! Chu Liu!* (Very fit!)' "

"Chu" was a great improvement on "su," but "very fit"
was overstating the case. For fifteen months Ho went from
jail to jail, loaded with chains, covered with scabs, surrounded by the lowest criminals, shackled to men under
sentence of death, one of whom died, one night, huddled
against him.

Were the Chinese seeking to persuade him to ally the
Vietminh with the docile Vietnamese nationalist groups
operating under Marshal Chang Fa-kwei and under his
counterpart in Yunnan Province, Marshal Long-yun? Or
was he simply a victim of the repressive measures which
were part of the system?

Ho marched from Nanning to Tsin-tsi, from Kweilin to
Luichow, sometimes with a yoke around his neck, often
with chained feet, surviving through sheer stubbornness.
And he wrote. It was during these months of acute hardship that he composed the poems later published under the
title *Carnet de prison* (Prison Notebook).*

Paradoxically, this ardent nationalist chose to express
himself at the time, not in Quoc Ngu, the national tongue,
but in Chinese—the beautiful classical Chinese of the great
Tang dynasty (7th–10th centuries) which is also used with
pleasure by Mao Tse-tung. Vietnamese critics sometimes
set Ho's work beside Mao's to show the subtlety, terseness
and elegance of their leader's verse.

The volume contains about a hundred short poems, all
very simple, charged with emotion, direct, and either
anecdotal or moralistic. Often, peasant humor will suddenly be replaced by the didacticism of the model militant.
Human warmth is combined with a stoicism that is typically
Vietnamese. It is open to question whether the prisoner

---

* Translated into French by Phan Nhuan (Paris: Seghers, 1963).

who wrote these poems is a great artist, at all events he is
a man—a stoic with a sense of humor.

From the very first words, we know what his moral standpoint is:

> It is your body which is in prison,
> not your mind. . . .

And we know that the importance he attaches to his
poems is relative:

> I versify until such time as I shall see freedom.

But the tone becomes more elevated, shifting from anecdote to points of morality:

> The rice-grain suffers under the pestle;
> yet admire its whiteness when the ordeal is over.
> It is the same with human beings in our time—
> to be a man, you must endure the pestle of misfortune.

Or again, as he watches his fellow prisoners sleeping,
covered with lice:

> Eyes closed, they all look honest and pure.
> Waking divides them into evil and good.
> Good, evil—no one is either by nature.
> It is what you become, mainly through upbringing.

Phan Nhuan, who translated Ho's work into French,
compares this utterance with one of the first sayings which
Vietnamese schoolteachers implant in children's minds:
"En naissant, l'homme est bon." Clearly, little Cung from
Kim Lien—now Ho Chi Minh—had progressed from Rous-
seau to Marx during his stay in prison.

Sometimes a cry of pain escapes him:

Four inhuman months
in the depths of this jail.
More than ten years' aging
has ravaged my body!

Or else he dreams, tenderly at first:

The rose blossoms and the rose
withers without awareness of what
it does. The scent of a rose has only
to stray into a prison
for all the world's injustices
to shriek within the prisoner's heart.

The dream has turned into an indictment. And further on we read:

The poems of our day must be clad in steel.
Poets too must know how to fight!

At one moment he is full of longing, at another full of barbs:

In the morning, the sun climbs the wall
and comes knocking on the door; the door stays shut;
night still tarries in the depths of the prison. . . .

. . . Being chained is a luxury to compete for.
The chained have somewhere to sleep,
the unchained haven't . . .
The State treats me to its rice, I lodge in its palaces,
its guards take turns escorting me.
Really, the honor is too great. . . .

True, this is not the voice of an André Chénier; nor does it match Oscar Wilde's in *The Ballad of Reading Gaol*. Yet something proud and tender shines through these words, which are a blend of Asian sensibility and French romanticism. They are curiously successful in conveying the personality, culture and remarkable destiny of Ho Chi Minh. As he sat in jail, drawing the beautiful, angular characters on stiff paper, he must have been haunted not only by memories of Nghe An and the great writers of the Tang dynasty, but also by his long hours of reading in the quai de Jemmapes, by the memory of his Parisian radical friends Jules Raveau and Georges Pioch.

His comrades had launched an intensive campaign to secure the release of the "old anti-fascist militant." What impact were such arguments likely to have on the leaders of the Kuomintang? Marshal Chang Fa-kwei, however, still had memories of 1925 and 1926 when he and the Communists had fought side by side in Canton; he therefore felt more of a bond with the revolution than the other warlords.

The marshal had other reasons for being somewhat lenient. With Ho safely out of the way, Chang had succeeded in setting up his own apparatus for an assumption of power in Vietnam; in 1942 he had founded (in direct competition with the Vietminh) a group called the Vietnam Cach Nang Dong Minh Hoi (Revolutionary League of Vietnam), a name soon shortened to Dong Minh Hoi. The heads of the Kuomintang had found a leader for it—an old Vietnamese nationalist named Nguyen Hai Than, who had lived in exile for so many years that he could no longer even speak his native tongue. Here was a tractable tool, and his docility was bound to be increased by the fact that President Roosevelt and Chiang Kai-shek were already devising a plan whereby northern Vietnam would be placed under China's trusteeship after the defeat of Japan.

Thus China was beginning to constitute a new threat at the very moment when France's colonial authority was reeling and when in Europe the Allies' successes against the Wehrmacht held out the promise of a new administration in Paris, one with which the Vietnamese revolutionary movement would be able to cooperate. It looked as though colonialism might well be replaced by the neoimperialism of Chungking. At this juncture Ho revealed himself as a great strategist. Seldom in his dramatic and strenuous career did he maneuver with such mastery and precision, and this despite the fact that he had just emerged from a debilitating stay in prison.

Before being released, he had informed Chang Fa-kwei that he was ready to collaborate with the "liberation" league founded by the Kuomintang. By this time, old Nguyen Hai Than had proved completely incompetent. The marshal still regarded Ho as a somewhat compromising figure in view of his associations with the Comintern, but the prisoner argued that he had altered his name and that there was no longer any such person as Nguyen Ai Quoc. Who had ever heard of Ho Chi Minh? Moreover, the new name sounded quite Chinese and would make a good impression in Chungking. And so the prisoner was appointed head of the Dong Minh Hoi, the organization which Chang Fa-kwei had built up for the express purpose of supplanting the Vietminh. Such are, then, the wonders of Chinese politics!

6

THE
LIBERATOR

In the spring of 1943 Ho suddenly found himself out of jail and working, under his new name, as head of the organization financed by the Chinese (at the rate of a hundred thousand dollars a month) for the twin purposes of fighting the Japanese and winning independence for Vietnam.* Two of his objectives had been achieved. As for the third—revolution—he was prepared to bide his time.

Hoang Quang Binh tells how the leader came to see him in Yunnan Province a few months after his release; Ho defended his policy of infiltrating the Dong Minh Hoi and outlined his hopes.

* Philippe Devillers, *Histoire du Vietnam*, p. 105.

He lay back and talked to me by the wan light of a gas
lamp. His cheeks had hollowed out, his eyes seemed to have
been thrust deeper into their sockets, and yet they still
flashed with joy. His blanket was shaking; the fever had not
yet gone. His beard was still dark, but already a few threads
of white showed in the unkempt mop of hair spread on the
sack which served as his pillow. We were overwhelmed at
seeing him like this. How was it possible to feel toward
things and people so great a love?*

The advent of Ho Chi Minh, the creation of the Vietminh—the movement's growing pains were over; it was en-
tering the arena of combat with banners, devices and *noms
de guerre* all in good order.

It was not long before Giap linked up, in upper Tonkin,
with the guerrillas of the Chu Van Tan Tho (a minority
group in the region), who had rebelled against the French
administration. He began to infiltrate toward Cao Bang
and Thai Nguyen, with the intention of staking a claim for
the future (since there was little hope of immediate occupation of the area). His troops met with increasingly effective
resistance on the part of the French.

Giap's activities had attracted the attention not only of
the authorities in Hanoi, where Admiral Decoux was official representative of the Vichy government, but also of the
French military mission sent to Kunming (capital of Yunnan Province) by the Algiers committee, which since June
1943 had been headed by General de Gaulle. A meeting was
arranged in Cao Bang between Boisanger, the admiral's
diplomatic adviser, and a member of the military mission.
Representations were made to the Chinese nationalist authorities, asking them to stop supporting the Vietnamese
revolutionaries. In addition, the anti-Communist elements
among the Vietnamese nationalists were angered by the

* *Souvenirs sur Ho Chi Minh* (Recollections of Ho Chi Minh), Hanoi:
Foreign Languages Publishing House, p. 147.

privileges accorded to Ho and his friends; it seemed to them that the Kuomintang was betraying its "real" friends and playing into the hands of the Communists. Marshal Chang Fa-kwei decided to avert a clash by working out a compromise between the rival Vietnamese factions. In March 1944 he called a conference in Liuchow, where a guerrilla-warfare training college had been established.

Ho Chi Minh and Pham Van Dong represented the Vietminh. Confronting them were the leaders of pro-Chinese, pro-Japanese and strictly nationalist groups—ranging from Nguyen Hai Than to Bo Xuan Luat, from Vu Hong Khanh to Truong Boi Cong, from Nghiem Ke To to Nguyen Tuong Tam. The Vietminh leaders were harshly criticised: they were charged with taking unauthorized initiative and monopolizing the movement for their own ends. The Chinese organizers' assessment of these allegations showed clear bias at the expense of the Communists. Ho was obliged to beat a retreat. In the "provisional government" set up at the end of the Liuchow conference under the premiership of Truong Boi Hong, an old friend of the Chinese, Ho was only one minister among many. But at least he had avoided the total elimination which his rivals had hoped for him. A link with the Sino-American effort was then essential to his purposes, and he had maintained it.

Ho's "allies" within this self-styled government at once started tearing one another to pieces; but already he was on his way back to the Indochinese border, where his men alone were exercising military pressure. Before long the Liuchow government disintegrated completely; but Ho, with his guerrillas and networks, survived—even though the news from the West was unfavorable.

On December 8, 1943, General de Gaulle spoke in Algiers of France's "need" to reestablish her authority in Indochina. This led to an immediate change in Vietminh propaganda, which had previously aimed a number of appeals at the "French democrats" and drawn a distinction between the "Franco-Nipponese fascists" and the Gaullists. In June a leaflet was distributed in Tonkin, declaring:

> So the French, themselves struggling against German domination, hope to maintain their domination over other peoples! We Indochinese Communists protest most strongly against the inconsistency of the Algiers committee. By working for the establishment of a broadly based antifascist front in Indochina, we want to deliver ourselves as well as anti-fascist foreigners from the oppression of the Nipponese fascist militarists. But to suggest that we are thereby sacrificing our national independence, in favor of domination by the Gaullists or anyone else, is pure sophistry.

Three months later a further pamphlet, oddly prophetic in tone, demonstrated that Ho and his colleagues were expert in the art of political analysis:

> Zero hour is near. Germany is almost beaten, and her defeat will lead to Japan's. Then the Americans and the Chinese will move into Indochina while the Gaullists rise against the Japs. The latter may well topple the French fascists prior to this, and set up a military government. . . . Indochina will be reduced to anarchy. We shall not even need to seize power, for there will be no power. . . . Our impending uprising will be carried out in highly favorable conditions, without parallel in the history of our country. The occasion being propitious and the factors favorable, it would be unforgivable not to take advantage of them. It would be a crime against the history of our country.*

At the end of July 1944 the revolutionary committee of the Cao Bang region, which took its lead from Vo Nguyen Giap, came out categorically in favor of launching an armed insurrection in northern Vietnam. In September, Giap

* Devillers, *op. cit.*, p. 111.

visited Ho in the cave at Pac Bo, to which the leader had returned. Ho quieted his young colleague's impatience, pointing out that Giap's decision was based on an analysis of the local situation and not on an overall view of the problem.

"The phase of peaceful revolution is behind us," he said, "but the time for general insurrection has not yet come." All the same, he suggested that Giap should set up a "brigade of liberation," whose aims should be more political than military. And the old leader went on to say, "We may not have strength on our side, but that is no reason for simply letting ourselves be crushed. . . ." And when he said good-bye to Giap, he insisted quietly, "Stealth, continual stealth. Never attack except by surprise. Retire before the enemy has a chance to strike back. . . ."*

Early in December 1944, Ho signed official instructions relating to the establishment of the "Propaganda Unit for National Liberation," formed from the nucleus of thirty-four fighting men who were then serving under Giap's command in upper Tonkin.

1. The Vietnam Propaganda Unit for National Liberation shows by its name that greater importance should be attached to the political side than to the military side. It is a propaganda unit. To act successfully, in the military field, the main principle is concentration of forces. Therefore, in accordance with the new instruction of the organization, the most resolute and energetic officers and men will be picked out of the ranks of the guerrilla units in the provinces of Cao Bang, Bac Can, and Lang Son and a great amount of weapons will be concentrated to establish our main force.

Because ours is a national resistance by the whole people, we must mobilize and arm the whole people. Therefore, when concentrating our forces to set up the first unit, we

* *Souvenirs sur Ho Chi Minh,* pp. 201-2.

must maintain the local armed forces, coordinate their operations and assist each other in all aspects. On its part, the
main unit has the duty to guide the cadres of the local
armed units, assist them in drilling and supply them with
weapons if possible, thus helping these units to grow unceas-
ingly.

2. With regard to local armed units, we will gather their
cadres for training, send trained cadres to various localities
to exchange experience, maintain liaison and coordinate
military operations.

3. Concerning tactics, we will apply guerrilla warfare,
which consists in being secret, rapid, active, now in the east,
now in the west, arriving unexpectedly and leaving unno-
ticed.

The Vietnam Propaganda Unit for National Liberation is
the first-born unit. It is hoped that other units will soon
come into being.

At first its size is small; however, its prospect is brilliant.
It is the embryo of the Liberation Army and can move from
north to south, throughout Vietnam.*

The first "regular" combat groups of the Vietminh were
soon ready. Under their protection, Ho moved deeper into
Indochinese territory on October 29, relinquishing the
border area of Pac Bo (things had changed since 1941!) and
setting up base amid the steep limestone slopes of Thai
Nguyen province. Ten months later he entered Hanoi; but
he often returned to the mountain base for shelter during
the years 1947 through 1954.

The Vietminh guerrillas, occasionally joined by small
groups of French troops fighting the Japanese and led by
Lieutenant Bernier, infiltrated the area and persuaded several garrisons to desert. They advanced into the narrow
mountain corridor of Dinh Ca, near Thai Nguyen, a sort

---

* Bernard B. Fall (ed.), *Ho Chi Minh on Revolution: Selected Writings,
1920–66* (New York: Praeger, 1967), pp. 141–42.

of land fjord where rebels had often taken refuge ever since the campaigns conducted by Gallieni.* Here they won three mountain villages over to their cause. Agitation was gaining ground.

This was primarily a period of indoctrination; militants and cadres were trained in jungle schools. Giap was the man in charge, under Ho's general supervision. Later he described how the leader would sometimes come and attend his courses—fording the nearby stream with his trousers rolled up to his knees. The visitor would interrupt and ask questions. At the end of a lesson, one young neophyte came up to Giap and said; "How odd to find that curious little old man here. He takes an interest in politics despite his age!"

In the minds of Vietminh militants, the formation of this guerrilla force in upper Tonkin is an enduring legend. It has brought Giap as much fame and glory as did his decisive defeat of the French forces at Dien Bien Phu in the culminating battle of the Indochinese War. Like membership in secret societies, guerrilla fighting is especially well suited to the romantic temperament of the Vietnamese: once fear and bewilderment were overcome, there was something undeniably poetic about living on the forest-capped slopes amid the greatest of dangers.

The French authorities in Hanoi decided to act. Officers and soldiers were chosen to take charge of the mopping-up operation in the highlands. The expedition was timed to begin on March 12, 1945. The French forces were more than adequate for dealing with Ho's forces and there seemed a strong chance that the Vietminh might go under. But three days before the French column was due to move north

---

* General Joseph Gallieni figured prominently in the French colonization of Indochina and Madagascar. Defending Paris against the Germans in August 1914, he sent soldiers to the front in the famous "taxis of the Marne."

from Hanoi, the Japanese army struck: at dawn on March 9, 1945 every Frenchman in Indochina with the smallest amount of authority was arrested and jailed. The gods were on Ho's side. Not only had the dismantlement of the French force prevented the destruction of the Vietminh's bases and networks and the probable capture of its leaders; it had opened the way to power. For the Japanese army, which now controlled the area, was far less skilled and efficient in coping with the revolution.

Meeting on the night of March 9th and continuing on the 10th the Permanent Committee of the Vietminh concluded that in assuming power Japanese fascism had become

> "the sole enemy of the Vietnamese revolution. In conse-
> quence, the Vietnamese revolutionaries must make contact
> with any French group sincerely desirous of fighting the
> Japanese fascists. The committee has decided to stage a
> series of local uprisings before launching the general insur-
> rection. A directive from the committee indicates the line
> to be followed and the courses of action best suited to this
> preinsurrectional period: the formation of further units of
> the army of liberation, all over the country, together with
> military committees, committees of liberation and people's
> revolutionary committees. But the situation does not yet
> favor a general insurrection.*

This did not prevent the commandos serving under Giap (Armed Propaganda Unit) and under Chu Van Tan (Army for National Salvation) from continuing their advance— or rather their infiltration—southward. At the beginning of April both forces, following separate paths, arrived in Thai Nguyen Province, linking up at Tan Trao. There was a general meeting of guerrilla leaders at Hiep Hoa, in the Bac Giang region, and the command was issued: popular revolt, and march to the south! At once Ho sent word to

* *Les Grandes Dates du parti de la classe ouvrière du Vietnam* (Great Dates of the Vietnamese Workers' Party) Hanoi: 1960, p. 48.

Giap that he wanted to see him. They met at Na Kieu in early May, just as Nazi Germany was capitulating.

Vo Nguyen Giap writes:

> I was so excited that I made my report to him there and then, speaking of the successes which had been achieved since he had instructed me to set up the Propaganda Unit. . . . He wore a meditative look as he listened, but I saw his face light up with happiness. He talked about the international situation, emphasizing how favorable it was. He wanted to choose a site which was politically secure and easy to defend so that he could set up a center for communicating with the outside world. . . .*

Nevertheless, Uncle Ho once again put his eager young lieutenant on his guard against overadventurousness, reminding him that no general rising could be started except on three conditions, which were not as yet completely fulfilled:

(a) the enemy must be in an untenable position;
(b) the people must be clearly conscious of oppression;
(c) the revolutionaries must have finished preparing the ground.

On June 4, 1945 Ho decided that the situation had evolved sufficiently to allow a modification in the Front's strategy. He therefore decided to regroup the various guerrilla bands, commando units and "liberated zones," and he signed an order stating that the six sectors controlled by the revolutionary groups were to unite in a single "free zone," while the various armed bodies were to unite in an "Army of Liberation." Giap would continue to serve as military coordinator.

It is to Giap that we owe the account of how preparations

---

* *Souvenirs sur Ho Chi Minh*, pp. 207–208.

were made in Tan Trao, the revolutionaries' small provisional capital. "After the capture of Nam Dao, we managed to salvage our first telephone. As a result, a line two hundred yards long ran between the President's office and my own . . . [Then Ho became ill.] For hours he lay in a coma. . . . Every time he came to, he would murmur: 'Now circumstances are in our favor. Independence must be wrested at all costs, even if all the Truong Son mountain chain has to be set on fire. In guerrilla warfare, one must take advantage of mounting upheaval and broaden one's bases. . . .' I refused to believe that he was imparting his dying thoughts. But afterward, looking back on the scene, I realized that he felt so weak that he was dictating his last instructions to me. . . ."*

Here again, one has to allow for idolatry. But the sketch is a compelling one and the observations convincing.

Ho and his colleagues had put out countless feelers in the hope of strengthening their "back areas" and broadening their bases. General Albert Wedemeyer, commander of U.S. forces in China, was in fact on the lookout for reliable allies to keep watch on the Japanese, who were threatening the air bases in Yunnan. In Chungking, the general staff was theoretically cooperating with the French military mission at Kunming; they had established links with the Gaullist networks (which took their lead mainly from Commandant de Langlade) and also, more closely, with the resistance organization created in the Sino-Tonkinese sector by Major Gordon, a Canadian who had been the Texaco Company's representative in Haiphong before the war and who was now in U.S. naval intelligence. Anxious to extend their activities, however, and systematically biased against any form of French presence in Indochina, the American special services contacted the Vietminh, even though its ideology was not unknown to them.

* *Souvenirs sur Ho Chi Minh*, p. 211.

Bernard Fall* states that Ho had made a personal visit
to Kunming in February 1945, with the object of meeting
Colonel Helliwell, area commander of the Office of Strategic
Services. Apparently, when the Vietminh leader asked for
arms and ammunition the American officer laid down two
conditions: that they should not be used against the French,
and that teams of American agents should be admitted to
the sectors controlled by the revolutionaries. According to
Colonel Helliwell, the Vietminh received only a few revolvers; yet several members of the O.S.S. have insisted that
Ho's men were given a fair amount of American light
armament at this time.

At all events, Ho's visit to Kunming had not been a waste
of time: his charm had made a deep impression on the
Americans, and for years afterward he retained friendships
within the ranks of the O.S.S. One of the American officers
who met Ho on this occasion is said by Robert Shaplen to
have remarked, "Ho was an awfully sweet guy. . . . If I
had to recall one quality of this old man sitting on his hill
in the jungle, it would be his sweetness. . . ."†

These contacts with the Americans were soon followed by
others. In July 1945, after lengthy discussions between
Nguyen Tuong Tam (one of the leaders of the V.N.Q.D.D.
nationalist movement, an "ally" of the Vietminh since the
Liuchow conference the year before) and Jean Sainteny,
head of the French military mission in southern China, the
Vietminh decided to inform France's representatives of its
political objectives.

This was done via Major Gordon and Lieutenant Phelan,
an officer in the U.S. mission attached to the Vietminh.
They delivered a memorandum in English to Sainteny and
the other members of his team (Léon Pignon‡ and General

* *The Viet Minh Regime* (Institute of Pacific Relations).
† "The Enigma of Ho Chi Minh," *The Reporter* (January 1955).
‡ Léon Pignon was director of civil affairs at the delegation of the
G.P.R.F. In 1950 he became high commissioner in Saigon.

Alessandri, who had escaped from the Japanese on March 9, 1945, at the head of six thousand men). The memorandum outlined the revolutionaries' aims in the following terms:

1. That there be universal suffrage for the election of a parliament to govern this country; that it have a French governor to act as president until independence is assured us; that this president choose a cabinet or group of councilors approved by Parliament. The precise powers of all these offices will be determined in the future.

2. That independence be granted this country within no less than five years and no more than ten years.

3. That the country's natural resources be returned to its inhabitants after making fair compensation to their present holders; that France be given economic concessions.

4. That all freedoms set forth in the United Nations be guaranteed to the Indochinese.

5. That the sale of opium be forbidden.

We hope that these conditions will be judged acceptable by the French government.*

Was the note of moderation which runs through this text merely a tactical trick, designed to get talks started as a prelude to extracting far more from the other side? When, only three months later, Pignon and General Alessandri asked Ho if this was the case, Ho (who in the meantime had become president of the provisional government in Hanoi) pretended that he had forgotten the terms of the document. But his general attitude throughout the subsequent negotiations had a spirit reasonably close to that of the July memorandum.

For lack of instructions, Sainteny and his colleagues were forced to give a noncommittal answer—though a very polite

* Jean Sainteny, *Histoire d'une paix manquée,* (Paris: Amiot-Dumont), p. 57.

one—to the Vietminh offers; they had no means of telling whether their message had been passed on by the special services. This was perhaps the first of many lost opportunities of achieving a settlement between Uncle Ho and Paris.

Suddenly after a gap of many years Ho was face to face with France again. The first phase of their relationship had ended in 1923, when the revolutionary had left Paris for Moscow. As a Communist, he had wanted to share in the life of the capital of Communism, to broaden his experience, to sharpen his knowledge of the doctrine and techniques of insurrection. Since then, he had traveled all over Asia, hunted, imprisoned and on the run; forever organizing and drawing up plans, recruiting new members, wooing the uncommitted, restraining the overzealous; forced to decide on eliminating X or Y, to order the execution of someone who had yesterday been a friend; always narrowly avoiding a trap or a noose. He had been living in a grim world.

And now came the chance to negotiate with the power which had long held sway over his country, which had outlawed and passed sentence on him, but which—fresh from its own experience of foreign occupation—now had a government composed of men who, a quarter of a century earlier, had been his friends.

True, the Vietminh did not receive much news of political developments in France, and such bits of information as arrived tended to provoke second thoughts about the new administration in Paris. Yet there could be nothing more natural than that this one-time contributor to *La Vie Ouvrière*, *Le Populaire* and *L'Humanité* should seek reconciliation with France the indestructible, whose newly appointed team of ministers included the Communist deputies Charles Tillon and Fernand Grenier, as well as several of their Socialist colleagues.

In Ho's words and deeds at this time and the warm welcome he extended to the Frenchmen with whom he came in contact, there could be sensed a nostalgia and, at times, jubilation—had he not always hoped that the liberation of his country would come by way of Paris, even if he was first required to negotiate the perilous paths of Asian revolution? But it would be wrong to overemphasize this behavior or view it in an idealistic light. Ho has never been guilty of excessive idealism, which might have kept him from resorting to drastic methods necessary to help him achieve his ultimate goal—the creation, by any course open to him, of a socialist and independent state of Vietnam.

Two Franco-Vietminh exchanges took place in the same month. On July 12, Commandant Revol, French officer in charge of the Tsin-tsi sector, met the Vietminh commander of the Soc Giang region. The latter offered to cooperate against the Japanese, but asked him for arms and ammunition.* Reporting back to Sainteny, Revol advised acceptance. Paris was consulted and expressed a provisionally favorable view. In an effort to make a more exact sounding of Ho's aims and potentialities, a Franco-American mission was parachuted in on July 16, led by Major Thomas and Lieutenant Montfort. There appears to be no written evidence of their meeting with the Vietminh leaders. But it was then that the plan for direct talks between Ho and Sainteny took shape.

It is not known whether it was one of the officers attached to this mission or the ever-resourceful Major Gordon, the man behind the entire operation, who informed the official representative of France that the Vietminh leader wanted to meet him, either in Kunming or else in an area of upper

* Sainteny, *op. cit.*, p. 58.

Tonkin controlled by Giap's forces. Jean Sainteny chose the second site; he felt that holding talks on Indochinese soil would serve to accentuate France's rights. However, Sainteny writes:

This plan could not be carried out because of the head-long pace of events and above all because of the torrential rain which ruled out any air activity in the region. It was later revealed to us by Allied officers who were at Vietminh headquarters at this time that the reception of a French dele-gate was keenly desired by the heads of the "Vietminh League," who had ordered tricolor flags and special streamers for the occasion, to welcome the representative of France. Apparently the Vietminh leaders would have liked, at this juncture, to enter Hanoi side by side with the French dele-gate, who had been entrusted by the provisional government of the French Republic with the task of taking possession of the Tonkinese capital after the surrender of the Japanese forces.*

There were several explanations for the desire of Ho and his colleagues to forge new links with France at this stage and to secure the country's political emancipation by process of agreement with their former masters. The first was admirably defined by Paul Mus in a telegram which he drafted after carrying out a mission in March 1945; this stated, in essence, that the behavior of the Vietnamese na-tionalists vis-à-vis France would be directly dependent on the position which Paris appeared to occupy in the world. And 1945 was the year which saw the final collapse of the Third Reich and the reemergence of France as a great power.

It was these fundamental facts which principally dictated the conduct of the Vietnamese revolutionaries, whose belief

* Sainteny, *op. cit.,* p. 59.

in making realistic appraisals had been sharpened by Marxist training. Another reason for their more "understanding" attitude toward Paris was the political complexion of the French government: a third of its members were Communists, and another third Socialists.

Finally, the Japanese—however weak their position—could not be dismissed out of hand. For a while at least, it was advisable to lean on the French "democrats" in the fight against "Nipponese military fascism." Negotiating from a distance with General de Gaulle was preferable to risking the immediate strangle hold of Field Marshal Count Terauchi.

On March 24, 1945, Paris announced its program for Indochina. The Vietnamese revolutionaries could not have been more sharply disappointed, for here was a plan to federate the *five* regions of Indochina—in other words, the French government was seeking to preserve the partition of the three Vietnamese regions, Tonkin, Annam and Cochin China, and keep them as separate as Cambodia and Laos. To a revolutionary patriot like Ho, the proposal was bound to seem a threat and an insult. Was this the best the "new" France could do?

But the pace of events quickened, upsetting all previously laid plans. On August 5, Japan was stunned by the bombing of Hiroshima; on August 15, the Tokyo government sought an armistice. The Japanese were dislodged only five months after they themselves had destroyed France's colonial apparatus. Ho and his colleagues must have lacked all religious sense, or they would surely have been struck by the miraculous nature of their rise to power. Some of them, however, had a sufficient knowledge of Hegel to see in these developments an instance of the "supra-determination of history."

Here we must pause a moment, for at this juncture we have the fullest revelation yet of Ho's political personality and of his strategy, which was inspired by Lenin. It is based on two concepts: the "favorable moment" and the "main adversary."

Nothing could be more characteristic of Ho than this preoccupation with the "favorable moment." Throughout his life, up to and including the second Vietnamese war in the sixties, he has deliberately sought the propitious moment for negotiating or acting. And now suddenly the future of his party, and perhaps of the revolution in Vietnam, was at stake.

For the past three or four months, certainly since March 9, his colleagues had been urging him to strike a major blow. With the French out of the way, why not launch an all-out attack on the Japanese fascists? But Ho had calculated the odds: locally they were still against the Vietminh, even though the international situation was in its favor because of the defeat of the Axis powers in Europe. They must wait until Japan was as weak in Vietnam as she was internationally. They must wait for Hiroshima—but they must act before France recovered.

As for the "main adversary," the important thing was not to focus on any one particular foe, since the enemy did not long remain the same one. In succession it was French colonialism, Japanese fascism, the Chinese occupying forces, American imperialism. What was important was to isolate the most dangerous of one's enemies and then to attack it with the help of other potential enemies.

On August 10, 1945, four days after Hiroshima, Ho Chi Minh, who was still not fully recovered from his illness, called a special conference in Tan Trao, Thai Nguyen Province. Sixty delegates attended, representing the various ethnic groups in the north and a number of shades of political opinion not yet incorporated in the Vietminh. This led to the formation, on August 13, of a National Liberation Committee of Vietnam, which "decided to seize power from the hands of the Japanese fascists before the arrival of the Allies" (the terminology is interesting). And even as Giap began to strike toward Hanoi, where he arrived after his local comrades had assumed control, Ho at last issued the call for a general insurrection:

> The Vietminh front is at present the basis of the struggle and solidarity of our people. Join the Vietminh Front, support it, make it greater and stronger!
>
> At present, the National Liberation Committee is, so to speak, in itself our provisional government. Unite around it and see to it that its policies and orders are carried out throughout the country!
>
> In this way, our fatherland will certainly win independence and our people will certainly win freedom soon.
>
> The decisive hour in the destiny of our people has struck. Let us stand up with all our strength to free ourselves!
>
> Many oppressed peoples the world over are vying with each other in the march to win back their independence. We cannot allow ourselves to lag behind.
>
> Forward! Forward! Under the banner of the Vietminh front, move forward courageously!*

And the document was signed, for the last time, "Nguyen Ai Quoc."

The call to arms was circulated in Hué and Saigon, as well as in Hanoi. And everywhere the fever was mounting. Nguyen Ai Quoc: the name conjured up so many hours of high drama! The Japanese forces of occupation, defeated, but still in control, were prepared to look the other way, as in the past the leaders of the Kuomintang had done in allowing Ho to go free—Asian revolution was preferable to European revenge.

When Jean Sainteny attempted to leave Kunming for the Indochinese capital with the object of asserting French rights there as soon as the defeat of Japan was confirmed, his movements were blocked by General Albert Wedemeyer

---

* Fall, *op. cit.*, p. 142.

of the United States Army, who would not allow him to travel until August 22. Meanwhile, Vietminh agents in Hanoi created a mood of unrest which reached boiling point on August 16, the very day when the Japanese (whose government had capitulated the day before) handed over all powers to the weak imperial government appointed five months earlier by Bao Dai. This time the adversary was no match for Ho and his associates.

On August 17, while Sainteny was still stranded in Kunming, the civil servants' union called a strike. In the stifling heat of Hanoi, which was relieved late in the day by heavy monsoon rain, tens of thousands of men in white shorts marched through the city and gathered outside the municipal theater. Beside the yellow and red imperial flag hung several scarlet standards bearing the gold star—the emblem of the Vietminh. A few hundred yards away, at the Senior Residency, the "Consultative Assembly of Tonkin," composed of men of wealth and position, was holding a hastily convened meeting. Events had obviously moved too fast for its members; they dispersed in bewilderment after a short debate.

The local Vietminh leaders had shown their hand. But they had not yet taken control of the uprising. To do so, they needed two more days of infiltrating, preparing, conditioning. August 18 was marked by renewed demonstrations, as prolonged and directionless as before. But on August 19, the "prerevolution" gave way to the "general revolution," to use the terms of the party's propaganda machine. The gatherings were larger, the crowds more mixed, with a higher proportion of coolies and women. The red flags with yellow stars fluttered almost alone along the front of the theater. A few fists, clenched in the traditional Communist salute, went up as the flags were hoisted, but the majority of people saluted as the French had taught them to salute the tricolor.

The night of August 19 and the next day saw the beginning of popular insurrection. French people were hunted down, and according to one estimate more than ten were killed. For the survivors, this was the start of a six-months' nightmare—briefer but bloodier in the south.

It was a triumph for the techniques of Communism: streamers, leaflets, microphones, slogans chanted in rhythm. The crowd was conditioned and molded, while the Vietminh's shock-troops occupied the public buildings and seized the arms and ammunition of the Indochinese Guard. The nationalist organizations seemed to have vanished. The Vietminh, gaining the support of the students' union on August 20, gained control of the city.

Meanwhile Ho's deputies were acting in Hué, the imperial capital. On August 25 they secured the abdication of Bao Dai, whose proclamation clearly invested the "Democratic Republic" with the same mandate from heaven which had been handed down to the emperor by his ancestors. And in Saigon, proceeding at a pace which caught the nationalists unawares, a small cell of Communists won control of the "Provisional Executive Committee of South Vietnam" on August 23, under the impassioned leadership of Tran Van Giau.

Thus, records Philippe Devillers, "on August 25, 1945, ten days after the Japanese capitulation, the Vietminh controlled the entire territory of Vietnam. With disconcerting ease, through the combined effects of negotiation, infiltration, propaganda and—above all—Japanese 'neutrality,' it had gained power. . . ."*

So far, Ho himself had remained in the background. Several members of the National Committee of Liberation, which had been formed under his leadership earlier that month, had arrived in Hanoi. With a few prominent left-wingers, they had set up a caretaker government. It had been agreed, however, that Ho should continue to lie low

* Devillers, *op. cit.*, p. 142.

until the local situation and the intentions of the Japanese
had become clearer.

The ordinary people were curious about the identity of
the man behind the uprising, and legends sprang up—not
always favorable ones. In his more or less autobiographical
novel, *Les Chemins de la révolte*,* Nguyen Tien Lang
records a conversation between the hero (then in jail) and
one of his cellmates: "Who is the head of the Vietminh?"
"They say it's a Chinese colonel, someone called Ho Chi
Minh. . . ." Meanwhile, French experts in Vietnamese affairs
were thinking hard. Some of them decided that the leader
of the rebellion must be the trade union leader Hoang Quoc
Viet, more commonly referred to as Ha Ba Cang in the
files of the *Sûreté*; crippled from hours of torture at the
hands of the police, he was a man of formidable reputation.

It seems that Ho reached Hanoi as early as August 21, a
day before Sainteny at last arrived in the city, only to be
interned by the Japanese. At first Ho lived quietly with
friends. One of his colleagues within the provisional government describes Ho's first encounter with his friends—or, at
any rate, with those who were not members of the Tong Bo
(politburo of the Communist Party). Nguyen Manh Ha,
president of the Association of Catholic Students, who had
just been appointed Minister of National Economy in the
first Vietminh government, gave me the following lively
account:

It seemed to us that the man called Ho Chi Minh, who
was rumored to be at the head of the uprising, was one and
the same person as Nguyen Ai Quoc, the revolutionary
whose name had haunted and fired our imagination when
we were young. . . . Giap, whom we had known at the university, and who appeared to have been directing the insurrection since August 20, used to call us together every eve-

* Paris: Editions du Seuil, 1952.

ning from eight until midnight for meetings of the inner cabinet at which public affairs were discussed. One evening he told us: "Tomorrow Ho Chi Minh will be present." That was on August 25 or 26.

Next day, as we stood chatting in the corridors, we saw a strange-looking figure coming toward us, clad in shorts, carrying a walking stick and wearing a most peculiar brown-painted colonial helmet. He looked like a real character. Who was he? A rural *can bo* (cadre) fresh from the paddies? A scholar from some outlying part? But our attention was caught by a detail which in those days was altogether unusual and which made it obvious that here was no ordinary party member—a packet of American cigarettes was sticking out of his shirt pocket. . . .

He came up to me and asked in a friendly way: "Aren't you Marrane's son-in-law?"*

That was how we first met. . . .

He was very easygoing at cabinet meetings. On September 1, the eve of the declaration of independence, he arrived with a scrap of paper on which he had drafted his proclamation to the people. He submitted it to us, passing it around, accepting amendments—though at this stage, before the anti-Communist nationalists came into the government, there was little that needed debating within the cabinet. . . .

The Vietminh held complete sway, and we seldom had any objections to raise. In essence, its policy was to reach agreement with France in order to keep the Chinese out and secure independence as soon as possible, without conflict. . . . How could anyone object to that? Things began to deteriorate in February 1946, when he was obliged to bring the ultranationalist V.N.Q.D.D. leaders into the cabinet. When he broke the news to us, he said: "We shall not be just a group of friends from now on. We shall have to stand up for our views. Several of us will have to give up their posts."

---

* Marrane was chairman of the Seine Regional Council at the time of the Liberation in August 1944. Nguyen Manh Ha left the Vietminh government after five months. First he retired to Phnom Penh and then to Paris, where he became one of the leaders of the campaign for peace and neutrality in South Vietnam.

He was crying into a large handkerchief. It was a deeply moving moment.

Only twice did I ever see him lose his temper. The first time was after the Minister of Propaganda, Tran Huy Lieu, the most bigoted of the Vietminh ministers, had a violently anti-French proclamation broadcast in the streets of Hanoi. Ho upbraided him at the cabinet meeting: "All right, so it's fun abusing the colonialists. And where does it get you?" On another occasion, the minister in charge of the postal services admitted that he was unable to produce the special stamps that the president had called for. Ho went for the poor man with surprising sharpness: "So! People clamor for independence, and yet it's too much bother to print a stamp!"

It was August 29 that the composition of the government was announced publicly. President Ho Chi Minh? Who was *he*, people wondered? Those who were best informed maintained that he was the Communist leader Nguyen Ai Quoc. Was this true? Questioned by journalists, the President was content to reply modestly, "I am a revolutionary. I was born at a time when my country was already a slave state. From the days of my youth I have fought to free it. That is my one merit. In consideration of my past, my companions have voted me head of government." The next day, Kunming radio broadcast a summary of the leader's life and career which, omitting all mention of Communist activities and associations, presented him simply as a devoted nationalist.

Within a few months Ho Chi Minh became "Uncle Ho" to a people still struggling to find their true identity. Note how he addresses first the "children" and then the "old people" in September 1945:

My children,
Today we start the first term of the Democratic Republic of Vietnam . . . Unlike your fathers and their fathers before them, you are lucky enough to enjoy the education afforded

by an independent state. . . . Eighty years of slavery have diminished our country's strength. Now we must retrieve the heritage bequeathed by our ancestors and catch up with the other nations of the world. Will Vietnam achieve fame and glory? Will her people occupy an honorable place on a par with the other peoples of the five continents? This will depend in large measure on your studious efforts. . . .*

The style is both dull and chauvinistic. But the words do contain a note of pride and affection which, in a society characterized as much by a sense of family as by nationalism and sentimentality, could not but please.

Of his "Letter to the Old People" only the opening words need be quoted:

> Gentlemen,
> It is as an old man that I address you. . . .

* *The Selected Works of Ho Chi Minh*, p. 80.

7

THE
NEGOTIATOR

Relations with France grew strained, of course. The abrupt collapse of Japan led Ho and his colleagues to imagine that they could rid themselves of "Nipponese fascism" without the help of "democratic France" and that their success in achieving a clean sweep in Indochina entitled them to deal less considerately with their former masters. And there were other considerations also: it was important for the Vietminh to launch a violent attack on colonialism to keep up with the nationalists, and to demand immediate independence, in view of Bao Dai's insistent championship of that cause, both before and after his abdication. (The ex-emperor was, in fact, about to be appointed "senior adviser" to Ho's government.)

On August 27, however, Vo Nguyen Giap called on Jean Sainteny—a week after France's representative reached Hanoi. Giap said he hoped to receive "advice and directives"* from him and was therefore greatly dismayed when Sainteny informed him in the presence of a senior American officer, Major Patti, that Chinese forces were about to move into the sector and take over from the Japanese the area north of the sixteenth parallel, roughly at the latitude of Tourane (Danang).

For the first time the Vietminh found an unexpected obstacle in its path. There was once again a practical reason for cooperating with France. But although Ho and his ministers must have reached this conclusion when they met that same evening, they did not moderate their remarks about France at the rally to mark the proclamation of independence on September 2. The situation was not helped when General Leclerc, commander in chief of the forces which were supposed to reestablish France's position in the Far East, issued a toughly worded statement in Ceylon, saying that France was determined to uphold her rights over Indochina even if she had to do it by force of arms.

It may be that tension and anxiety were partly responsible for the violent anti-French speeches made at the rally on September 2. Even Ho Chi Minh, who was always toning down the attacks made on France by some of his colleagues, delivered a harangue which—after a brief introduction (which will be mentioned later)—was one long outcry against France.

The crowd was drawn chiefly by the prospect of seeing the man of mystery whom a few hectic days had established as its leader. Throughout the day-long organized demonstrations, there was little display of feelings of hatred against

* Jean Sainteny, *Histoire d'une paix manquée* (Paris: Amiot-Dumont), p. 86.

France. Jean Sainteny emphasizes in his book that "several hundred thousand people took part in this rally . . . including a good many Catholic priests."* He calls attention to the "orderliness of the procession" and the "absence of any seditious outcries." Even though the itinerary of the procession included the avenue running past the governor general's palace, a symbol of colonialism which had become Sainteny's home, he and his colleagues "observed not a single hostile gesture."

He even remarks that already Ho "seemed anxious to figure as a moderating influence." Be that as it may, there was nothing very moderate about the speech which he delivered that afternoon from a platform erected in the Place Ba Dinh. His beard blowing in the wind, and his voice heavy with emotion, he said:

> . . . for more than eighty years, the French imperialists, abusing the standard of Liberty, Equality, and Fraternity, have violated our fatherland and oppressed our fellow citizens. They have acted contrary to the ideals of humanity and justice. In the field of politics, they have deprived our people of every democratic liberty.
>
> They have enforced inhuman laws; they have set up three distinct political regimes in the north, the center and the south of Vietnam in order to wreck our national unity and prevent our people from being united.
>
> They have built more prisons than schools. They have mercilessly slain our patriots; they have drowned our uprisings in rivers of blood. They have fettered public opinion; they have practiced obscurantism against our people. To weaken our race they have forced us to use opium and alcohol.
>
> In the fields of economics, they have fleeced us to the backbone, impoverished our people, and devastated our land.

* Sainteny, *op. cit.*, p. 92.

They have robbed us of our rice fields, our mines, our forests, and our raw materials.* They have monopolized the issuing of bank notes and the export trade.

They have invented numerous unjustifiable taxes and reduced our people, especially our peasantry, to a state of extreme poverty.

They have hampered the prospering of our national bourgeoisie; they have mercilessly exploited our workers.

For these reasons, we, members of the provisional government, representing the whole Vietnamese people, declare that from now on we break off all relations of a colonial character with France; we repeal all the international obligation that France has so far subscribed to on behalf of Vietnam and we abolish all the special rights the French have unlawfully acquired in our fatherland.

The whole Vietnamese people, animated by a common purpose, are determined to fight to the bitter end against any attempt by the French colonialists to reconquer their country. . . .†

Anyone who has met Ho since that time is bound to view these lines with some surprise and to wonder what can have led so shrewd and self-controlled a man to give vent to his old bitterness at the very moment when he was about to take on the responsibilities of power. Paul Mus,‡ who knew him well, gives the following explanation: this first official act of international importance on the part of President Ho Chi Minh was, at the same time, the last revolutionary act on the part of the old outlaw Nguyen Ai Quoc—one might call it a legacy, the celebration for Ho of the transition from revolutionary to head of government.

Another episode at this stage demonstrated that a great

* The wording here is almost identical with that of Ho's speech at the Tours Congress.

† Marvin E. Gettleman (ed.), *Viet Nam: History, Documents, and Opinions on a Major World Crisis* (New York: Fawcett World Library, 1965), pp. 57–58.

‡ *Vietnam, sociologie d'une guerre,* p. 88.

deal still needed to be done to improve relations between France and the Vietminh. The French delegation in Calcutta had appointed two "Commissioners of the Republic:" one for the South, an official named Cédile; the other, Messmer, for the North. Both were parachuted into the country on August 22. But whereas the former reached Saigon without too much difficulty, the latter was captured by a Vietminh unit after landing on a mountainside near Thai Nguyen. He was treated roughly—imprisoned, chained and dragged from place to place. One of his companions, Dr. Brancourt, had a heart condition and died after taking some "medicine."

With Marmont, his wireless operator, Messmer managed to escape on October 18, while the villagers to whom they had been entrusted were busy celebrating the moon festival. Stumbling through the rice fields in the pitch dark, harassed by the alarm gong, they waded for ten hours before finally giving their pursuers the slip and reaching the Chinese, the lesser of two evils, in Bac Ninh. From there, Messmer made for Hanoi and conferred with Jean Sainteny, who in the meantime had been instructed to deputize for him. He was so exhausted that he asked Sainteny to take over officially and then returned to France by way of Saigon. Seven months later he came back to Indochina as leader of the delegation sent to negotiate with the Vietminh in Dalat.

Difficulties that began to accumulate did not encourage early moderation. The new masters in Hanoi were inclined to blame their French predecessors for all the problems they had to contend with in early September, especially the consequences of the terrible famine which had occurred in the winter of 1944–45.

On September 3, Ho persuaded his government to adopt a series of economic and financial measures aimed at softening the effects of the famine: a public subscription, fasting on every tenth day, a ban on distillation of liquor from rice and maize, orders for the intensive cultivation of food crops;

everywhere, production was to be stepped up to the maximum.

When considering the Vietminh's relations with France at this time, and the harsh regime which Ho and his ministers inflicted on their people, it must be remembered that jubilation at achieving political freedom was all but stifled by the horrors arising from that appalling famine. Two million dead, according to the Vietminh; four hundred thousand, according to French and Japanese sources. Whatever the figure, it was a terrifying ordeal which drove the revolutionary authorities to introduce fasting (the word itself has an oddly religious ring). But whether one speaks of "fasting" or "rationing," the situation was a tragic one and accounts for many of the excesses perpetrated then, and for the unrelieved austerity of the Vietminh government.

On November 25 the Central Committee laid down the following directives: "The main enemies of the Indochinese peoples are the French colonialist aggressors; therefore our efforts must be concentrated against them. The fundamental task of our people at present is to consolidate the power of the masses, combat the French colonialist aggressors, stamp out internal treachery and raise the general standard of living."

So the "main enemy" was no longer (for a very good reason) Nipponese fascism. Nor, as yet, was it Kuomintang militarism. It was "French colonialist aggression" again.

All the same, circumstances were about to compel Ho to reestablish contact with France. By now, General Leclerc's expeditionary force was well on its way to Saigon, where British forces had, pending its arrival, taken over from the Japanese. The hungry Chinese battalions led by General Lu Han were marching on Tonkin, and in their train they brought the Nationalist leaders whom the President had spent twenty years fighting in Kwangsi and Yunnan and with whom the settlement at Liuchow had achieved no more than a temporary reconciliation. In addition, various

anti-Communist organizations—the Dai Viet, for instance
—were undermining Ho's position in Vinh Yen and Phuc
Yen. France began to seem an inevitable and useful counterbalance to these developments.

But Ho and his cabinet were unwilling to confront De
Gaulle's representatives until they were sure of the goodwill
of the United States. The Soviet Union was too far away,
and in any case Ho was anxious not to turn to her for aid at
present—there would be plenty of time for him to acknowledge his real friends later. On August 26 an American mission of inquiry arrived and was given a welcome by the
Communists which was disconcertingly enthusiastic even by
the standards prevailing before the Cold War. As the American national anthem rang out that day, Vo Nguyen Giap
was observed saluting the Stars and Stripes with a clenched
fist.

The Vietminh leaders succeeded in establishing close, if
not deeply sincere, bonds with the United States representatives in Hanoi. They exploited to the full the anticolonialist
spirit which was then the basis of American thinking with
regard to Asian politics. Major Archimedes Patti, Captain
Farris and even General Gallagher were often to be
seen with Ho and his cabinet during the great Franco-
Vietnamese dispute, which was now imminent.*

The dispute has to be seen in its true historical perspective: the start of a general process of "decolonization," ex-
emplified by the Indonesian uprising, the approaching independence of India and the progress made by Chinese
Communism. The political climate is also an important
consideration. France was now ruled by a government
which had as its deputy premier Maurice Thorez, while
Mao Tse-tung was still confined in the northwestern provinces of China, thousands of miles from the Tonkinese
border. Finally, the strategic situation must be taken into

* See Chapter 12.

account. Four Yunnanese "armies" were fanning out on
Tonkinese soil, ostensibly to supervise the Japanese departure but in fact with the aim to settle there; and in the
meantime General Leclerc's expeditionary force, which had
already gained a footing in the south, was about to head
northward.

Let us now consider the pieces on the chessboard: first,
still nervously feeling its way, a Nationalist–Communist
government in Hanoi—bold measures had brought it to
power, but weak resources and a lack of trained men made
it a target for the militant hostility of rival organizations;
second, a French force advancing on Tonkin and preceded
by a political delegation representing a regime which had
fought against fascism and which contained several members who had long been friendly with Ho; third, a pillaging
Chinese horde let loose on Tonkin by a government which,
as everyone knew, was doomed to collapse before long, but
this horde had an appetite and a lack of discipline which
threatened to bring anarchy and ruin to northern Indochina. These were the fundamentals, summarized by Paul
Mus* as the "politico-military triangle" of 1946.

Now we must see how the problem was resolved by the
two men who were to remain the key figures throughout
these tense and crucial months—Sainteny and Ho Chi
Minh. To highlight them is not to minimize the part played
by such people as General Leclerc (whatever is said here
about Sainteny may equally well be applied to him) or
Admiral d'Argenlieu, or Moutet, or General Lu Han; but
each of these participants plays, with a greater or lesser
degree of freedom and talent, the part dictated by his status,
his situation, his past. On the other hand it was sheer determination and perspicacity which brought Sainteny, the
French nationalist, to a viewpoint which was in those days
stunningly new; while Ho Chi Minh, the Vietnamese Marx-

* *Vietnam, sociologie d'une guerre*, p. 74.

ist, resisted the temptation to play the romantic revolutionary and supported instead a middle-of-the-road solution
appropriate to the demands of the time. It should be noted
that in agreeing to talk terms with Sainteny, Ho was resisting those instincts that would prejudice him against a
man who was not only a son-in-law of Albert Sarraut, former
Governor General of Indochina and despite his compar-
atively liberal attitudes a favorite target of *Le Paria*, but
also a friend of Jean Laurent, director of the Bank of Indochina. The Vietminh leader was capable of looking beyond
this conservative background and recognizing Sainteny's
integrity—which is saying a great deal for Ho himself.

Sainteny, like Leclerc, had come from Paris with the
prime objective of reestablishing France's assets in Indochina. He considered that these assets had been weakened, if
not ruined, by Japan's triumphs, by Admiral Decoux's policy of collaboration and by the humiliation inflicted on
March 9, 1945. One such asset was armed strength. But as
soon as France's "prestige" was restored, this must be employed to secure negotiation, not domination. He had
quickly assessed France's resources in the Far East, the feelings of her allies, the terrain on which any war would have
to be fought and the strength of feeling behind the revolution. All these things warned him against plunging his
country into what he saw, even then, as a chancy under-
taking.

He realized he should avoid getting bogged down in any
situation, that he should leave himself a line of retreat and
accept the unavoidable while retaining his own freedom
of action. Some would accuse him of showing strategic
know-how rather than profound political thinking, pragmatism rather than liberalism. And why not? When strategy
is carried as far as this, accurately gauged necessity can be
equated with wisdom. What, after all, is the value of liberalism when it amounts to no more than an abstract distaste

for coercive methods? In politics, true moderation is knowing when exactly to draw the line between showing strength
and resorting to force.

Sainteny wanted Leclerc's tanks inside the Vietminh
capital so that he might secure recognition of France's
rights; at the same time, he was ready to acknowledge Vietnam's claim to independence. As we shall see, it was Leclerc
who first uttered the word independence, opening up
broader avenues for Sainteny and his two principal collaborators, Pignon and Salan, even before Paris had given
its blessing to this audacious step. And the general certainly
did not envisage granting independence to ghosts and pup-
pets—he cabled his contacts in Hanoi that the operation
would meet with no success unless he found a "real government" waiting to put its case to him. Sainteny and his team
believed that a political force strong enough to offer genuine
resistance was also strong enough to depend on. Hence they
chose the path of negotiating with the hard-core Vietminh
rather than doggedly trying to disunite the revolutionary
movement by encouraging the rivalries existing between
the pro-Chinese nationalists, the pro-Japanese elements, the
"progressives" and the Communists.

When Ho, on his side analyzed the situation, he took full
account of the Chinese threat and the opposition from the
more extreme Vietnamese nationalists; he considered the
pressure of public opinion, the people's strong thirst for
immediate emancipation; he weighed the military might of
General Leclerc's expeditionary force, the memory of
French colonial rule and of Chinese invasions over the
centuries; he realized that although the three-party coalition in Paris encouraged hopes of genuine Franco-Vietnamese cooperation, it was frail and ready to equivocate;
he assessed the opportunities for economic and technical
development which France could offer the new republic in

the light of underdeveloped China's and Russia's failure
(at this stage) to offer help. Past, present and future were
all pulling in different ways. The scales tipped back and
forth between idealistic passions and hard realities, between
old grudges and new longings. A choice had to be made.

In his continually illuminating *Vietnam, sociologie d'une
guerre,* Paul Mus quotes a remark which Ho is said to have
made at this time: "It is better to sniff the French dung for
a while than eat China's all our lives."* An observation
worthy of Henry IV of France, which might well serve as an
epigraph to the agreement of March 6, 1946. But is is difficult to regard the decision which Ho came to as mere
political opportunism.

It was not in vain that his political judgment had been
molded in France, that he owed his early grounding in
Marxism to Jean Longuet, Paul Vaillant-Couturier, Jules
Raveau and Jean Duret, or that Tours had been the setting
of one of the most important decisions in his life. Nor was
it any accident that he now secured the participation,
throughout the exchanges, of Caput, Bousquet and Babut,
a trio who—though on the left or even the extreme left—
still guaranteed that the voice of France should be heard,
sharp and clear, from beginning to end.

After enduring harsh ordeals since his early days in
France, after being a Comintern agent for three decades,
after studying and teaching, first in Moscow and later under
Borodin, after roaming Asia for twenty years under twenty
different names and experiencing the terrors and intrigues
of the Kuomintang, it was only natural that he should be
more intensely alive than ever to the things that bound
him—over and above his memories of colonialist oppression—to the French revolutionary tradition.

"Better to sniff the French dung for a while than . . ."
Yes, but there was more to it than that, as will emerge

* Paul Mus, *Vietnam, sociologie d'une guerre,* p. 85.

clearly from his dealings over a period of many months with
Sainteny, with Salan, with Leclerc, with French journalists,
and with the peasants of the Basque country. It was no
mere mood of resignation which impelled Ho to seek agreement with France, no mere computer-like assessment in
terms of "objective realities:" he was driven by a longing
to reunite two disjointed halves of his own life and training,
a schism which was reflected in the destiny of his people.
And he must have been conscious—why deny it?—of a
sense of fellowship as well.

But there is something else which must not be forgotten:
in attempting to achieve emancipation by friendly means,
the man who had once edited and managed *Le Paria* was
obviously mindful of the other French colonies. His anxiety
to avoid an irreparable rift with France was in part dictated
by the hope of establishing a precedent, acceptable to Paris,
which would sooner or later earn freedom for the Moroccans
and Madagascans and Senegalese, in whose aspirations and
resentments he had shared years ago. However intense his
patriotism, however strong his commitment to purely
Asian causes, it would be quite wrong to underestimate
Ho's more general aims and beliefs. The author of *Le
Procès de la colonisation française* was only too conscious
of the global character of the colonial problem; it was not
likely that he would forget, especially now, that events had
put him in a position of arguing with the French authorities on an equal footing.

Finally, it must be remembered that although his leadership might be unchallenged within the revolutionary
government, he had to deal with opposition on two sides.
On the right there were the nationalist groups, who were
as delighted as he himself was displeased to see the Chinese
armies advance toward Tonkin, and who did not hesitate
to shed blood in their efforts to destroy his regime. On the
left his policies were challenged by a powerful faction inside
the Tong Bo (the politburo of the Vietminh), made up of

the crippled Hoang Quoc Viet, broken by colonial oppression, who had good reason for his intransigently anti-French attitudes; Ho Tunk Mau, a member of the Chinese Communist Party for the past twenty years; and Tran Huy Lieu, a former nationalist militant who had now implanted his bigotry in the heart of the Vietminh. Not to mention the ex-Emperor Bao Dai—now Vinh Truy, senior adviser to the cabinet—who was ready to denounce the government for being too moderate, as a means of restoring his public image.

In late February 1946, only a few days before the agreements were signed, I saw much evidence of Ho's predicament. A series of interviews which I concluded with several of the protagonists, and finally with the President himself, made me realize the scale of the dilemma confronting him. Tran Huy Lieu was hard-eyed and stony-faced, with a face like old furrowed leather beneath a shock of tousled hair; he was taut with bitterness and rejection—all he could talk about were France's "crimes." Bao Dai, wearing a bored expression, told me how skeptical he was about any agreement with Paris. Vo Nguyen Giap, the President's right-hand man, did not quite rule out the possibility of a settlement but reminded me that the Vietnamese had the power to force France's hand and would not hesitate, under pressure, to carry out a scorched-earth policy. (The way he said it, nodding that round head with its huge brow! His eyes blazed, and his voice was like a slap in my face.)

Ho Chi Minh talked a different language, or at least took an entirely different tone. As far back as September 1945, in the first interviews with French journalists, it seemed that his desire to come to an understanding with France outweighed even his unshakable determination to secure recognition for Vietnamese independence.

He told the French newspaperman Jean-Michel Hertrich, "France and Vietnam were married a long time ago. The marriage has not always been a happy one, but we have nothing to gain from breaking it up. . . . France is a strange country. It is a breeding ground of admirable ideas, but when it travels, it does not export them. . . ."* And to another reporter, André Blanchet, he observed, "If Frenchmen were sent here in a spirit of peace, anyone who tried to molest them would do so over my dead body!"†

Early in January 1946, on the very day when highly organized general elections had given the Vietminh a ninety-seven per cent majority, he assured P. M. Dessinges, special correspondent of *Resistance:* "We feel no hatred whatever for France and the French people. Together we mustn't let other countries tell us what we ought and ought not to do—we must reach a private settlement together. But mark my words—if we are forced to fight, we are determined to fight to the end."

I didn't see him enter, I didn't even hear him. His sandals, like a mendicant monk's, seemed to glide over the shiny floor of the palace previously occupied by France's senior resident in Tonkin. "It was kind of you to come, monsieur." The voice was thin, with the suggestion of a lisp, and there was something in his tone which prevented him from sounding, as Vietnamese do, like the echo of a rally in a game of ping-pong. The accent was as close to a German one as to Chinese.

At that time I was steeped in the legend of the man, having attempted to read every word that had been written about him by journalists, detectives, hagiographers and propagandists. But even without that background, I would have been fascinated by the figure who had just come into the room. I had expected him to be taller and more bent, less calm and contented-looking. I was surprised that he

* *Tribune des Nations,* April 14, 1956.
† André Blanchet, *Au Pays des balillas jaunes,* p. 193.

was not more bitterly marked by his experiences—the years on the run, the long spells in jail.

The first thing that struck me, apart from his unexpected kind air, was the extraordinary glow in the eyes beneath his bushy brows, huge forehead and tuft of grey hair; it was so shaggy that he would have looked ridiculously like a circus "funny man" had it not been for the inviolable dignity of his features and bearing. The expression in those remarkable eyes would have invited the word "ingenuous," except that I knew things about him which precluded any possibility of thinking that.

I detected a touch of awkwardness in his courtesy and kindness. When he asked me to have a cup of tea, or drew up a chair for me or offered me a cigarette, it was as though he were making apologies for living among all the trappings of a colonial governor. Since then, people have assured me this awkwardness was an act, carefully studied and rehearsed, designed to make him seem just another poor Communist born on the wrong side of the track. But can mere artifice have produced such an engaging manner and extraordinary gift for making contact, a gift which at once brought a warm and direct exchange of views and gave a startlingly fresh ring to commonplace words?

How can I have retained so incomplete a memory of what was said that day? My recollection of our remarks is wholly overshadowed by that of his warm attentive gaze continually resting on me, though I was young, a stranger, a person of no consequence. Sitting sideways on the broad couch, with his feet positioned side by side, he talked in his unreal voice, the voice of an ironic ghost:

A race such as yours, which has given the world the literature of freedom, will always find us friends whatever it may do. If only you knew, monsieur, how passionately I reread Victor Hugo and Michelet year after year! There is no mistaking the tone of their writings: it is the tone of the ordi-

nary people in your country who are so curiously akin to the
ordinary people in ours. . . . So different, on the other hand,
from the Frenchmen who have misrepresented your country
here. . . . Ah, monsieur, colonialism must certainly be evil
if it has the power to transform men to such a degree!

His beard quivered, his hands moved eloquently, his
voice became shrill. But suddenly he checked himself, for
fear of embarking on a diatribe which might give offense to
his guest. An odd smile came over his face and drew the large
cheekbones up toward the sparkling eyes, which—for the
moment—really had lost their ingenuous look. His puck-
ered smile, affording the sudden revelation of a sorry-look-
ing row of teeth, made me sense that there were limits to
the man's charm. But this fleeting approximation of the
manner of a Chinese pimp was quickly erased, and once
more I was treated to the disarming gaze of a Franciscan
Gandhi.

In his threadbare, sand-colored tunic, reminiscent of Sun
Yat-sen's and at the same time of those old-fashioned uni-
forms still occasionally worn by ancient ex-colonials living
on their pensions in little harbor towns along the Provençal
coast, Ho looked like a venerable mandarin of old Annam
who had chosen to be reincarnated in a revolutionary's
attire.

In response to some remark of mine about France's role
in Tonkin, he said sharply, "But we are no longer living in
the days of *les papillons noirs*. . . ."* Was this artless rejoinder premeditated or was it a mental lapse, a phrase
picked up at evening class? Without pausing for breath,
he gravely summed up the nature and purpose of the Vietminh, depicting it as a simple, nationalistic, democratic

---

* *Les pavillons noirs* (black flags) meant "pirates" to the French, and
"patriots" to the Vietnamese, who resisted French colonialization at the
end of the nineteenth century. Ho's expression here means "black butter-
flies," and figuratively "gloomy thoughts."

front in which his Communist friends did not play a predominant role, even though they were the majority group.
I might almost have imagined that I was listening to some
astute radical explaining away an electoral alliance or a
parliamentary coalition designed to secure the adoption of
a budget vote.

But his skill in presenting himself as a moderate was
exceeded by his ability to sidestep questions when he felt
them to be awkward or premature. In these closing days of
February 1946 the negotiations between himself and
Sainteny had entered their final phase. But when I tried to
draw him out on the subject, he parried repeatedly, slipping
in a word of praise for General de Gaulle, recalling Paris in
the early twenties, alluding to André Malraux, questioning
me about the French press. "There is a chance we may
reach a settlement," he said finally, with a smile, "M.
Sainteny is such a likable man. . . ."

That was all I could get out of him. But like a good many
others, some of them less well disposed toward him, I was
spellbound.

And indeed, a settlement was in sight. Léon Pignon,
Sainteny's immediate subordinate, and General Alessandri,
commander of the French forces in the north, had established first official contact with Ho on September 28.

The Vietminh leader was affable, but promised nothing.
And when his visitors, venturing to the heart of the problem, reminded him of the memorandum which the "Vietminh League" had sent to Kunming in July, calling for
independence in "a minimum of five and a maximum of ten
years," Ho stared at them in surprise. He said he had no
recollection of the episode. Plainly, the provisional government now securely installed in Hanoi no longer stood by the
terms proposed by its members when they were still
struggling revolutionaries. But this did not deter the two
Frenchmen from cabling Chandernagor, France's head-

quarters in Asia, that Ho had impressed them as being a "sound and honorable" man.

Negotiations got under way as soon as Ho and Sainteny met on October 15. On a personal level, all went well. In his *Histoire d'une paix manquée,* Sainteny writes:

> From my first dealings with Ho Chi Minh I derived the impression that this ascetic man, whose face reflected a mixture of intelligence, guile and subtlety, was a person of the highest caliber. . . . His intelligence, vast culture, unbelievable energy and total unselfishness had earned him unparalleled prestige and popularity in the eyes of his people. His talk, his deeds, his bearing—everything about him served to convince one that a solution by force of arms was repugnant to him. There can be no doubt that he had aspirations, throughout this period, of becoming the Gandhi of Indochina.*

But both men had a long way to go. Especially because they began from such different starting points. In the eyes of Ho Chi Minh, independence had existed since September; a government was in office; real negotiation was impossible until these basic facts had been acknowledged. But for Jean Sainteny, lawful establishment of any new regime could stem only from the recognition of France's sovereignty and of her rights over Indochina.

Furthermore, progress toward agreement was being slowed down by internal conflicts on both sides. Ho, as already stated, had to reckon with nationalist opposition and the intransigence of his colleagues within the Tong Bo. Sainteny, himself, had been convinced from the early summer of 1945 that there was no question of France's reasserting her old authority by force of arms. A visit to Marshal Juin in Paris, at the beginning of August had been determinative. "We would need three hundred thousand

* Sainteny, *op. cit.,* pp. 164–66.

men," he told the Chief of Staff, who merely shrugged his shoulders. "So we shall have to negotiate?" he persisted. Juin did not say a word.

Sainteny was aware that even if he had been promised three hundred thousand men there was no means of transporting them. France no longer had the military resources, still less the maritime resources, to conduct a strong-arm policy in Asia. The United States, which was opposed to such a policy, had the power to block her initiative and, if need be, meet force with force. And then there was the newly reassembled China. Decidedly, France's presence in Indochina would have to take a new form.

All this was obvious to Sainteny, but what of his team? It was a strange mixture of elements. On the one hand there were a number of former colonial administrators, highly experienced and able but patently biased against the Vietminh; some of them tended to think that the "revolution" which had brought it to power was a nine-days' wonder. On the other hand, there were the young officers in the special services, more warmly disposed toward the Vietminh, whose youthfulness and courage impressed them deeply.

Then again, Sainteny had somehow to win acceptance of his views from the High Commissioner, Thierry d'Argenlieu—who thought solely in terms of "the grandeur of France," yet did not rule out the use of methods liable to tarnish his purpose beyond redemption—and from the Paris government, where the admiral found constant support until the departure of General de Gaulle on January 20, 1946. True, once the general had been replaced by Felix Gouin, and Soustelle (Minister for Overseas Territories) by Moutet, things became somewhat easier for the "liberal" group.

As we have seen, Sainteny's view was shared by the commander of the expeditionary force, General Leclerc. The latter had followed the same line of reasoning: he was aware that any military effort by France at this time would be subject to strict limitations, and he had related the problem to its Asiatic context. An inclination to act as a soldier had been curbed by his highly intelligent adviser: Colonel Repiton, his head of intelligence, and Paul Mus, an internationally renowned expert in Asian sociology, both of whom had made him realize the strength of the nationalist movement and the likelihood of its attracting support in the area.

Leclerc saw the objectives as follows: first, he must reestablish French military presence at various strategic points, so that a political solution could be worked out from a position of reasonable strength; second, the Chinese must be evicted from northern Indochina, which they were preparing to appropriate; third, in consultation with a local government having real authority over the area, a privileged relationship must be defined and established between the new state and France. This must be done quickly, for the peaceful landing which he hoped to effect in Tonkin could only be carried out, because of tides, in late February or early March.

On February 13 Admiral d'Argenlieu left Saigon for Paris, apparently to advocate an entirely different policy: France would come to terms with the local dignitaries and eventually restore the monarchy. The very next day, General Leclerc—who was the acting high commissioner—sent a cable to his government, stating that a settlement with the Vietminh was a matter of urgency and that to obtain it they must be prepared to voice the word "independence" without further delay. Immediately afterward he told Sainteny, who was in Saigon on official business, that the business should be brought to a conclusion as swiftly as possible.

But the talks in Hanoi were making slow progress. They were conducted in Chinese fashion, with mediators attending and contributing. Whenever he saw fit, and especially if a deadlock seemed imminent, Ho would draw on the

services of Caput, an old Socialist militant; Babut, a friend
of long standing; Bousquet, a one-time associate of Abel
Bonnard* and later a Communist; and on occasion even a
certain Soloviev.†

There were two main stumbling blocks. The first was
how to define and delimit the *doc lap* proclaimed in Hanoi
on September 2, some six months after a similar proclamation in Hué. Some translated it as "freedom," others as "independence"—Ho and his colleagues clearly favoring the
second interpretation.‡ The second stumbling block concerned the adjustment of Vietnam's new sovereignty to
allow some form of French overlordship. Sainteny claimed
that the solution to the problem lay in her joining the newly
formed French Union and the Indochinese Federation,§
which was then being established.

On February 16, 1946, Ho informed Sainteny that he was
ready to negotiate on the basis of membership of the French

---

* He was Minister of National Education under Marshal Pétain. Though
condemned to death by the Resistance, he was not executed.

† This extraordinary figure is a fairly apt symbol of the political climate
then prevailing in Hanoi. After serving as an officer in the White Russian
army, he had crossed China on foot and taken refuge in Japan. Later he
joined the Foreign Legion in Tonkin and went back to Russia with the
last military mission attached to Admiral Kolchak. Then he went to
France and qualified as an agronomist. As a naturalized Frenchman, he
returned to Indochina and settled in Hanoi.

In 1941 the intelligence service run by Admiral Decoux's Vichy-con-
trolled administration sent him on a curious mission to the Soviet embassy
in Chungking. He was entrusted with the task of negotiating a secret trade
agreement with Moscow under which Indochina would supply rubber,
the U.S.S.R. war materials. He is said to have been warmly received by
the Soviet ambassador only a few days before the Germans launched their
attack on Russia on June 22. At the next meeting, on June 23 or 24, the
ambassador is alleged to have told him, not without sorrow, that his country was no longer in any position to sell war materials; in fact she must
buy all she could, at no matter what price.

‡ Linguistically, they were certainly right. *Doc lap* means "to stand
alone."

§ The French Union was an association of Metropolitan France and its
overseas territories, loosely analogous to the British Commonwealth. The
Indochinese Federation included the states of Vietnam, Laos and Cambodia.

Union; but he made no mention of the federation, nor did he abandon the demand for independence. Sainteny passed the news on to Leclerc, who urged Paris to accept. The Gouin government eventually replied that France was prepared to recognize an autonomous Vietnamese government on two conditions: first, it must afford a friendly welcome to the French armed forces when they arrived to take over from the Chinese; second, Cochin China (Nam Bo)—to which Hanoi had staked a claim—must be free to determine its own future by referendum.

The conditions for a settlement were almost realized. But to avoid taking all the responsibility on his own shoulders, Ho made drastic changes in the composition of the cabinet, bringing in the Nationalists. The very next day, February 26, a communiqué issued by the Vietminh announced:

> President Ho Chi Minh has met with M. Sainteny, the official representative of France, concerning the possibility of opening official negotiations between Vietnam and France. The President again emphasized that Vietnamese policy is one of "independence and cooperation." M. Sainteny stated that France agreed to recognize Vietnam's right to have her own government, army and treasury within the French Union.

The way seemed open at last.

However, the Chinese still had to be persuaded to withdraw. Efforts to this end were being made by Achille Clarac, Admiral d'Argenlieu's diplomatic adviser, in association with Meyrier, France's ambassador in Chungking. Officially the matter was concluded on February 28, when the Chungking government agreed to recognize French sovereignty over Indochina and the right of French forces to take over from the Kuomintang by March 31, in return for France's abandoning her concessions in Shanghai, Canton, Tientsin

and Hangchow, and giving up her lease of Kwangchowan.*
But suddenly the Chinese military authorities found they
could not make any such agreement without General Doug-
las MacArthur's consent or without first coming to terms
with the Vietnamese.

On March 2, 1946, the National Assembly, holding its
first session in Hanoi, voted in support of a new coalition
government headed by Ho Chi Minh and called the *Union
des Forces*. His aging pro-Chinese rival, Nguyen Hai Than,
became deputy premier, while the two anti-Communist
leaders, Nguyen Tuong Tam and Vu Hong Khanh, were
given the ministries of foreign affairs and defense. Eighty
deputies belonging to the Viet Nam Quoc Dan Dang and
other ultra-nationalist parties now had seats in the assembly,
although they had taken no part in the January elections.

Ho completed his strategy by approaching the Vatican. In
those days the Holy See was represented by an apostolic
delegation accommodated in the old imperial capital, Hué.
Nguyen Manh Ha was due there in early March; he was to
study the problem of conveying rice from the south to the
north. The President handed him a letter of introduction to
Monsignor Drapier and gave him verbal instructions to
sound the prelate as to the possibility of his paying a visit
to Hanoi and even taking up residence in the north.

Ho clearly thought such a gesture would make a good
impression on the pious High Commissioner, Admiral
d'Argenlieu, and on the M.R.P. members of the French government, while encouraging fuller cooperation from the
Catholics at home. But Monsignor Drapier, whose views
were openly monarchist, turned the suggestion down, saying it was contrary to the interests of security.

Uncle Ho has the knack of turning setbacks to advantage
and employing them as weapons against his present
enemies. "How can I commit myself when the opposition

* *Renamed Chankiang by Communist China.*—Ed.

prevents me? I have to take all trends and pressures into
account. . . ." Ho's attitude hardened; he clung to his demand for Cochin China and refused to have anything to do
with the Indochinese Federation. The whole future of the
talks was in jeopardy.

On March 4 it was learned in Hanoi that the French
convoy carrying General Leclerc and his troops was on its
way to Haiphong. The Chinese took fright and urged the
Vietnamese to adopt a more moderate line.

Next day, March 5, 1946, the Central Committee of the
Vietminh met at Huong Canh, on the outskirts of Hanoi,
and ruled as follows:

> At this juncture, the best way of insuring the country's
> salvation is not to burn bridges but to preserve peace. The
> Vietminh resists two misguided inclinations: (a) to wage
> war, whatever the cost, and (b) to imagine that difficulties
> will be over once an agreement has been signed with France.
> It puts people on their guard against the threat of provoca-
> tions by Chiang Kai-shek's troops and by the local reac-
> tionaries.*

That night Ho, Sainteny and Pignon met for a long discussion. The Vietminh leader conceded that *doc lap* might
legitimately be construed as "freedom," and that he did not
entirely rule out the possibility of Vietnam's joining the
Indochinese Federation. But Cochin China must automatically be incorporated in the new state. Exhausted by
futile attempts to make Ho cede this point, the Frenchmen
eventually gave up and left at about midnight, advising
him to think the matter over carefully. The French fleet
was already in the Gulf of Tonkin.

Hanoi was in a state of fever, and I shall never forget the
hours I spent there that night. War seemed likely. French
people attempting to buy firearms from the Chinese mer-

* *Grandes Dates du parti de la classe ouvrière du Vietnam*, p. 56.

chants found the price had risen to a prohibitive level.
Among European families there was talk of a wholesale
massacre. The French garrison, confined to the citadel ever
since the Japanese coup, was preparing for the worst.

At dawn on March 6, however, one of Ho's colleagues
roused Sainteny and told him, "The President is ready to
accept your conditions." (Alarmed at the prospect of an
immediate French landing, General Chow of the Chinese
Army had just brusquely advised Ho to "come to an understanding with the French.") It was decided by mutual agreement that the papers should be signed that afternoon. Yet
this late settlement was very nearly destroyed by events in
Haiphong. As they sailed into the harbor, the first French
ships were fired on by the Chinese, whose commander, General Gaston Wang, claimed he had not been informed of
the Sino-French agreement. Only after the loss of twenty-
four lives did General Valluy order his men to shoot back;
in doing so, they destroyed the munitions which the Kuomintang generals had planned to appropriate as war booty.

When Ho and Sainteny held their final meeting at noon
to put the finishing touches to the text of the agreement, the
President made no allusion to this incident in Haiphong.
His mind was made up, and he had realized the resolution
of the French. They arranged to meet again at 4:30 P.M.
For Sainteny, Pignon and General Salan (the new commander of the French forces in northern Indochina, who
had participated in the final phase of the negotiations with
both the Vietnamese and the Chinese) these were hours of
grim suspense; they had to keep a sharp eye on developments in Haiphong. Fortunately the shooting stopped
shortly after midday.

The handful of journalists present in Hanoi sensed that
the end was near. As they strolled between the Hotel Metro-
pole and the building which housed the head of government, they suddenly saw trayloads of champagne being
taken into the paymaster general's villa, where Ho was liv-

ing. The journalists hurried inside but arrived too late to witness the initialing ceremony, which had been conducted in the presence of American, Chinese and British observers and, at Ho's insistence, of Louis Caput, the French Socialist.

Now everyone posed for the official photographer. Ho stood dwarfed between Sainteny, on one side, and Pignon and Salan, on the other. The Vietminh leader had been assisted by his senior foreign affairs adviser, Hoang Minh Giam, by the nominal chief of the Vietnamese diplomatic service, Nguyen Tuong Tam and by Vu Hong Khanh, leader of the V.N.Q.D.D., or Vietnamese Nationalist Party. This last figure, whose hostility to France was well known, countersigned the agreement as a guarantor.

The document stipulated that France "recognize the Republic of Vietnam as a free state having its own government, its own parliament and its own finances, and forming part of the Indochinese Federation and the French Union." As for the future of Cochin China, the French vowed to honor the wishes of the local people, as expressed by referendum. The government of Vietnam declared that it was ready to "give a friendly welcome to the French army when, in conformity with international agreements, it relieves the Chinese army." Finally it was agreed that "frank and friendly" negotiations should be opened, concerning the future status of Indochina and of French interests in Vietnam.*

Jean Sainteny relates how, when he turned to Ho and told him of his satisfaction that armed conflict had been avoided, he met with the answer: "I'm not so pleased, for really it is you who have benefited; you know perfectly well I wanted more than this. . . . Still, I realize one can't have everything overnight." With which sentiment, he embraced

---

* This text was complemented shortly afterward by a military agreement concerning the cessation of hostilities, signed by General Salan and Vo Nguyen Giap. A joint declaration by Ho and Sainteny was pasted on walls all over Hanoi, announcing the imminent arrival of the French expeditionary force.

Sainteny and Pignon and said, "Friendship is my one con-
solation." These exchanges were strongly indicative of how
relations between the two countries were likely to develop.

Ho feared disappointment or bitterness at his compro-
mises among the opposition and a good many of his own
militants. Could this have been avoided? Paul Mus asks the
question in cogent terms. Would it not, he asks, have been
to Ho's advantage to "stay in the background and let [the
French] hang themselves on Chinese cord?" In support of
this theory, he quotes the remark addressed to him by one
of the French negotiators: "Circumstances have given the
Hanoi government a pistol loaded with one bullet. To
permit the presence of Leclerc and his army was to fire in
the air and remain empty-handed. . . . What would they
have lost by biding their time?" To which the author of
Vietnam, sociologie d'une guerre replies, "Perhaps everything. By coming to terms with us, Ho wanted to provide
against a Franco-Chinese deal on the basis of the agreements
which had just been signed in Chungking, and which did
not even refer to the Hanoi government. A local deal
between Leclerc and General Lu Han? Caught between
the jaws of such a vise, the Vietminh would have been
smashed. . . ."

The initial reaction of the people of Hanoi to the Franco-
Vietnamese agreement was so cold and suspicious that Vietminh headquarters decided to put all their cards on the
table. They invited everyone to assemble the following day,
March 7, and hear what the leaders had to say. Whatever
may be one's ultimate view of Ho and his colleagues, it is
impossible not to be impressed by this anxiety to explain
to the masses and to act in harmony with them. The mixture of conviction and technique makes one think of Lenin.

The scene in the huge Place du Théâtre, however, was
more reminiscent of *Julius Caesar*. Furious outcries and
dark rumors of assassination flew among the enormous,
overexcited crowd. One by one, the leaders of the govern-

ment came out on the theater balcony. When Giap, the veteran warrior, appeared and raised his fist in salute, a menacing silence came over the gathering. Borne by the loudspeakers, the voice of the little war leader rolled like thunder: ". . . We decided to negotiate as a means of creating conditions favorable to the struggle for complete independence. . . . In 1918 the USSR signed a treaty at Brest-Litovsk in order to halt the German invasion and gain time, under cover of truce, to strengthen her army and her political power. Did she not become very powerful as a result of that treaty?"

A friend and I exchanged glances; the words seemed unbelievably cynical. And yet they were right on target. The crowd was brought to heel. Now it must be stirred, fired—and at this point the old leader made his appearance. Standing there, slightly stooped, in that shabby old tunic, with his tuft of gray hair ruffling in the breeze, he looked frail and paltry beside the giant red flag with the gold star. Our ears still rang with the charges that had been leveled at him in the streets of Hanoi for the past twenty-four hours (he was a traitor, a puppet, a hostage, a Communist who had sold his country into the hands of his French comrades), so we were completely taken aback by the tremendous ovation which now rose to greet him. He thrust both hands toward the crowd, as though to ward off this wave of enthusiasm, and then began to speak in his rather harsh voice: "It testifies to our intelligence that we should negotiate rather than fight. Why sacrifice fifty or a hundred thousand men when we can achieve independence through negotiation, perhaps within five years?" He concluded with the remarks: "I, Ho Chi Minh, have always led you along the path to freedom; I have spent my whole life fighting for our country's independence. You know I would sooner die than betray the nation. I swear I have not betrayed you!" We were too far from the balcony to see the tears flow down his cheeks, but we could hear them in his voice. The impact on the crowd was extraordinary and popular acceptance of the agreement was won then and there.

Simultaneously, the party machine was defining the new line. For the trained, hard-core elements, the directives issued by the Tong Bo that same day were the counterpart of what had been said to the crowd in the Place du Théâtre.

> The struggle in which our nation is engaged is now linked with that of the French nation, just as it was previously linked with that of the Chinese nation. . . . Our main enemy is the French reactionary element. . . . We must collaborate unreservedly with those Frenchmen who are sincerely democratic . . . and achieve, insofar as is possible, a Franco-Vietnamese democratic front.*

This could scarcely be imparted to the masses yet.

The Vietminh's efforts to carry out this program met with strong opposition, and most of it was inspired by the government's so-called "senior adviser," Vinh Thuy or Bao Dai, who had obstinately refused to join in the negotiations with Sainteny, even though he had known the Frenchman well for many years. He thought it intolerable that France had negotiated with these "Reds" rather than with him. He was not content with simply boycotting the talks; as soon as the agreements were signed, he decamped and took up residence in Hong Kong.

Bao Dai was soon leading a gayer life there than in Hanoi. The gossip columnists discussed his private life. A few months after his departure he received a rather curious letter from Ho which said, "Do not forget that you symbolize Vietnam and its history. Let your life be worthy of the name you bear, of the land we share, and of the independence we have acquired at long last. . . ." It was as though Robespierre were writing to a Louis XVI who had avoided arrest in Varennes and inherited the tastes of Louis XV.

---

* Devillers, *op. cit.*, p. 231.

But in March 1946 there were two bigger problems: the return of General Leclerc's forces, which might give rise to incidents, and the "frank and friendly" negotiations which were to define all that had been left vague by the agreement of March 6: the future of Cochin China, the composition of the French Union.

Only a fortnight earlier, there had been much talk of exterminating the French troops if ever they set foot in the Tonkinese capital. Now they arrived quite peacefully, and the former commander of the Second Armored Division was well received by the Indochinese Communist leaders. Happy outcomes such as these defy prediction based on political analysis. True, the crowd which feted Leclerc on March 18 was made up of those Frenchmen who for a whole year had been living lives of painful insecurity; but the Vietnamese behaved impeccably amid these wild celebrations. They did not demonstrate against the sudden influx of French tanks and armored cars—and indeed these were decked with the crossed flags of France and Vietnam.

General Leclerc, however, could not keep from frowning and muttering at the terms in which Vo Nguyen Giap welcomed him to Haiphong: "As a Vietnamese resistance fighter, I salute you as a great French resistance fighter. . . ." But he certainly had a broad smile on his face at 5 P.M. next day (March 18) when I saw him charge up the steps of Ho's villa, clasp the hand of his host and exclaim in his deep, hoarse voice: "Well, *monsieur le Président,* so we meet as friends?" A few minutes later this traditionalist, nationalist and intransigent Gaullist seemed almost to shock Sainteny by the zest with which he laughed, over the champagne, at some retort by the old Communist leader. And for the second time he called out at the top of his voice: "Long live France and Vietnam within the French Union!" In the next room Giap, spellbound, stood mumbling to us: "Now we must forge ahead. . . ." True, the remark was open to more than one interpretation; but at the time it sounded like a promise to work as partners.

The encounter passed off so pleasantly that a few days later President Ho observed to my colleague P. M. Dessinges: "Leclerc? He is a loyal, upright man—a *chic type*, as you say in French. If only one could always talk things over with men like that."* Meanwhile the general, as concrete evidence of his good will, stipulated that two-thirds of the platoon acting as his personal escort should be fighting men of the Vietminh, who, for this purpose, would have to be supplied with new weapons.

Nobody needed to be reminded that Admiral d'Argenlieu, in Saigon, took a thoroughly unfavorable view of the line taken by Sainteny and Leclerc. Strangely cut off from the north, he was impervious to its problems.

It is said that in the course of a stormy interview with the commander-in-chief, the admiral even went so far as to compared what had happened in Hanoi with Munich.† But there was nothing to be gained from being hostile to an agreement which had been favorably received in Paris and the rest of the world‡ and which brought a conspicuous sense of relief to the people of South Vietnam. The high commissioner expressed his satisfaction with this "sound treaty" and decided to hold a formal meeting with Ho as a means of showing acceptance. Reluctant to venture into the lair of so recent an enemy or to receive him in Saigon, the admiral suggested that the meeting should take place aboard the cruiser *Emile Bertin,* in the wonderful setting of Along Bay.

On March 24 Sainteny took Ho on his seaplane to the

---

* *Paris-Saigon,* March 31, 1946.

† Subsequently, in conversation with (among others) Mendès-France and Sainteny, the admiral denied talking to Leclerc in such a way. But several witnesses testify to the authenticity of the remark.

‡ Compare the British, American and Indian press of March 7–8, 1946.

meeting with the High Commissioner. The two men were
photographed at the time of the flight. The President wears
a sidelong look beneath his sun helmet; his lips are set tight,
his hands clenched on the bamboo walking stick. He is not
the same person who so cheerfully entertained Leclerc; he
has become the stock character of old-fashioned Hollywood
films—the Oriental conspirator hatching some intricate
plot. Yet those who witnessed the meeting—including
Sainteny himself—report that the initial exchanges between
the revolutionary and the admiral were courteous, almost
cordial. They were observed holding private discussions
on the foredeck, for long periods at a time. But it was
through the intercession of Leclerc and Sainteny that Ho
obtained his wish: the "frank and friendly" negotiations
provided for in the agreement of March 6 which were to be
held in Paris.

In acceding to this request, the French were counting on
the magic power of the capital to rekindle the old leader's
memories and fire the dreams of his young companions.
Surely the visitors would sense how much was to be gained
from preserving their links with France? Thus on April 16,
a Vietnamese parliamentary group was given quite a warm
welcome on arrival in France.

Meanwhile a preliminary conference opened in Dalat,
the hill station in the south. Its purpose was to begin to
define future relations between the two countries, for it
was obvious that these could be founded neither on the
outburst of bitterness of September 2, 1945 nor on the warm
embraces of March 18, 1946. The talks were conducted in
the tiny, austere hall of the Yersin lycée, and later in the
elegant rooms of the Lang Bian Palace. But the two delega-
tions—headed respectively by Vo Nguyen Giap and Pierre
Messmer—were unable to achieve anything more than a
"cordial disagreement," as Giap subsequently described it.

The disagreement may have been cordial, but it was deep
on two fundamental points. The first was the nature of the

formal link between the two countries. Ho and his colleagues had regarded the statement of March 6 ("a free
state within the Indochinese Federation and the French
Union") as a promise of equal association, between sovereign countries, whereas most of France's representatives
took the view that by signing the Hanoi agreement the new
state had incorporated itself—at the Indochinese federal
level—in a pyramid buttressed from base to tip by the
French Republic.

The second source of misunderstanding was more dramatic. It concerned Cochin China. For the Vietminh, the
referendum agreed to on March 6 was a mere formality,
since "the masses" were obviously in favor of being absorbed
into an undivided, independent state. The French, on the
other hand, regarded Cochin China as a surety which would
guarantee the autonomy of the south, if nothing else. Moreover, it was legally a French territory and could not be
"ceded" without the approval of parliament.

It was this question of Nam Bo (Cochin China) which led
Giap to spark the only serious incident at the conference.
The pathetic picture he painted of the possible sufferings
of people in the south at the hands of the French army laid
him open to some tart rejoinders, especially from Messmer,
concerning the atrocities perpetrated in Saigon in September 1945, and the fate which might yet befall the French
in Hanoi under the administration in which he served as
Minister of the Interior.

Before the two sides went their separate ways, I had the
opportunity to ask Giap and Messmer for their verdicts. It
was clear that the spirit of reconciliation which had prevailed in March—the near-miracle worked by Ho, Leclerc
and Sainteny—was now a thing of the past. But there endured a rationally based desire to settle differences; the
discussions had brought to light as many mutual needs as
points of friction. And when I appeared to cast doubts on
Giap's confidence in a lasting settlement, reminding him of

his reference to the Treaty of Brest-Litovsk at the rally on March 7, he seemed amazed and annoyed that I should still remember it and did his best to persuade me that arguments put forward at a rally could not possibly be binding for a cabinet minister.

The negotiations proper were due to be held in France. The Vietnamese delegation would not be headed by Ho, but by Pham Van Dong. The President was to travel to Europe with his colleagues, however, on a good-will mission aimed at achieving the right psychological effect. He hoped that his Parisian friendships, the memories of the left-wing militants and also his personal charm would help create a favorable climate for the negotiations; and if his own team's enthusiasm for a settlement needed stimulating, he wanted to be there to stimulate it.

On the eve of departure, however, he met with a discouraging experience. Georges Bidault had entrusted the leadership of the French delegation to his friend Max André, an influential figure in the M.R.P. (*Mouvement Républicain Populaire*). André came out to Hanoi on a mission, and Nguyen Manh Ha—an ex-minister in Ho's government and a Catholic like André—held a reception at which visitor and President could meet. Ho was unimpressed. "What is his background?" he asked his host, after André had left. He was told that he used to be a bank clerk. "I'm not surprised," said Ho. "We certainly won't get far with people like that!"

8

THE
VISITOR

On May 30, 1946, Ho boarded the plane for Paris. He was muffled up in a brown tunic because of the rain. At his side was General Salan, one of the authors of the agreement; the general's presence was regarded as a shrewd reminder of the spirit of March 6.

On the evening of June 1 the plane flew over Damascus. It was then the President learned, by radio, that the Republic of Cochin China had been proclaimed in Saigon, on Admiral d'Argenlieu's instructions, as "a free state having its own government, its own parliament, its own army and its own finances, forming part of the Indochinese Federation and the French Union"—the exact phrasing Ho had finally managed to secure for the whole of Vietnam on

March 6. True, it was stipulated that Cochin China's status was defined as "subject to the referendum provided for in the covenant of March 6," but the desire for a fait accompli which would determine the future of Nam Bo (Cochin China) was so obvious that the Vietminh leader felt completely stunned and bewildered—especially because the move had been made the very day after his departure and constituted a challenge which might cause his deputies in Hanoi to react with violence.

When he then learned that his plane had been diverted from Paris to Biarritz and that he would be obliged to remain there until a new French government had been formed (following the elections of June 2), he began to wonder whether some sort of trap had not been laid for him, whether the March agreement had not been merely a diversionary tactic on the part of the French, whether in short he had not been duped.

To Jean Sainteny, who came to welcome him at Biarritz airport, he confided bitterly that he could no longer see any point in staying in France, that the time for negotiating was past and that the only thing he could do was fly straight back. He seemed more crestfallen than angry, and his confusion was obvious. Sainteny soothed his feelings, assuring him that Admiral d'Argenlieu's measure was purely temporary, that the referendum would take place without question and that the High Commissioner's hand had been forced by an express demand from certain circles in Cochin China—whether those groups were representative or not, would be shown by the way people voted.

So Ho moved into the Hotel du Palais. Within a few days he had recovered his equanimity, developed a liking for the Basque country and fallen into the manner of a carefree vacationer, gossiping with the fishermen and peasants. ("The soil is good here. Where I come from it is even better, but there are so many mouths to feed. . . .") He went on a few sea trips and visited Lourdes. And when Charles Tillon, Air Minister and at that time a highly influential member of the French Communist Party, arrived to investigate the circumstances in which he was being "penned up" in a "second-class hotel, undergoing repair," Ho replied with a smile that he had experienced worse ordeals than living in such a sumptuous hotel.

On June 22, Ho and Sainteny finally left Biarritz for Paris, where a new government had been formed under the premiership of Georges Bidault, leader of the M.R.P. Sainteny writes:

> By four o'clock we were flying over Paris. The landing field at Le Bourget was black with people. The French government was represented by Marius Moutet, Minister for Overseas Territories, and he had a host of civil and military dignitaries with him. Above the airport building, the French and Vietnamese colors fluttered together. I looked at my guest. All the blood had gone from his face. His eyes shone, and he was so tight in the throat that although he obviously wanted to say something to me he could not get the words out. When the plane came to rest on the runway, he clutched my shoulder hard. "Whatever you do, don't leave me," he said. "There are so many people here!"

The other side of the picture is given by Jacques Dumaine,* head of protocol:

> The landing at Le Bourget was full of diplomatic risks. . . . We all heaved a sigh of relief when the new head of state was safe inside his car, with sixteen motorcycle police around him. All kinds of serious incidents might have occurred. It was obvious that Ho Chi Minh was playing the role of Gandhi—and moreover seemed to be practicing the deceit with some sincerity. Did he genuinely want a settlement or was he merely playing for time? His most hotheaded support came from Vietnamese living in France. They were

* *Quai d'Orsay*, p. 97.

unaware of the local difficulties and of Ho's powerlessness to govern Tonkin. . . . Moreover, their activities were being surreptitiously managed by the French Communist Party. Nothing seemed to bode well for the visit. . . ."

Among those who turned out to welcome him was Paul Rivet, the Socialist deputy, director of the Musée de l'Homme and ardent anticolonialist, renowned as a champion of the Vietnamese cause. The two men embraced. "Comrade greets comrade," said Rivet. Ho pointed out that they did not subscribe to the same Internationals; but this did not prevent him from telling Rivet shortly afterward: "With men like you, I would make peace at once," or from spending more of his time in Paris with left-wing members of the Workers' International than with the leaders of the Communist Party. To Jean Rous, one of the most influential among them, he even went so far as to say, "I get along better with you than with them." (But Rous points out with a smile that both of them were aware, without commenting on it, that the words contained something of that "pious fraudulence" which Nietzsche attributed to the saints.)

Ho stayed at the Royal-Monceau. He turned it into a kind of embassy and received a regular flow of callers. One day it would be the Algerian guerrilla leader, Ferhat Abbas—he still had the same preoccupation with securing worldwide emancipation of the colonial peoples—the next it would be David Ben-Gurion, who at that time was merely head of the Jewish Agency, or Paul Bernard, director of the Bank of Indochina.

Not all these visitors called to pay homage, however. An interesting document has survived, revealing the state of mind of some of the Vietnamese immigrants referred to by Jacques Dumaine: the text of an "Open Letter to Comrade Nguyen Ai Quoc," which had a great emotional impact on the one-time editor of *Le Paria*. The signatories declared:

We are the remnants of the handful of men trained by you in 1925. Your ideas made a deep impression on us. . . . We saw you as the symbol of all the young workers in Vietnam. . . .

Little did we suspect that we should have to renounce all hope after March 8.* You have signed an agreement to accept self-government, not independence! The strength of our faith in you in the days when your name stood for the great revolutionary idea is equaled today by the rage in our hearts —we are ashamed that we should have chosen the wrong elder. . . .

But the Vietnamese people never lose hope for long. . . . They will continue along the path which you have been unable to follow to the end. . . .†

Ho insisted on talking to the signatories of this crushing attack. Later I suggested to one of them that the President might simply have been trying to fool France. Did he, I asked, try to defend himself along these lines? "Not at all," he said. "He tried to convince us that France was the best partner available to Vietnam in her present state of disorganization and weakness, that the chosen policy was the one which would cost the nation least, and that the task of reconstruction must come before all else. . . . He almost won me over. . . . It was not until long afterward that I realized he was right."

On June 25 he held a reception in the Royal-Monceau, presenting a flower to every lady who attended. The reporter of *Le Monde* judged him "quiet and pleasant" and credited him with the appearance of a "minor mandarin." At a press conference on July 13, Ho declared: "I have always lived in hiding. I did not emerge from hiding until August 20, 1945." Had he ever been in jail? "Yes—here and there." For long? "Time spent in jail is always long. . . ."

---

* An allusion to the agreement of March 6.

† Jean Sainteny, *Histoire d'une paix manquée* (Paris: Amiot-Dumont), p. 97.

Paris was delighted by his artful simplicity, his felicitous social manner, his spontaneity, his "ingenuous" expression, his quips, his original ways and dress, his knack of making the appropriate gesture; the city adopted him as its own. And not only the poor, industrialized Paris with which he had identified himself, but also—for all the reserve unaccountably shown by General Leclerc, despite Sainteny's entreaties—a world which he had been fighting all his life, the world of the French ruling class. Daniel Guérin,* that intractable high priest of anticolonialism, has written an interesting account concerning this subject:

> At a garden party in the Bagatelle rose garden I was privileged to see a beaming Ho Chi Minh, deserting the arms of beribboned generals only to receive the embraces of M. Francisque Gay. These effusions of friendship were disproportionate and alarming. A heavy sense of awkwardness hung over the gathering . . . [Guérin's judgment of the scene was obviously colored by a conversation which he had just had with Ho:] . . . The pleasure which I took in paying my respects to him and rejoicing with him in the liberation of his country was darkened not only by our ideological disagreements but by the memory of Ta Tu Thau. Some overzealous Stalinists, close to the leader, had recently slain the former municipal councilor of Saigon on account of his "Trotskyite" views.
>
> "He was a great patriot and we mourn him," Ho Chi Minh told me with unfeigned emotion. But a moment later he added in a steady voice, "All those who do not follow the line which I have laid down will be broken."

The remark reveals a great deal about Ho Chi Minh, especially as it was addressed to an influential left-wing figure at a time when the President was deliberately wooing French opinion.

Yet his visit was proving very successful as an exercise in

* *Au Service des colonisés.*

public relations. So far as official exchanges were concerned, he could feel well satisfied. On July 2 he met the new premier, Georges Bidault, for the first time, in an atmosphere of cordiality. The former leader of the National Resistance Council, though unable in private to conceal the antipathy which the old revolutionary aroused in him, declared in a short speech: "We are going to work together in good faith, guided by a deep shared sense of that humanism which Confucius and the western philosophers alike have established as the basis for a new conception of the relations which should exist between free and mutually dependent human beings." And on July 14 the President of the Democratic Republic of Vietnam laid a wreath of flowers on the Tomb of the Unknown Soldier. In this moment he was consecrated as an official guest of France. One wonders what were the inner thoughts, during the ceremony, of the man who as Nguyen Ai Quoc had founded *Le Paria* and inveighed so strongly against the use of Asians and Africans as "cannon fodder." A reference to the dialectics of history sheds great light on such moments. At that time French political circles were full of men who would soon be forced to engage in meditations similar to Ho's.

Jacques Dumaine's observations* on all this are an inimitable, almost comical, mixture of professional curiosity and mild distaste.

We were obliged to supervise the official visit of Ho Chi Minh. Age and calm have lent polish to his goodhearted manner, and he conducts himself with native ease and a certain dignity. . . . He caused me an additional headache on Bastille Day, when we had to decide where he should be seated for the review. M. Bidault did not want him at his side. Uncle Ho insisted on being next to the President. The positioning of his chair in the official stand was a detail which I had to calculate to the last inch. The Communist

* *Quai d'Orsay*, pp. 99–102.

leaders, Thorez and Tillon, were dissatisfied. . . . [A further encounter, a few days later, is summarized with a shrewdness which *almost* overrides Dumaine's somewhat esoteric social attitudes.] We had luncheon in private with Ho Chi Minh. One can only admire the mastery with which this self-taught man controls his language, conveys his thoughts and endows his designs with the semblance of moderation and the stamp of courtesy. Those about him are high-strung, fanatical and unmindful of their behavior. He, on the other hand, gives the impression of being wise and perspicacious. If he can obtain a little more than the possible, perhaps he will not ask for the *im*possible? Would not that be the lesser of two evils?

As remarked earlier, Ho had relatively little contact with the French Communist leaders at this time. Perhaps he wanted to avoid involvement during the talks, for fear of awakening hostility to Vietnam in conservative and Catholic circles. Perhaps he was disappointed to discover how little they knew about Asian politics. Perhaps he was still irked by the memory of Maurice Thorez's remarks to General Nguyen Van Xuan earlier in the year: the general secretary of the French Communist Party is said to have observed that he "ardently hoped to see the French flag flying over every territory in the French Union" and that he "had not the slightest intention of being held responsible for a sellout of France's positions in Indochina." Whatever the truth of the matter, a member of the Vietnamese delegation was to declare, on returning to Hanoi, that the French Communist Party had no clearly defined position on overseas problems.*

Relations between the Vietnamese Communists and their French comrades had been anything but simple. The latter had taken a hostile view of the Indochinese Communist Party's willingness to collaborate with the Trotskyites in

* Philippe Devillers, *Histoire du Vietnam*, p. 292.

1935 and had been disagreeably surprised to hear of the party's dissolution ten years later. At the time, André Marty had branded this second event as a "sellout decision," but the French were now ready to accept Ho's argument that it had been a mere survival tactic made necessary by the sudden encroachment of the Kuomintang armies.

The truth is, the French Communists were (a) hampered by their nationalist strategy in Metropolitan France and (b) still undecided on what their colonial line should be.

Ho's most cordial relationship during this period was with a fellow traveler of the Communists, Raymond Aubrac, former Commisioner of the Republic in Marseilles, whose wife, Lucie, was then a member of the National Assembly. Ho met them at a reception one day, and when he heard them say they lived in the country, he immediately thought of a possibility: Paris was so noisy and overcrowded, would it be possible for him to stay at their house? As a result of this chance exchange, he and eleven colleagues moved to the Aubracs' villa in mid-August and remained there until his departure on September 15. Every morning he got up at dawn and, in typical Vietnamese fashion, perched uncomfortably on a stone for three hours while he read the Paris newspapers. Afterward he received a succession of callers before driving back to Paris.

By this stage, however, the Franco-Vietnamese conference begun at Fontainebleau on July 6 had failed. Paul Mus has drawn attention to the despondency induced in the Vietnamese delegates by the choice of Fontainebleau—a chilly setting, far from Paris—and by the character of the French delegation; it was made up of talented experts (apart from Max André, who had made such a poor impression on Ho in Hanoi and was looked at askance by his own colleagues), but it did not contain a single politician of a rank and reputation equal to the demands of an international conference; even the Communist Party was represented only by a secondary figure, Lozeray. Until then, Paris and French political life had continued to hold a magic, in the eyes of Ho's companions, which might have acted as a powerful psychological weapon.

Furthermore, the gulf between the two basic approaches to the problem had not narrowed since Dalat. The Hanoi team still tended to regard Franco-Vietnamese relations in terms of international law, while the Paris team viewed them as a domestic matter. For the former, the issue was one of independence coupled with alliance or association; for the latter, one of self-government within a French block, which was the sole custodian of sovereignty.

This fundamental disagreement had been seriously exacerbated by friction over Cochin China (Nam Bo), resulting from the proclamation of the "autonomous republic" in Saigon on June 1, and from the French occupation of the Moi plateaus in the weeks that followed. Then, as though he had not already done enough to compromise the future of the talks, Admiral d'Argenlieu—yielding to the entreaties of high-ranking people in Saigon—administered what was more or less the deathblow by announcing that a "federal conference" would meet in Dalat on August 1 to define the roles of Cambodia, Laos and Cochin China itself in the Indochinese Federation. Could anyone still claim there was going to be a referendum?

This announcement resulted in the suspension of the Fontainebleau talks. The French leaders at the time simply do not seem to have realized that, in the interests of securing *unity* for Vietnam, Ho and his colleagues were prepared to make substantial concessions regarding *independence*. In exchange for an immediate regrouping of Vietnamese territories, they would have agreed, for the time being, to relinquish some of their claims to sovereignty. (The same problem, in different terms, created a barrier between France and the African territories in 1958 and led to the breach with Guinea.)

Ho issued statement after statement, sometimes bitter,

often conciliatory. On July 12 he had declared that he was "determined to prevent the Indochinese Federation from becoming a sort of governor-generalship in disguise." But on August 15 he told *Franc-tireur:* "I came here to make peace, I am not anxious to return to Hanoi empty-handed. I want to go back there in France's company—in other words I want to take home to the Vietnamese people concrete results, the certain knowledge of the collaboration which we are hoping for. . . ."

A few days later he sent a cable to Hanoi, where celebrations to commemorate the anniversary of the revolution and the proclamation of independence were due to be held on September 2, insisting that the festivities be devoid of any anti-French connotations. And on September 11, though the failure of the Fontainebleau talks was now an accepted fact, he told an Associated Press correspondent: "There is no real dissension between us. Our differences are of the kind which are to be found in every family. . . ."

The Vietnamese delegation, however, had already left Paris, after insisting, in a prepared statement, on its "firm desire to conclude, in local consultation with the representatives of the French authorities, limited agreements on specific questions and to give active proof of its wish for understanding and cooperation with France."

Ho wanted something more than this declaration of intent. He felt the need to give new life to the "miracle" of March 6 by means of a positive declaration. He held almost daily discussions with the Minister for Overseas Territories, Marius Moutet. It was Moutet who had welcomed him to France in June, and Ho had lost no time in reminding the minister of his efforts before World War I, as a young lawyer and a friend of Jaurès, on behalf of political detainees in Indochina—including Ho himself and his colleague Phan Chu Trinh. Ho had embraced him and said, "You are my oldest friend in France."

Ho was clearly anxious to secure a formal agreement

which would assure him of public success and set the seal on the policy which he had adopted in the face of contrary opinion at home. "Don't let me go back empty-handed," he kept saying; "arm me against my own extremists." But he was infuriatingly fussy over points of detail, and the minister felt quite worn out before the end came.

These discussions reached their climax on September 13 and 14. On the evening of the 14th, Moutet went home, feeling quite disheartened. At about midnight he received a telephone call. It was Ho Chi Minh: "I think we have almost reached agreement. There are just a few details that need settling. Expect me at any moment." Moutet felt too weak to endure any more at present. "I'll see you tomorrow," he said, for the sake of peace and quiet. But an hour later the telephone rang again: "I'm on my way to you, all ready to sign. . . ."

Ho arrived in the middle of the night, and—under the convergent gaze of a Vietminh bodyguard and a statuette of Buddha—Moutet sat on the bed in his pajamas and signed the document which was afterward known as the "modus vivendi of September 14." The text summarized in broad outline the provisions laid down in March, provided safeguards for French interests in the north and stipulated that the "democratic freedoms" were to be respected in Cochin China. It provided for a cessation of hostilities in the south, which was partially applied to both sides.

Ho had succeeded in preserving the lifeline, but at the cost of giving way on several points of detail. These concessions entailed risk, for attitudes had hardened in Vietnam as a result of the measures announced in Saigon by Admiral d'Argenlieu. There were many powerful opponents to the policy of peace through negotiation, and they had been quick to argue that d'Argenlieu's moves had been the inevitable outcome of the deception to which Ho had been an all too ready victim.

After more than three months in France, the Vietnamese

head of state set sail from Toulon on September 19, aboard the sloop *Dumont d'Urville*. He was rumored to be a deeply troubled man, convinced that in signing the text of the modus vivendi he had thrown away his prestige and perhaps his whole future. But the commander of the sloop has since stated that his guest was in excellent spirits throughout the month-long voyage and proved the liveliest of table companions, discussing a wide variety of subjects and even trying to tease the ship's chaplain about the existence of God. Far from seeming like a man with his back to the wall, he gave the impression of being very sure of himself.

High Commissioner D'Argenlieu had expressed a wish to meet him on the journey home, and a rendezvous was arranged in Camranh Bay, off the Annam coast. In the late afternoon of October 18, I and a party of journalists aboard the cruiser *Suffren* saw the sloop approaching. Uncle Ho was standing on deck, instantly recognizable by his narrow frame, tuft of gray hair, threadbare tunic and Spartan-style sandals. For over two hours he and Admiral d'Argenlieu talked in the privacy of the *Suffren*'s wardroom. Then they called the journalists together. D'Argenlieu watched closely, with tight lips and a frown, as Ho—laughing almost and wearing his most innocent expression—told us: "The admiral and I consider that the Saigon and Hanoi newspapers, French and Vietnamese alike, are too fierce in tone. We cannot always be exchanging bouquets but why hurl abuse at each other? Do what you can, my friends, to calm troubled minds. . . ." He went on to say that he deplored the acts of terrorism still being perpetrated in the south and that the faithful implementation of the modus vivendi of September 14 would help pave the way for the next conference which, following the one at Fontainebleau, was to be held in January.

At this point the admiral, bringing his thin smile into play for the first time, observed, "I believe a step has just been taken along the road to agreement. . . ." Then something very surprising happened: we saw Ho turn to the High Commissioner and embrace him. The look on the admiral's face at that moment had to be seen to be believed.

Traveling back to Saigon that evening in the High Commissioner's seaplane, my colleagues and I tried to weigh the significance of this strange encounter. In an attempt to fathom d'Argenlieu's attitude, I asked his nearest associate who or what the admiral considered he was dealing with when he came face to face with Ho Chi Minh. Vietnamese nationalism? Asiatic revolution? The downtrodden colonial peoples? Communism?

"Communism, of course," he assured me, without hesitation.

For Ho Chi Minh, this was not an easy homecoming. He was even more conscious than in the hours immediately following the agreement of March 6 that he was being branded a traitor by the opposition, if not by certain militants and cadres within his own party. But he was fully determined to stand up for his policies, and in this drawn-out attempt to guarantee a bloodless revolution in friendly accord with the colonial power, were perhaps his finest hours.

Indeed, the proclamation which he addressed to his people on October 23 is one of the most significant documents he ever drafted. Excerpts follow:

Compatriots throughout the country,
. . . I have the following statements to make:

On my way to France, during my stay in France, and on my way back from France, the French government, to show its desire to cooperate with Vietnam, received me ceremoniously. Out of sincere friendship for our people, the French people received me fraternally.

On your behalf, I have the honor to thank the French government and people. . . .

Answering the kind invitation of the French government,

I went to France with the purpose of solving the question of Vietnam's independence and the unification of the north, center, and south. Due to the present situation in France, these two questions have not yet been settled. We have to wait. . . .

We took Vietnam's flag to France. The French government and people and foreign residents there looked on our flag with respect. . . . We caused a great many Frenchmen to become friends of the Vietnamese people. . . . The French in France are very friendly toward us. So the Vietnamese in Vietnam should also be friendly toward the French people. . . . All this is to show the world that we are a civilized people. . . . Acts of reprisal are forbidden. Toward those who went astray, our compatriots must display a generous policy. We must let them hear the voice of reason. Everybody loves his country. It is only for petty interests that they forget the great cause. . . .*

One of the French dignitaries who turned out to welcome him home and who spent the whole day at his side, describes the occasion as follows:

There was delirium in Haiphong. I had never seen anything like it. When he stepped ashore, he called on the crowd to sing the "Marseillaise." I was struck by the fact that Eurasian children had been placed in the front row. . . .

The sixty-mile train journey from Haiphong to Hanoi took us twelve hours. Every half mile, the train would stop in open country, and the *nhaqués* [peasants] would rush forward and cheer him. It was indescribable. . . .

Old Ho, who was quite calm while talking to us—I've never seen anyone so self-controlled—would bound to the door, take out a red handkerchief and wipe his eyes. . . . What a marvelous actor! [I saw him do the same thing a few days later, at the theater in Hanoi, while a speaker from the south was describing the bad treatment suffered by the in-

* Bernard B. Fall (ed.), *Ho Chi Minh on Revolution: Selected Writings, 1920–66* (New York: Praeger, 1967), pp. 168–71.

habitants of the area. Seated beside Giap, confronting the assembly, he took out his large red handkerchief and sniveled loudly with emotion. . . .]

I'm quite certain that he then believed he could come to an understanding with France. He distinctly told us so on the train. . . .

In Hanoi, where he was received with great popular acclaim that same evening, Ho again called for cheers in support of "Franco-Vietnamese friendship"; but the phrase was wearing thin, and the press conference which he gave shortly afterward sounded like a summing up for the defense in a case that was going badly. By now his confidence was blunted. He had returned to find an atmosphere of mistrust and criticism at the very heart of the politburo of his own party. His two ablest lieutenants, Giap and Dong, had come home in a mood of profound disappointment—one from Dalat, the other from Fontainebleau. Giap was now regarded as one of the leaders of the "intransigents" who had exercised the realities of power while the leader was away. For over three months he had behaved as though he considered a trial of strength inevitable, and he had been making careful preparations for it. Indeed, the chapter devoted to this period in Philippe Devillers's *Histoire du Vietnam* is entitled "Giap Forges His Armory."

And yet he had been on quite good terms with France's representatives in Vietnam. The departure of Leclerc, in July, had alarmed those Vietnamese, especially Giap, who had put their trust in him. His successor, General Valluy, declared, "We must honor the agreements and resolutely brush aside those self-confessed or crypto-colonialists who are determined to sabotage them,"* but the question remained: would he put theory into practice?

Another retirement which occasioned anxiety was that

* General Marchand, *Le Drame indochinois,* p. 65.

of Jean Sainteny. The latter felt that he had fulfilled the temporary mission which had been entrusted to him and that as a private individual he ought, with the war now over, to put an end to his official duties. He had therefore tendered his resignation in Paris. It had not been fully accepted. No successor had been appointed; there were only "temporaries"—first, Colonel Crépin, one of Leclerc's men, and then General Morlière. Each had shown goodwill and understanding, even to the extent of helping the Vietminh against its nationalist opponents, a policy which had provoked severe criticism among Admiral d'Argenlieu's staff.

Further, the joint commissions set up by the French and Vietnamese were doing valuable work. In the March, 1950, issue of *Les Temps modernes,* J. H. Roy gives a firsthand account of the functioning of the two-nation patrols. "The mutual distrust shown at the beginning had vanished," he writes, describing how he, a French soldier, presented arms to Ho Chi Minh when the Communist leader paid an official visit to the Hanoi fortress.

But too many people were determined to show that the agreements were "a dangerous piece of deception on the part of an implacable enemy who is bent on evicting us"—to quote one of Admiral d'Argenlieu's colleagues. Momentary friction between the overlapping armed forces might at any time spark a major incident which would result in an open conflict.

Early in August a French column making its way up toward Bac Ninh, in the central region, was attacked by Vietminh elements, which escaped with the pay that was to have been delivered to the garrison at Lang Son. The attack resulted in five deaths. There was some evidence to suggest that the attack may have been a deliberate act of provocation engineered by anti-Vietminh elements or—as I was assured by a French official dealing with the case—by southerners serving in the Vietminh army but hostile to agreements which paid too little heed to Nam Bo, or Cochin China. All the same, it was a serious warning of what might happen.

On October 30 hostilities more or less ceased in Cochin China as a result of the modus vivendi of September 14. During a visit to the underground forces in Nam Bo, toward the end of September, I had gathered the impression that the southern leaders were anxious to stand by the terms of the modus vivendi and that they were confidently looking forward to the referendum. Ung Van Khiem and Pham Ngoc Thuan, both destined to become ministers in Hanoi, talked in terms of agreement and cooperation. Only one person of any consequence seemed opposed to a settlement; this was Huynh Phu So, the "mad monk" who had founded the Hoa Hao sect and whose extraordinary personality made a deep impression on me. A few weeks later he disappeared.

But when the French and Vietnamese began talks (as they immediately did) in an effort to insure a return to lasting peace in the south, they were held up at every turn by the opposition of Nguyen Binh, military leader of the Vietminh organization in the south. This Tonkinese, an anti-Communist whose views were to cost him his life three years later—he was liquidated while on a mission to the north—refused to allow his troops to be regrouped, still less disarmed. As it turned out, however, the conflagration began, not in his area, but in Haiphong in the north.

On November 11, Ho protested to the Prime Minister Georges Bidault, against the unilateral decision to open a French custom house in that port to control external trade —a step which, he claimed, was contrary to the terms of the modus vivendi of September 14 and which "might have particularly grave repercussions on the talks . . . which the Franco-Vietnamese joint commissions are about to open with the object of cementing the policy of friendly co-operation between the two countries." Against this, the French argued that the very existence of the Indochinese

Federation, which Vietnam had chosen to join (though the constitution adopted by the national assembly in Hanoi on November 12 made no reference either to the federation or to the French Union), gave the central authority the right to supervise all trade carried on by its member states and to check incoming shipments which, it was suspected, "often involved arms and ammunition."

On November 20, following a clash between Vietnamese and French forces in Lang Son, a Chinese junk, laden with undeclared motor fuel and (or so it was claimed) military supplies, sailed into Haiphong harbor. French military security ordered it to be stopped and searched just as the crew was preparing to unload their cargo at a wharf in the Chinese quarter. A Vietnamese guard intervened at once, firing several shots at the French launch. The launch fired back. Barricades were set up all over the harbor and then in the city itself. Eventually the Franco-Vietnamese joint commission succeeded in ending the exchange of fire.

But Colonel Dèbes, officer in charge of arms, who heartily loathed the "Viets" and was solely concerned with restoring the army's prestige, gave orders for the barricades to be removed and sent a bulldozer to hasten the process. The vehicle was greeted with bullets, whereupon Dèbes decided to "purge" the European quarters of all the Vietnamese elements that had moved into the area. The operation was unbridled, especially after a French officer was killed in the middle of the afternoon.

In Hanoi, the Vietnamese and French authorities conferred in a mood of great urgency, both hoping for a quick end to the crisis. The joint commission ordered an immediate cease-fire and the withdrawal of both armies to their respective quarters. Ho had talks with de Lacharrière, the federal commissioner for legal affairs, who was on a mission to the north, and suggested an emergency meeting of the Franco-Vietnamese committees dealing with customs and external trade. Finally, General Morlière sent three of his aides to Haiphong—Lami, Colonel Herckel and Commandant Fonde, head of the joint commission—with instructions to localize the disturbance and obtain a cease-fire, which was signed on November 21.

But on the evening of the same day Colonel Dèbes received a cable from the acting high commissioner in Saigon, General Valluy, ordering him to secure the "evacuation of the Vietnamese armed forces from Haiphong." This extraordinary directive from a man who had previously been regarded as a "liberal" has been the subject of much comment.

It was true, however, that only a few weeks earlier, in Paris, Bidault had advised the general to use artillery if the Vietminh proved too venturesome. As a result, Colonel Dèbes considered himself released from the promises given by Lami and Colonel Herckel; the need for restraint was further lessened the following night when a telegram from the acting high commissioner reached General Morlière in Hanoi, enjoining him to "exploit this serious incident to the full as a means of improving [his] position in Haiphong."

It was almost as though Saigon were deliberately seeking a rift. On the morning of November 22, General Morlière telegraphed a reply. He pointed out that demanding the evacuation of Haiphong was tantamount to a decision to occupy the city; such a decision implied the total abandonment of the agreement of March 6, and the fighting would be bound to extend to all French garrisons in Tonkin. Morlière argued that there was a chance of obtaining adequate guarantees without the need to generalize the conflict. A few hours later, Morlière received a further telegram from Valluy which took away his last remaining doubts: "In face of premeditated aggression . . . your honorable attempts at conciliation are no longer appropriate. . . . The time has come to give a harsh lesson to those who have treacherously attacked us. . . . By every means at your disposal, you must take control of Haiphong and bring the government and the Vietnamese army to repentance. . . ."*

On November 23, Colonel Dèbes, feeling thoroughly reinforced in his "firm" attitude and taking note of the dense concentration of Vietminh forces in the Chinese quarter, demanded the immediate evacuation of this sector, failing which he would open fire. Three hours later, having obtained no satisfaction, he ordered his men to shoot at the fringes of the Vietnamese quarter and sent in an armored column. Meeting with resistance, he called for naval artillery support. The *Suffren*'s gunners saw a line of people fleeing in the direction of Lach Tray and mistook them for a military unit. The six-inch shells tore into the straw huts, destroying them and their inhabitants—it was total carnage.

There has been some dispute over the extent of the Vietnamese losses. Paul Mus, whose objectivity and sources are as unchallengeable as his scholarship, maintains that there were six thousand dead. This figure was based, among other things, on an estimate by Admiral Battet. The admiral has since died, but his testimony is borne out by several of his friends including Jacques Raphaël-Leygues,† who fought with the expeditionary force. After this, it was not surprising that the policy which led to the March agreements should be regarded as null and void in Hanoi.

But Ho Chi Minh still appeared to be clinging to a hope. French journalists and officials who called on him in late November and early December came away with assurances that all could yet be saved, provided there was genuine willingness in Saigon and Paris. He was impatiently awaiting the return of Jean Sainteny who, in response to appeals

* G. Chaffard, *Carnets secrets de la décolonisation* (Paris: Calmann-Lévy, 1965), pp. 70–74.
† Raphaël-Leygues is at present France's ambassador in Abidjan, the Ivory Coast.

from several members of the government (and, curiously enough, from Admiral d'Argenlieu), had agreed to come to Hanoi again. The hero of the March negotiations left Paris on November 23, but when he reached Saigon he was kept under a mild and friendly form of house arrest for six days by the acting high commissioner, General Valluy. Plainly, in view of the policy of intimidation in which the general was then engaged, with the active support of the French premier, he could well do without the presence in Tonkin of the man who had declared his firm belief in the possibility of working things out with Ho. In a semiofficial note, Valluy argued that it was better to keep Sainteny in reserve until the resumption of talks, when he would serve a more useful purpose.

Sainteny finally reached Hanoi by air on December 2. He was told by members of the French delegation and by American and British consular officials that the situation was almost beyond hope and that nothing could now save it except perhaps the trust which had been established between himself and Ho. An official banquet was given to mark his return; the optimism he dutifully showed would not, he writes, have fooled anyone.

Only a day after his return, Sainteny received a note from President Ho: "I should be very glad to see you between five and six this afternoon. In view of my present state of health, it will of course be a personal meeting between old friends." Sainteny* gives an account of their meeting:

> I found Ho Chi Minh in bed. His eyes shone and his hands, which held on to mine for a long while, were feverish. Hoang Minh Giam and Nam were with him. They did not retire from the room, nor did he ask them, as he usually did, to leave us alone. We talked about his health and my journey. . . . Finally he alluded to events in Haiphong and showed every sign of being deeply upset by them; he hinted

* *Histoire d'une paix manquée*, p. 217.

that these grave events were not unconnected with the illness which kept him confined to bed.

"You see," I said to him, "I was right to show concern in Paris at your decision to spend so long away from home."

"True," he replied, "but then your own return was overdue."

We let the subject drop.

He received a number of other Frenchmen in the days that followed, including Bernard Dranber of *Paris-Saigon* on December 7 and Ageorges, the Agence France Presse correspondent, on December 17. To them, he seemed increasingly agitated and despondent, but not desperate. He even told Dranber: "This war is something we wish to avoid at all costs. We long passionately for independence, but for independence within the French Union. War doesn't pay. The reestablishment of Vietnam will not allow this slaughter, these sufferings. . . .* And when Sainteny told Hoang Minh Giam, the most influential of the President's aides, how alarmed he was to see important posts being assigned to men who were notoriously anti-French, Ho invited him (again through Giam) to name any ministers and officials who were considered undesirable from the French point of view.

On the same day (December 7) as his interview with Ho Bernard Dranber was assured by Sainteny: "President Ho Chi Minh, for whom I feel more than friendship, has only to make his colleagues appreciate the full gravity of the consequences which would result from a rift, and the worst can be avoided. . . . France still stands by the agreements of March 6. . . ."†

Ho had grounds for supposing that the hand he still extended was about to be grasped at the eleventh hour: on December 12, the Chamber of Deputies in Paris called on

* *Paris-Saigon,* December 12, 1946.
† *Ibid.*

Léon Blum to form a government. The President regarded the aging Socialist leader as an old comrade, a symbol of the French left to which he was still bound by so many ties. Furthermore, only two days earlier Blum had published an editorial in *Le Populaire* calling for a "sincere agreement [with Vietnam] on the basis of independence." And one of his first actions as premier was to send Marius Moutet, Minister for Overseas Territories and cosignatory of the modus vivendi, on a mission to Indochina. All could be saved, even now. On December 15, Ho addressed a memorandum to Blum suggesting a return, on both sides, to the positions held prior to November 20.

It was too late, and there were too many obstacles to this belated attempt to salvage the situation. The memorandum, which had to be relayed via Saigon, was "delayed in transmission" and not brought to the premier's notice until December 26, by which time the situation was irreparable.*

The number of incidents increased sharply. Several French civilians were slain between December 15 and 20. On the seventeenth a French paratrooper opened fire in a densely crowded street, the rue des Vermicelles, in a working-class neighborhood; more than ten people were killed. That same day Sainteny received a message from Hoang Huu Nam, one of Ho's immediate deputies, making an "urgent appeal to [his] political understanding." He replied, two days later, with a very sharp letter to President Ho demanding appropriate punishment for those responsible for a further outrage, which had resulted in the deaths of two more Frenchmen. Sainteny admits, however, that "with things as they were, it is uncertain whether this letter reached its addresses."†

For on December 18 the situation had grown worse than ever. Barricades and trenches erected and dug by the Viet-

---

* Philippe Devillers, *Histoire du Vietnam*, p. 352.
† *Histoire d'une paix manquée*, p. 352.

namese were razed and filled in by the French. Shots were
exchanged. It was Haiphong all over again. But this time,
responsibility for the trouble lay far less with the military
leaders of the French than with those of the Vietminh. A
month ago, the major share of blame had to be placed on
Colonel Dèbes and General Valluy. In Hanoi, the explosion
was obviously triggered by the vengefulness of Giap (as head
of the "people's army") and of the commander of the Tu
Ve, or militia.

Can it be said that Ho himself worked to the end to
avoid a showdown? For several days he had anticipated the
worst. On December 17 he asked Hoang Quoc Viet: "Are
you sure all the children have been evacuated?" Even supposing that his manifestations of pro-French feeling had
been feigned for tactical reasons, many of his private remarks at this time make it clear beyond doubt that he
wanted to spare his people the sufferings of total war, however convinced he may have been of a favorable outcome.

But he had spent a whole year campaigning for a peaceful solution, and in the past month his policy had met with
more and more setbacks. He felt worn-out and disappointed
as he waited in vain for a reply from "Comrade Blum." All
around him, even in the heart of the Tong Bo (the politburo) those who were against a compromise settlement were
able to advance increasingly persuasive arguments.

Then came news of Marius Moutet's arrival, which
seemed to promise the extension of the policy of March 6
and September 14. The opponents of the "Ho line" argued
that the visit was just another attempt to put them off
and keep them dangling while the French improved the
positions of their armed forces. In Haiphong, the French—
with their fleet to support them—were strategically placed;
the Vietminh in Hanoi were not. To strike now was not to
choose war rather than peace, reasoned Ho's adversaries,
but merely to redress the balance by driving the French
from Hanoi as Giap's men had been driven from Haiphong.

Afterward it would be possible for the Vietnamese to argue as equals, command respect, dictate conditions of their own.

And preparations for a coup were being made at a far less exalted level than the Tong Bo. Feelings ran high among the ordinary militia, the Tu Ve. No doubt the mood was fostered by *agents provocateurs* working for the nationalist opposition, and perhaps also by Japanese cadres, whose presence was reported by several observers, including Paul Mus. In an attempt to account for the brutal decision taken by Giap and his companions, Philippe Devillers* writes: "Acute anxiety; determination to break out, at all costs, from a position which they saw as untenable; violent anti-French feeling; revolutionary dialectics—each of these played its part. . . ."

From the late afternoon of December 18 onward, not an hour went by but that General Morlière's or Sainteny's staff was warned to expect an immediate attack by the Tu Ve. The likelihood of such an attack was increased by the harsh measures taken by the French command on the eighteenth and nineteenth: the premises of the Bank of Indochina were taken over, and the Vietminh militia was ordered to disband. It was generally anticipated that the attack would be launched at 8 P.M. on the nineteenth.

The "tip-off" was too plain, too precise. Sainteny hesitated, especially when he received the following letter from Ho at noon that day:

Monsieur le Commissaire et cher ami,
    The atmosphere is becoming more and more strained at present. That is very regrettable. Pending the decision from Paris, I am counting on you to work out with M. Giam some way of improving the climate. Please accept my kindest regards and convey my respects to Madame Sainteny.
                                                        Ho Chi Minh

* *Histoire du Vietnam*, p. 353.

Also at noon, Giap asked General Morlière to lower the
tension by canceling the order confining troops to barracks.
At 5 P.M., however, the information became more precise
and the threats more specific. Sainteny and Morlière agreed
that the French troops of the Hanoi garrison should remain
at action stations. It was further agreed that as soon as a
shot was fired the two men should meet at the citadel and
direct operations from there.

Sainteny himself describes the ensuing events:

> At 8 P.M. an exceptional calm came over the city. The clock
> over the Yersin Hospital, next to the French commissioner's
> office, slowly tolled the hour. "It doesn't look as though we're
> in for trouble tonight," I said to my colleagues. "I'm going
> home for a while." I got into my car. A moment later there
> was a low roar, and the city was abruptly plunged into dark-
> ness. The electric powerhouse had been blown up. It was
> exactly 8:04 P.M. The first shots began to sputter, rending the
> shadows which enveloped the town and engulfing all our
> hopes and efforts. . . .

Sainteny scrambled out of his private vehicle and boarded
a light armored car, intending to join General Morlière at
the fortress, but in the rue Paul-Bert the armored car ran
over a mine. Though seriously wounded, with twenty pieces
of shrapnel lodged inside him, he managed to struggle free
from the blaze and was picked up by a patrol. The following
night, he was operated on in a hospital besieged by Vietminh militiamen, who shot at the patients from the shelter
of nearby trees.

General Morlière and his troops fought back with vigor.
Giap failed to "sweep the French out of Hanoi overnight"
in keeping with a boast which he is alleged to have made.
(Actually, his chief objective seems to have been to plant a
permanent thorn in their side, as a means of reestablishing
himself in a position of strength.) On the afternoon of
December 20 he and the President had the utmost difficulty

in escaping from the senior residency before it fell to the French troops. They headed back towards the rice fields and the remote regions of the north, from which they had set out sixteen months earlier. That same evening, Ho issued a proclamation:

> Compatriots all over the country!
>
> As we desired peace, we made concessions. But the more we made concessions, the further the French colonialists went because they are resolved to invade our country once again.
>
> No! We would rather sacrifice all than lose our country. We are determined not to be enslaved. . . .
>
> Men and women, old and young, regardless of creeds, political parties, or nationalities, all the Vietnamese must stand up to fight the French colonialists to save the fatherland. Those who have rifles will use their rifles; those who have swords will use their swords; those who have no swords will use spades, hoes, or sticks. Everyone must endeavor to oppose the colonialists and save his country.
>
> Even if we have to endure hardship in the Resistance War, with the determination to make sacrifices, victory will surely be ours.*

And the following day he turned his attention to his opponents and to international opinion:

> French people! We have affection for you and sincerely want to cooperate with you within the framework of the French Union because we have a common ideal which is freedom, equality, and independence. . . .
>
> Peoples of the Allied powers! The French reactionaries . . . are waging an aggressive war in Vietnam. . . . The Vietnamese people ask you to intervene. . . .†

* *Ibid.*, p. 174.
† Bernard B. Fall (ed.), *Ho Chi Minh on Revolution: Selected Writings, 1920–66* (New York: Praeger, 1967), p. 172.

By this time, Vo Nguyen Giap had ordered fighting on all fronts. In general he was obeyed. The French army had contrived to avert real disaster in Hanoi, but already it was semibeleagured, already it was caught in the toils of a war from which it did not extricate itself until ninety-one months later, and only then at the price of a costly political settlement.

The end of the year 1946 marked also the end of a policy and the collapse of a hope which had long been nurtured, not only by a few Frenchmen but by Ho Chi Minh as well. Now began the conflict between the tiger and the elephant which he had described, back in September, to the American journalist David Schoenbrun: "If ever the tiger pauses, the elephant will impale him on his mighty tusks. But the tiger will not pause, and the elephant will die of exhaustion and loss of blood." And to a French Socialist minister, at a time when he was still hoping to achieve a peaceful solution, he had summed up the war as follows: "You would kill ten of my men for every one I killed of yours. But even at that rate you would be unable to hold out, and victory would go to me. . . ."

9

THE
GUERRILLA
LEADER

In Paris it was widely held that the ordeals to which the Vietminh must now return, following the collapse of Ho's policy of gradual independence through friendly negotiation, were bound to lead to his fall. He was now wide open to charges of "rightist deviationism" and "bourgeois opportunism." Surely his extremist opponents in the Tong Bo would strip him of all real power, or even arrange for his physical "elimination"? Communists, the experts said, simply did not forgive mistakes on such a scale.

Yet when Paul Mus was sent on a mission to the Vietminh leader in April 1947, he was particularly struck by the fact that Ho had preserved his power to make decisions. Without bothering to call the Tong Bo together to consult his

principal colleagues, he provided Mus with information
concerning the fate of the Vietnamese resistance for years
to come.

Not long afterward I met a man in Hanoi who, until he
left the movement, had been in charge of popular education
in a Vietminh zone and had attended a conference of "cultural cadres" held near Phu-Tho. Ho had acted as chairman
and played a lively part in the discussions. "The old man
is as active as ever," he said. "He remains the boss, or rather
the arbiter. Life in the resistance still takes its style from
him, with his shabby tunic, his sandals and the simplicity,
homeliness and cordiality of his speech. He has a hold
on people's minds, his personal popularity is undimin-
ished. . . ."

In the bush around Tuyen Quang, as in the cave at Pac Bo
five years earlier, his personal magnetism was proving even
stronger than in the relative calm and stability of Hanoi.
Here he seemed the living embodiment of the myth of
"undivided resistance."

The legend lived on. Despite his own previous advocacy
of a tougher line, Vo Nguyen Giap describes Ho's bearing
in the period following the collapse of the 1946 policy with
unfailing admiration and with more fervor than realism:

Before the campaign in the northeast, he drew up the "Eight
Commandments" of the government of the Democratic Republic of Vietnam and had them distributed among the
troops who were going to liberate the area. All who were
present well remember how he arrived at the rally held to
mark the opening of the campaign. Torrential rain had been
falling for several days. The streams were bursting their
banks and flooding the roads. But nothing could deter
Uncle. A crowd of people stood beside one such torrent,
waiting for the water level to go down. Without hesitation
Ho looked for the best place to ford and carried on as though
nothing were wrong. When they saw this, all the villagers
followed in his footsteps. We didn't need to be told of the

dangers of crossing a stream in the rainy season. President Ho arrived in time for the meeting, and it was an invaluable lesson to those about to go into battle. . . .

Scarcely on a par with Moses and the Red Sea, of course, or even with Mao vying with the waters of the Yangtze— but exactly what was needed to awaken new ardor and loyalty in the villages. And there are numerous other scenes which testify to Ho's serenity and stoicism at this time and to the other qualities which had been molded by thirty years of fighting for the revolution: visual impressions of him standing outside the crude hut in which he habitually slept, not far from his soldiers; sitting deep inside a cave and typing out an order of the day for the troops; inspecting a volunteer commando group and wearing a scruffy lumber jacket, with his beard and hair blowing about in the wind; climbing a steep slope in the highlands, stick in hand. Always himself, always in the right place at the right time, always midway between the Mao of the Long March and Gandhi at the spinning wheel.

Hoang Quoc Viet, another of his lieutenants opposed to the idea of negotiating a settlement with France, recalls:

In the early days of the resistance he used to live among the peasants, wear brown cotton clothes like theirs, and live by the same restrictions as everybody else. . . . When a bomber appeared, he used to do what the peasants did: run and hide in the fields. . . . Later, at Quang Nap, he lived in a hut, built on piles, with a very low roof right in the middle of the jungle. . . . It stood exposed to the four winds and was completely bare except for his "baby" portable, some colored pencils and some writing paper. His sole companion, a dog, had fallen victim to the tigers which prowled about at night. . . .

Later still, he lived in a small house surrounded by a garden. Here he used to tend his morning glories, his mustard seeds, his cabbages, his pumpkins, his sweet potatoes. . . . He did exercises and played volley ball. And whenever he passed the ball to a teammate, he would shout: "There's diplomacy for you!"

Several times I tried to question him about his private life, but he wouldn't tell me anything; he would instantly hand me some documents and tell me to study them. . . . I always found it very hard to tear myself away. Glancing back, I would catch him staring after me, delaying the moment for retiring into his hut and getting on with his work.

It is true that *La Résistance vaincra* (The Resistance Will Conquer), the most important piece of doctrine published by the Vietminh leadership at this time, was not written by Ho but by Truong Chinh, General Secretary of the party (which had officially been dissolved); but this fact was due to a division of responsibility and not to the failure of Ho's policy. Ho—and we shall be returning to this—has never been a theorist like Truong Chinh, some of whose writings had already appeared in *Truth,* the organ of party doctrine, even before the breach with France. The leader was more concerned at the time with war—and with peace.

For here is further proof of how high his standing remained; efforts to come to terms with France did not cease after December 19. We may find it hard to accept the idea of a strategy which coupled attacks on Hanoi with appeals for negotiation, but this was exactly what Ho was attempting.

He provided his own summing-up of these approaches to France in an interview given on March 27, 1947.*

Since December 19, I have issued appeals to the French government and people . . . on December 21 and 23, 1946, on January 1, 7 and 10, 1947 and on February 18 and March

* *The Selected Works of Ho Chi Minh* (Hanoi: Foreign Languages Publishing House, 1962), II, 102–3. (The identity of the interviewer is not given.)

5, 1947, some of them being entrusted to the good offices of the consular representatives of third powers. Yet Premier Ramadier claims that the letter which I addressed to Premier Blum carried a forged signature and that the French government has not received any further communication from me. If the representatives of France are deliberately hushing up these messages, they bear the responsibility for it. Minister Moutet claims that no one has set eyes on me since December 19, and that there can be no telling whether I am still alive or not! Fortunately I am still alive and well, and look forward to seeing him again shortly.

On April 26, Ho put forward yet another offer aimed at securing the cessation of hostilities. He expected this one to have more effect, for it was issued in the name of Hoang Minh Giam, whom he had just appointed Minister of Foreign Affairs and who was not a Communist but a Socialist, like most of the members of the French government at that time. These two factors wrested a reply at last. But at this point we must go back a bit.

On the French side, there had always been voices in favor of resuming talks, even after the tragedy of December 19; and not all these voices were Communist. But nothing came of such views. Toward the end of December, General Leclerc and Marius Moutet came to Indochina on a mission assigned to them by Blum. The Minister for Overseas Territories stopped off at Phnom Penh, where he implied that the French had not ruled out the possibility of reopening talks: "If anyone has propositions to transmit to us, they will be examined with care." General Leclerc, who arrived in Hanoi before him, received the offer (dated December 23, 1946) of a meeting with Ho. One of his officers describes how the former commander in chief strode furiously about his office, thumping the floor with his stick and saying, "It is imperative that we go, it is imperative that we do not let the opportunity slip. . . . Oh, if only

Moutet were here. . . . I cannot do anything without his approval. . . ."

But after his brief visit to Cambodia the minister had called at Saigon, and here he received the same treatment from Admiral D'Argenlieu as Sainteny had received from Valluy a month earlier: the High Commissioner placed him under friendly restraint and did his best to brainwash him in his own way that is, in the manner of a grand inquisitor. It was not until January 2 that Moutet reached the Tonkinese capital, where sporadic fighting was still going on, and where he came under fire at times. The Vietminh radio, maintaining that Ho had set up his headquarters in Ha Dong, some six miles from Hanoi, broadcast a personal message from the Vietnamese leader to Léon Blum, congratulating him on his decision to send Moutet and offering to meet the latter at once.

But Moutet insists today that he never received any message confirming these intentions. Nor, it is true, does he now have any recollection of an offer by members of the army to trap Ho and his colleagues, whose hideout had been spotted. The minister turned the suggestion down with the words: "A Socialist government does not behave like a bunch of gangsters."

As it was, Moutet spent little more than a day in Hanoi, clearly not long enough to establish contacts at such a troubled period. He did not even have time to take cognizance of Ho's communication of December 23, which had so keenly aroused Leclerc's interest. (Chief among Ho's proposals were that the two armies should return to the positions laid down in the agreement concluded between Salan and Ho on April 3, 1946, and that the Vietnamese head of government and the French Minister for Overseas Territories should meet and work out a permanent settlement on the basis of the agreement of March 6.

Moutet was shocked and distressed by the warlike atmosphere in Hanoi, and genuinely indignant at the "coup of

December 19," of which he had been given a somewhat
distorted account by Admiral d'Argenlieu's staff. He had
arrived with a genuine desire to negotiate, but when he left
Saigon he insisted that the appeals broadcast by the Vietminh radio could not be taken seriously and that the men
who really held power in the Vietminh (an allusion to the
"elimination" of Ho Chi Minh) did not want a settlement.
He then traveled south to Ban Me Thuot, where he told
General Marchand, the area commander, that he had in-
controvertible proof that the attack by the Vietminh had
been premeditated. At which point Admiral d'Argenlieu,
relieved that he should have been so well understood by a
man with whom he got on so badly, assured *France-Soir* on
January 2: "From now on it is impossible for us to treat
with Ho Chi Minh. . . ."

Which is why no answer was ever sent to the astonishing
letter which Ho addressed to Sainteny on January 24, 1947,
while the latter was still convalescing:

> Dear friend,
>
> I have just learned that you are about to return to France.
> I send you and Madame Sainteny my wishes for a good
> journey and good health.
>
> I am sure that you, like me, are profoundly sorry that our
> mutual efforts for peace should be destroyed by this fratri-
> cidal war. I know you well enough to say this: you are not
> to blame for this policy of force and reconquest.
>
> That is why I am anxious to tell you again that, despite
> what has happened, you and I are still friends. And I can
> assure you that our two peoples are still friends too.
>
> We have already had enough death and destruction!
> What are we to do now, you and I? France has only to recog-
> nize the independence and unity of Vietnam, and at once
> hostilities will cease, peace and trust will return, and we
> shall be able to get down to work and start rebuilding for
> the common good of our two countries.

For my part, I am ready to work for peace, a just and honorable peace for our two countries. I hope that you, on your side, will be working toward the same goal.

May God grant us success!

Your devoted
HO CHI MINH

The document is exceptionally revealing of Ho's character—an inimitable mixture of cunning (Ho takes the credit for exonerating Sainteny from a "policy of force" for which, as he well knows, his own colleagues are equally to blame) and spontaneous warmth. It even concludes with a reference to a Creator with whom the founder of the Indochinese Communist Party had not been unduly concerned since the declaration of independence on September 2, 1945. It was, however, to remain a dead letter for the diplomats and politicians, if not for the biographers and dabblers in psychology.

The French army secured control of Hanoi and drove Vietminh headquarters back toward the highlands. And at this point, Admiral d'Argenlieu offered his resignation which, to his surprise and resentment, was accepted. He had made the gesture as a tactical maneuver. Now he was obliged to step down in favor of Bollaert,* an influential radical who took his lead from Pierre Messmer, the man who had negotiated for France at Dalat and Fontainebleau, and from Paul Mus, former political adviser to General Leclerc.

On April 26, acting on Ho's behalf, Hoang Minh Giam sent the new High Commissioner a message speaking of "Vietnam's friendship for the people of France" and pro-

---

* A leader of the Radical Socialist Party, who had been chairman of the Resistance movement in occupied France.

posing "the immediate cessation of hostilities and the opening of negotiations with the object of reaching a peaceful
settlement to the conflict."

The initiative was exactly what was needed to give rise
to a major shift of opinion in France. But two occurrences
in Paris—one public, the other private—brought fundamental changes in France's Indochinese policy. Following a
clash with Premier Ramadier* about workers' wages, the
Communist ministers were sacked by him—and there was
no nationwide storm of protest against their dismissals.
Now, it was obvious that "the key to the situation in Indochina lies in the political situation in France," as Ho told an
American journalist at the time. Suddenly the Vietminh was
shorn of immediate allies within the French government.

Besides this depletion of the forces in favor of negotiation, another disquieting obstacle arose. Bollaert and his
two advisers had made little effort to conceal their intention of trying to reopen negotiations. But at the beginning of April they received a very sharp warning from
General de Gaulle, who was then attempting to build up
the "Rally of the French People" as the voice of French
nationalism; anyone responsible for the "loss" of a "French"
territory, said the general, would sooner or later be brought
before the High Court. It so happened that Bollaert had
served as de Gaulle's representative in occupied France, and
Messmer too was an ardent Gaullist. No more telling blow
could have been dealt to the policy of negotiated independence. The general had sealed off all possible openings.

And so, when Paul Mus was sent on a mission to the
Vietminh leader (some form of meeting was unavoidable
after Hoang Minh Giam's message of April 26, Bollaert
instructed him to lay down conditions for a cease-fire which

---

* Succeeded Léon Blum as head of the Socialist government in early
1947.

—as Mus was well aware from his sound knowledge of the
men he was dealing with—were bound to be rejected outright. The Vietminh was required to "hand over all its
weapons . . . agree to allow French troops freedom of movement throughout Vietnam . . . concentrate its disarmed
forces within given perimeters . . . and deliver all non-
Vietnamese into [French] hands. . . ." These terms demanded outright capitulation, the surrender of a defeated
army, and as an added humiliation the final clause introduced a note of contempt which one would like to think
was not deliberate.

Mus was received by Ho in the last remaining undamaged
villa in Thai Nguyen, a small town about eighty miles from
Hanoi, set among steep limestone slopes, which made it
easy to defend; it had been the site of the Vietminh headquarters in the early summer of 1945, before the move to
Hanoi. Mus had no illusions as he delivered the message
entrusted to him, and he was totally unsurprised by Ho's
rejoinder, which afterward became famous: "There is no
room for cowards in the French Union, and a coward is
what I should be if I accepted these conditions." The argument dragged on after this heroic, or almost mock-heroic,
pronouncement; but at no time was there the smallest hint
that a compromise might be arrived at. Mus was much
distressed at the absurdity of the line of action to which
he was committed. As we have said, he came away with the
impression that Ho was fully in command of his team, free
to make decisions without approval by others, and confident of how the battle would end.*

Mus has described how he was conducted back to the
French lines by a young Vietminh officer who had until
recently been a law student in Hanoi. "Is it to be war?"

---

* And yet the mission had been awaited optimistically by the Vietminh
leaders. Mus states that his hosts had believed in the possibility of agreement, to the extent of putting champagne on ice in case it was needed.

asked the young man. Mus nodded gravely. "So I shan't be finishing my studies in Paris after all," said his guide.

For seven years there was to be silence between Ho and the West, except for an occasional interview with a foreign journalist (with Andrew Roth, for instance, who was told in the autumn of 1949 that the Vietminh did not rule out the possibility of remaining neutral between the two great blocks), or a broadcast appeal to the "forces of peace" and the "democrats" of France, or a visit by a French Communist delegation.

But in 1949 an event occurred that was still more significant to the future of the Vietminh than Ramadier's dismissal of the Communist ministers in the spring of 1947. This was the defeat of the Kuomintang by Mao and his associates, who then assumed control of China. Soon afterward, the Communists were at the Tonkinese border. Marxist Peking became so strong a pole of attraction that the "revolutionary" complexion of Paris seemed of far less importance.

In terms of the political and military triangle which had existed between Paris, Hanoi and Chungking in March 1946, the French political world had seemed closer to the Vietminh and above all more sympathetic than the Kuomintang. But the triangle had now assumed different proportions. Even while French Radicals and Socialists and "Popular Republicans" were bickering over power and dividing it up (all within the framework of an ardently anti-Communist policy and strategy), Peking—capital of the biggest country in Asia—had fallen to the Communists. In 1946, Maurice Thorez had been deputy premier in Paris, Chiang Kai-shek ruler of China (officially at least), Mao a rebel fighting an underground war; in 1950, Mao was in Peking, Thorez in opposition, Chiang in Formosa.

All this gave an entirely new aspect to the situation. Paris no longer held the key to the Indochinese problem, nor was it the fountainhead of "democracy." These altered circumstances were highlighted, on January 18, 1950, when the Chinese revolutionary government decided to recognize Ho's administration and exchange ambassadors with it; in this, the Chinese anticipated the Kremlin by a fortnight.

Vietnam had been subject to varying degrees of Chinese overlordship for tens of hundreds of years. Now China was strong again and belonged to the same ideological block as the Vietminh. The time had come to reconstitute the Indochinese Communist Party. The decision to disband it in 1945 had been even less popular among the Chinese comrades than among the party leaders in Paris.

On February 11, 1951 a revolutionary congress* attended by two hundred delegates was treated to a remarkable historical survey of the political scene by President Ho Chi Minh and a report by the General Secretary, Truong Chinh, concerning "the party's political experience and the immediate tasks of the democratic revolution of national liberation." The congress then voted in favor of setting up the Viet Nam Dang Lao Dong (Vietnamese Workers' Party). According to the political program of the new party, "the fundamental tasks of the Vietnamese revolution are as follows: to drive out the imperialist aggressors, to win independence and unify the nation, to abolish the colonial regime, to obliterate feudal and semifeudal vestiges, to give the land to the peasants, to develop popular democracy as a basis for Socialism."

The Central Committee elected by the congress was headed by Ho Chi Minh, whose summary of the growth of

---

* Some North Vietnamese publications refer to this as the Eleventh Congress of the Indochinese Communist Party, as though the latter had not been disbanded in 1945. Others call it the First Congress of the Lao Dong. In *The Selected Works of Ho Chi Minh* (p. 219) it is strangely described as the Second Congress of the Lao Dong.

the revolutionary movement included a careful justification of the breakup of the I.C.P. in 1945.

But however strong the influence of Peking had now become, Ho did not neglect his relations with the French left—this is why he extended such a friendly welcome to Léo Figuères, leader of the French Young Communists, in March 1950.

For three years, dealings between French and Vietnamese Communists had of necessity been limited; the Vietminh had been quite cut off from the outside world except for brief missions sent through Laos, Burma and India. Contacts could only be reestablished after the Chinese People's Army arrived at the Tonkinese frontier in January 1950. It was mutually agreed that the Vietminh youth conference due to be held at the end of February would be the best opportunity for a resumption of contact. Hence the importance of Léo Figuères's visit.

The young envoy left Paris at the end of January and traveled via Moscow, Peking and Hankow. It was not until early March that he arrived at his destination in the same truck as the first ambassador appointed by the Chinese People's Republic. The youth conference was over, but the Vietminh leaders were waiting for him.

Even though a war was raging, Ho welcomed him with great warmth. "You've picked the right moment," he said, "I've just received some champagne from the troops. . . ." The reception was held in the leader's private residence. Figuères noticed that, beyond the geniality which Ho was so fond of showing, various signs—the aide-de-camp, the bodyguard, a degree of ceremoniousness—served as reminders that the host was no ordinary guerrilla leader, but a head of state. This did not prevent Ho from showing the visitor his vegetable garden, where he spent hours among the tomatoes and sweet potatoes, or from taking him down to the "swimming pool" which he had improvised at the bend of a nearby stream.

Three things made a particular impression on Figuères during his talks with Ho and in the course of his visits to other party leaders and to the Vietminh installations in the wooded, mountainous area with many rivers around Tuyen Quang. First, there was the determination to check disorder and insure that the state retain its organized structure even in such primitive conditions; second, the skill shown in decentralizing this structure to the smallest detail so that it was effectively hidden in the jungle; third, the anxiety to re-create conditions which would make possible a negotiated settlement with France.

Ho suggested to Figuères that the exchange of prisoners might well provide the opportunity for preliminary contacts which would eventually lead to a political parley. Ho's desire to be in touch with Paris again was obvious. However, he made it quite plain to his guest that if the survival of the Vietminh between late 1946 and early 1950 had been entirely due to their great energy, obstinacy, ingenuity and adaptability, there was now a new asset, the victory of Chinese Communism, which radically changed the picture.

Ho pointed out that until the advent of the new China he and his colleagues had lived in a state of siege in the mountains, stubbornly trying to create a state from a guerrilla force which was cut off from the outside world; but now they had allies, they were recognized by ten or a dozen states, and they had a common frontier with the Socialist world.

When Figuères reported back to Paris, the French leaders dismissed all such pronouncements by Ho as mere political scheming. But a deep impression was made on the Vietnamese side by this resumption of contact and by the new impetus which it gave to the French Communist Party's campaign against the war. It is noticeable that in *Great Dates of the Vietnamese Workers' Party* Vietnamese historians single out as a major event of the period the speech which Maurice Thorez made at the Twelfth Congress of the French Communist Party in April 1950, following Figuères's return to Paris. Thorez declared: "It is precisely because we are patriotic Frenchmen, workers fired with the spirit of internationalism, that we are campaigning against the foul war in Vietnam. It is precisely because we love France that we suffer and are ashamed to learn that Frenchmen have been guilty of crimes. More than ever we feel the accuracy and truth of that observation by Marx: 'Any race which oppresses another cannot be free.' "

But nothing came of the few attempts which were made to reestablish contacts of a less peripheral nature. Alain Savary, adviser to the French Union, failed in his bid to meet Ho in 1952. Jacques Raphaël-Leygues and Professor Buu Hoi (later to become Saigon's ambassador to various African states) got no further than Bangkok; an attempt by Nehru at mediation—inspired from Paris by Jean Rous, who with Fenner Brockway was the animating spirit behind the Congress for the Independence of the Colonial Peoples —aroused some interest on the Vietnamese side, but had little appeal for French official opinion.

10

THE
VICTOR

While Ho and Giap—*General* Giap now—assembled the machinery for their "counteroffensive," the year 1953 was marked by the emergence in France of an irrespressible desire to put an end to this remote and dubious engagement in Indochina. Everyone could see that this colonial campaign which had turned into a civil war, and then into an anti-Communist crusade, was giving rise to a degree of international dissension that could lead to a third World War. The death of Stalin, in March, had opened up new vistas in the whole area of East-West relations. It was essential to find a way out of the dilemma, and the answer certainly did not lie in the "Bao Dai solution"* which, since 1949, had merely added a further dimension to the problem. But what was Ho Chi Minh really after?

Among the many people asking themselves this question was a Swedish journalist, Sven Löfgren, Paris correspondent of *Expressen*. One day, after listening to a debate in the Chamber of Deputies concerning the possible intentions of the Vietminh, he was struck by the fact that none of the arguments put forward had been based on the smallest scrap of up-to-date and specific information. He promptly decided to send a questionnaire to Ho Chi Minh, via Sweden's ambassdor in Peking. At the end of October he forwarded a set of queries regarding possible conditions for a cease-fire and a political settlement.

On November 26, Löfgren received a reply. It was even more favorable than he had hoped:

> The war in Vietnam was launched by the French Government. The Vietnamese people are obliged to take up arms and have heroically struggled for nearly eight years against the aggressors, to safeguard our independence and the right to live freely and peacefully. Now, if the French colonialists continue their aggressive war, the Vietnamese people are determined to carry on the patriotic resistance until final victory. However, if the French Government has drawn a lesson from the war they have been waging these last years and want to negotiate an armistice in Vietnam and to solve the Vietnam problem by peaceful means, the people and government of the Democratic Republic of Vietnam are ready to meet this desire.†

* *Bao Dai had been "emperor" of Annam during the Japanese occupation. Under the "Bao Dai solution" in 1949 the French recognized Bao Dai as emperor of all of Vietnam, as a counter to the Vietminh government.*—Ed.

† Bernard B. Fall (ed.), *Ho Chi Minh on Revloution: Selected Writings, 1920–66* (New York: Praeger, 1967), p. 256.

Ho's answers were published two days later in *Expressen*.

His statement may have been less explicit than the statements which the Vietminh leaders had addressed to the French government back in 1947. But in the atmosphere of bitterness and foreboding which now surrounded the war, it awakened keen interest. Löfgren was informed tartly at the Quai d'Orsay that "diplomacy is not conducted by means of classified advertisements" (the remark was Georges Bidault's); but public opinion would not allow Premier Joseph Laniel's government* to neglect any opportunity, however slight, of getting the country out of its difficulties in Indochina. This feeling was intensified when, on February 18, 1954, the Berlin Conference (attended by Russia, the United States, Britain and France) decided to call another four-power meeting in April, this time devoted to Asia.

Meanwhile René Pleven, the Minister for National Defense, was anxious that Ho should spell out his intentions more clearly. He asked Alain Savary to establish contact with the Vietminh leader. As we have seen, the Socialist deputy had already tried and failed to do exactly this in 1952. This time his attempt, though approved by the President of the Republic, was vetoed by Foreign Minister Bidault. "The Vietminh is at the end of its tether," argued Bidault, "your efforts will restore its confidence and give it sustenance. . . ." "You are taking a terrible responsibility upon yourself," retorted Savary. Three months were wasted in this manner, and when Bidault at last lifted his veto the battle of Dien Bien Phu had already sealed the fate of France in Vietnam. The Savary sounding-mission, which would have been very useful in November, had by then lost all purpose. Savary proceeded no further than Moscow.

* The Laniel government (1953-54) was distinctly rightist; its members included Georges Bidault and Paul Reynaud.

It is very hard to tell exactly what part was played by Ho in the long negotiations first broached at the Berlin Conference, officially begun at Geneva on May 7 (the very day when the entrenched camp of Dien Bien Phu fell to Ho's guerrillas), brought to a head on June 9 when the military delegate of the Vietminh openly presented a provisional plan for partitioning Vietnam, and finally concluded on July 21, 1954. But however little we may know of the behind-the-scenes discussions which resulted in the Vietminh leaders' decision to attend the Geneva talks, in their choice of delegates and statement of conditions, and finally in their readiness to cut their losses by offering to accept partition in exchange for a return to peace, we have only to recall at random any previous phase in Ho's career to sense that it was again he who had taken the lead.

Now that an opportunity had come at last to rekindle a little of the spirit of March 6 under all the ruins and ashes, he must have exerted all the pressure he could in favor of starting negotiations. He may even have thought of coming to Europe himself, as in 1946. The fact that Pham Van Dong, his trustiest disciple in the past thirty years, was appointed head of the Vietminh delegation shows the extent of Ho's eagerness that his own ideas should take precedence over the labors of the emissaries from the Democratic Republic of North Vietnam.

And as for proposing partition—even on the assumption that it would be temporary and that reunification would eventually be achieved by referendum—one cannot help feeling that no one else could have imposed such a sacrifice on his colleagues at a time when they were elated over the victory at Dien Bien Phu. Indeed, the whole tenor of the Vietminh's behavior at this time—its comparative moderation, its ingenious proposals, its flexibility, its tactical shrewdness—betrays the hand of Ho Chi Minh.

Moreover, the President did play a direct part in the debate. Immediately after his meeting in Berne with Mendès-

France on June 23, Chou En-lai set out for the Far East to confer with his colleagues and other Asian leaders. After visits to Nehru and Nu, he had long talks (July 3–5) with Ho Chi Minh on the Sino-Vietnamese border. As soon as he and the Vietnamese President had decided on the minimum conditions for a settlement, Chou En-lai flew back to Geneva.

On July 13 Chou saw Mendès-France again. The latter questioned him about Ho's current frame of mind. "I found an equal desire for peace among all the people I talked to," he returned with a suave smile. And in a style worthy of Ho himself Chou added: "Each side would need to step toward the other. . . . Which is not to say that each has an equal number of steps to make. . . ."*

Whatever the "steps" agreed on between Ho and Chou, the Vietnamese leader had to get them endorsed at the sixth meeting of the Central Committee of the Lao Dong Party, on July 15, 1954.

There are few more revealing documents than the text of Ho's address to the members of the Central Committee that day; and although the appeal was made in secret and not published until seven years later, it constitutes one of the best pieces of evidence of his determination to secure the reunification of his country without the use of force.

In the new combination of circumstances, the former watchword "resistance to the end" must be replaced by "peace, national unity, independence, democracy. . . ." When people embark on negotiations, they have to make reasonable mutual concessions. In the past we used to talk of driving out the French expeditionary force and annihilating it; now the French have agreed to withdraw their army at a given date. . . . Hitherto, the French Union did not

---

* It was three days later that Chou En-lai communicated to Eden the new Vietnamese conditions which saved the negotiations from deadlock; the Vietminh offered to accept partition at the sixteenth parallel—pending the demarcation at the seventeenth.

exist in our eyes. Today we are prepared to discuss the question of joining the French Union, freely and on an equal footing. . . .

And explaining the temporary partitioning of Vietnam, already agreed to by Hanoi's delegates in Geneva, Ho declared:

To demarcate those areas within which forces are to be regrouped is not the same thing as to divide the nation: this is a provisional measure aimed at the successful reunification of the country. . . . Our compatriots dwelling in hitherto free regions which will now be temporarily occupied by the enemy* will have grounds for discontent; some will take a black view, they will despair and possibly allow themselves to be exploited by our adversaries. We must make them realize clearly that, in the interest of the whole country, in its lasting interest, they must be capable of enduring the present. Doing so will bring them honor. The nation will be grateful to them.

Was this an incitement to subversion or an appeal for patience? The next part of his address reveals even more about the man, his conceptions and his strategy (it should be borne in mind that the author of these words had just won a victory of unhoped-for magnitude):

The following errors might occur: leftist deviationism— people intoxicated by our continual victories will want to fight at any price, fight to the end. Like men who cannot see the woods for the trees, they are mindful of the enemy's withdrawal yet pay no heed to his maneuverings; they see the French but not the Americans; they are full of enthusiasm for military action and underestimate diplomatic action.

* Under the terms of the agreements of July 21, 1954, the Vietminh were reassigned about twenty per cent of the territory which it controlled and more than a million and a half inhabitants.

They do not understand that side by side with armed battle we are carrying on our campaign at the international conferences, with the same objective in view. They oppose new watchwords, regarding them as evidence of rightism, as ill-considered concessions. They put forward excessive conditions, unacceptable to the other side. They want to rush everything and do not realize that the struggle for peace is hard and complex. If we yield to leftism we shall be isolated, cut off from our own people and from the people of the world, and we shall end in failure.

Rightist deviationism takes the form of negative pessimism and unprincipled concessions. Having no faith in the strength of the people, the rightists weaken its will to fight. They have got out of the habit of enduring hardship and no longer aspire to anything but a quiet and easy life.*

Ho's words afford a highly revealing glimpse of the wranglings inside the Central Committee of the Lao Dong just before the Geneva agreements were signed. The amount of attention which he devotes to "leftism" and "rightism," respectively, testifies to the nature of his own position and of the opponents whom he had to convince. Even the best behind-the-scenes reporting could not tell us as much about the role the old leader played at the time. Against the "leftists" who "opposed new watchwords" (the wrangling was keen and sustained), Ho fought in favor of a compromise solution—and he won.

That men who had reaped so heady a military success as Dien Bien Phu after eight years of exhausting effort and extreme privation, who controlled two-thirds of the national territory and who sensed that their prestige in the Cochin China region in the south was continually gaining strength—that men in such a strong position should have decided in favor of relinquishing much of the ground they had won and of leaving the best and richest areas in the

* *The Selected Works of Ho Chi Minh* (Hanoi: Foreign Languages Publishing House, 1962), pp. 458–62.

hands of their foes can be explained only in terms of the intervention of a great national figure.

The leaders of the Democratic Republic of North Vietnam were so self-assured at this stage that the advice of the two great Communist—but foreign—powers may not have been sufficient to steady them: the wisdom of such a sacrifice had to be affirmed by one of their own number, and indeed by the man whose word carried most weight. Ho may not have confronted Mendès-France physically in Geneva on July 21, as he had confronted Sainteny on March 6, 1946. But the spirit of the man and his personal touch were unmistakably present.

What can he have thought when news of the signing of the agreement at last reached Hanoi, during the night of July 21, 1954? That he had cut his losses again, as in March 1946, and surrendered a great deal in the process? That the end of fighting was worth the giving up of land? That tomorrow he would start rebuilding, and that sooner or later a massive vote on the part of the people in the south would join the divided nation?

The experience of forty years' relentless fighting had convinced him that a man has never altogether won or altogether lost, even when sprawling in the depths of a Kuomintang jail or standing as an honored visitor above the Tomb of the Unknown Soldier. Only a few days earlier, when Vo Nguyen Giap had told him of the fall of Dien Bien Phu, he had retorted gently, "However great the victory, it is only a beginning. . . ."

On October 10, 1954, eight years after the outbreak of war, five months after Dien Bien Phu, two months after the Geneva agreements, Ho arrived back in Hanoi at last. Even then, the return was a quiet one: the only cheering was for Giap and the "People's Army." There was little to celebrate, when so much lay in ruins.

But what sort of man would the French send as their representative now that peace—or at least a truce—had been established? A few weeks earlier, while sailing off the coast of Italy, Jean Sainteny had received a cable from his premier, asking him to come to Paris at once. Next stop Hanoi. The news gave Sainteny pause for thought. True, he had never sought to wash his hands of the matter, and in the difficult days of 1953 and 1954 he had expected Bidault or Pleven to send him back to Indochina with the perilous objective of getting talks started again. And his refusal to act as go-between for Bidault in the days immediately prior to the Geneva Conference had been inspired solely by the belief that there was insufficient time for him to reestablish his credit with the other side. Now that peace had been achieved, however, was there much point in sending him out there? Mendès-France was emphatic in his arguments and highly persuasive.

On November 7 he arrived in Hanoi as special envoy, designated as *délégué général*. Next day he called at Ho's residence. Would the man who greeted him be the same as before—the same both physically (for there had been so much talk of his elimination) and politically? Suddenly the two men found themselves face to face once more. After a moment's hesitation, Ho stepped toward him and with tears in his eyes embraced him as he used to in the old days. Immediately afterward, Sainteny cabled Mendès-France: "The man I saw is certainly Ho Chi Minh."

The heads of the Vietminh were plainly delighted at Sainteny's appointment and anxious to establish relations with France. Apart from providing them with a gateway to Europe and the West, such relations would enable them to import goods at favorable tariffs, enjoy the benefits of the more useful French "capitalist" firms operating on Vietnamese soil (though they would now of course be subject to the control of the Vietminh), receive assistance from the experts and technicians who would be sent out from

Paris, and successfully offset Vietnam's reliance on China and the Soviet Union. Others besides Jean Sainteny were wooed. One of his military aides, General de Beaufort, was told by Ho and Dong: "We have knocked each other about a good deal. Now we must work together on a fifty-fifty basis." And Giap observed to another French army officer: "Past wrongs can be attributed equally to either side; future exertions must also be shared equally. . . ."

But Sainteny himself was the principal target of this intensive campaign of charm. Despite the modest nature of the title and duties which Paris—bound by promises to the nationalists in Saigon—had seen fit to confer on him and which made him a kind of consul general rather than an ambassador, he was constantly treated as doyen of the diplomatic corps and seated without fail on the President's right. And Ho went even further: at one of the innumerable receptions given by the diplomatic missions of the eastern countries, he caught sight of Sainteny and, ignoring all others, walked across the room to him with outstretched hands. Then, turning to Lavrichev, the Soviet ambassador, he asked him to improvise a few words of French. The Russian diplomat apologized in confusion—he was unable to oblige. Ho burst out laughing. "He can't speak French?" he cried. "How very peculiar!"

Sometimes the President would telephone the *délégué général* at the last minute and say, "Do come around to dinner this evening. Just the two of us. We can settle a few things while we chat. . . ." But that was the trouble: *nothing* was ever settled. To avoid a rift with Saigon and to facilitate the task of General Ely, whose responsibilities in the south were very heavy, the Paris government dared not establish full diplomatic relations with Hanoi; it refused to receive a counterpart to Sainteny's delegation. As for the French public utility concerns, the owners decided to take measures—panic measures, in some cases—to insure that their property did not suffer the fate which Mao and his colleagues had inflicted four years earlier on similar establishments in Shanghai.

The almost idyllic harmony which had been carefully fostered for a whole year between Sainteny's team and the Hanoi government could not fail to turn sour. Certainly the old leader retained his personal liking for the signatory of the March 1946 agreements. But the weight of events was too great for anything to come of the mission. And after seven cruel years of war Ho could not be expected to take the same risks as in 1946, staking his prestige and authority on the off chance of reaching agreement with France, so distant geographically and so reluctant to commit herself. Moreover it soon became apparent that the promise given by the Nine at Geneva to organize general elections as a preliminary to the reunification of the country in July 1956 was not going to be honored. And France gave the impression of being none too mindful of the responsibilities inherent in her position as sole signatory of the Geneva agreements, under which she was duty bound to persuade Saigon and Washington to carry out the electoral experiment.

In November 1955, Ho agreed to receive a delegation from the French Senate, composed of Michelet and Léo Hamon; this was one of the last encounters with visitors from Europe which seemed to hold out any hope of a resumption of talks. The senators, who had come to Hanoi to look into the possibility of maintaining France's economic and cultural interests, had a long conversation with the President. They came away with the impression that Ho continued to think longingly of his years of understanding with France, that he deeply regretted the widening rift between the two countries, and that he would have responded fully and imaginatively to any genuine initiative from Paris. Yet what proposals could Paris make which would not scandalize Washington and look like betrayal to Saigon? For the French governments of the period these were major obstacles.

Sainteny's third mission to Hanoi ended with an incident which came close to ruining any future chances of negotiation. In October 1956 the uprising in Budapest against the Stalinist regime of Matyas Rakosi elicited an enthusiastic response among the small group of Hungarian experts who had been sent to assist their Vietnamese comrades. There were only eight of them, but they made no secret of their views. Consequently, as soon as Imre Nagy was defeated, the Hungarian authorities ordered them back to Budapest. Sensing what was in store for them, the men asked the French *délégué général* for political asylum.

Sainteny, who was in Paris at the time on official business, decided to accede to their request. And even as the North Vietnamese authorities informed Budapest that the eight Hungarians were being repatriated, a French commando group (unarmed, of course) intercepted them on the way to the airport and escorted them to the French headquarters where Sainteny, after a hasty return, made arrangements for their protection. Ho was furious and threatened to employ coercion. Whereupon Sainteny dictated the whole story to the Agence France Presse correspondent in Hanoi and warned the Vietnamese government that if any attempt was made to "recover" the Hungarians by force the entire world would be informed within minutes.

Making the most of the short respite which this warning gave him, Sainteny managed to smuggle his eight "guests" out of the city in empty gasoline drums bound for the French military mission in Laos. Ho did not at all relish the trick his friend had played on him and refused to have anything more to do with Sainteny. There was not even a farewell meeting between them when the Frenchman finally returned to Paris. As Ho saw it, Sainteny had flouted

Vietnamese sovereignty and jeopardized relations with a sister state.

Ten years later, however, Sainteny's fourth mission to Hanoi—of which more later—was marked by an atmosphere of renewed friendship. Never had Ho been more cordial. Eight Hungarians were of less account than the future of Vietnam and the role that France might be induced to play in it.

11

"HO CHU TICH MUON NAM!"

So here was Ho Chi Minh confronting his people in the immediate aftermath of victory—a man of sixty-four, moving among the ruins and the dead as leader of a temporarily divided Vietnam. What kind of human being was he at this time, and how extensive were his powers?

People who had known him before the war and who saw him again later say that the long, hazardous period of retirement in the forests of Tuyen Quang had evidently had a restorative effect on him. Gérard Tongas* writes, "He looked ten years younger than the man I remembered from 1946. I could not believe my eyes as he stood there before

---

* *L'Enfer communiste au Nord-Vietnam* (Paris: Debresse), p. 83.

us—jovial, smiling, the soul of geniality, glowing with health and vitality. . . ."

Jean Sainteny, who had known him better than anyone else from the West since his accession to power, considered that after this long interval Ho was "his old self, in good health, hardly a day older. . . ."

As for his power, there was some question as to whether the war, errors in judgment and above all the new, dramatic concession he had made—the partitioning of the country for two years, until the referendum—might not have harmed his prestige. A number of observers foresaw a quiet withdrawal to the political sidelines and a change in personality resembling Lenin less than Aesop and or Gandhi. Six months after his return to Hanoi the offices of prime minister and head of state, which he had hitherto combined, were separated; thereafter he was simply the President. Was this just a decorative, high-sounding title for an old hero, dreaming by the fireside?

To make such a negative appraisal was to discount his incredible vitality, the power of the legend surrounding him, the general affection for him—and events requiring his unique services. In 1956, a savage and hastily implemented land-reform policy brought the Democratic Republic of Vietnam to the brink of catastrophe. The Cabinet lost no time in begging the old pilot to return to the helm; he took over as party secretary from Truong Chinh, who became the scapegoat for leftist excesses. In fact, many of the tasks of this key post were soon assumed by Le Duan, who became official holder of the office in 1960. But the episode is still significant. In the hour of crisis it was to Uncle Ho that the party turned because the people were crying out for him.

Even supposing that his star had dimmed for the Vietnamese, surely his international reputation, his acknowledged stature and his position in Communist circles abroad and in most of the "uncommitted" countries of Asia would have sufficed to maintain his prestige and authority. Nehru considered him a friend. When he went to Peking for the anniversaries of the Chinese revolution, he was seated at Mao's right hand. And when he attended a Communist congress in Prague in 1959, he was surrounded by admirers, and militants from other states were greatly impressed.

Ho Chi Minh is first and foremost a man of original and personal style, a man with a distinctive relationship with the people. I have already quoted a few examples of the way he talks to children and to militants, to party cardres and to the aged. The subject is worthy of more attention, for it is crucial to any understanding of him.

In *The Selected Works of Ho Chi Minh,* the text which appears immediately after the declaration of independence —the first, therefore, which he drafted as head of state in the autumn of 1945—was not addressed to the soldiers, or to the workers, or to the militants, but to the children. To some the words will seem preposterous, but not to those who realize how important the family unit is in Vietnamese society:

My dear children,
Today is the mid-autumn festival. Your parents have bought you lanterns, tambourines, crackers, flowers and lots of other toys as well. You are as happy as can be!
. . . You are rejoicing, and your Uncle Ho rejoices with you. Guess why? First, because I love you very much. Second, because last year, at this same mid-autumn festival, our country was still living under oppression and you, my children, were still little slaves, whereas this year Vietnam has won back its freedom and you have become the young masters of an independent nation.
Today, enjoy yourselves as much as you like. Tomorrow,

I hope you will give your minds to your studies. Do you all know the Vietnamese alphabet? Those who do not know it should learn it. . . .

Next mid-autumn festival, we shall organize parties both for the children and for the old. What do you think of that?

This year I have no present for you. I just send you my loving kisses.

Hardly the kind of thing one would find among the collected speches of Joseph Stalin or Winston Churchill or Charles de Gaulle. Not that Ho was incapable of devising solemn words to match solemn events—as witness the appeal of December 20, 1946, or the political report of February 1951. But the tone of this militant Aesop is to be found even in his directives to combatants and cadres, and those dated April 1948 and entitled "What to Do and What Not to Do" provide a compendium of Vietnamese cultural values and practices. After putting the militants on their guard against any action which might "damage the inhabitants' gardens and crops, houses and furniture," and against such social blunders as "taking live fowl into the homes of our highland compatriots" or "lying down before ancestral altars, stepping on hearths, playing music indoors," Ho urges them to "tell bright stories, though without giving away any secrets of national defense" and "teach the alphabet and up-to-date ideas on hygiene." And at the end he even breaks into verse:

> Where's the mystery
> in these twelve points?
> No one with a grain of patriotism
> could ever forget them . . .
> A tree's sturdiness depends on the root.
> The palace of any victory
> is built upon the whole people.*

* *The Selected Works of Ho Chi Minh*, II, 129–31.

Ho did not alter his style with the return of peace. It remained genial and easy. Nor did he reserve that particular tone for the very young and the very old; he was quite capable of employing it on occasions which were generally considered serious. Early in 1960 the National Assembly held a debate about the wording of the new constitution. Ho sat listening in silence while the speakers had their say. Then he observed, "Well, if you want my opinion, I consider Clause A incomprehensible, Clause B inexplicable, Clause C a bit naïve. . . ." His objections had such punch and were so unceremonious that the deputies burst out laughing. "Oh, so you're laughing?" said Ho. "In that case I've won my point. One has only to achieve such an atmosphere, and half one's problems are solved. . . ."

A few years earlier, at the closing session of a "course in political education for intellectual cadres," the President began his speech with the words: "Today we shall gaily conclude our political course. . . ."* "Gaily" is not a word that anyone but Ho would think of applying to a course in Marxist reforms, given for the benefit of cadres in a besieged country; nor would anyone else make such a genuine attempt to inject this promised gaiety.

Hence the extraordinary character of the relationship between Ho Chi Minh and the Vietnamese people, a relationship summed up by two words which are invariably tacked on to Ho's name by the Vietnamese press and government propaganda: *cu,* "the revered," and *bac,* "uncle."

"Cu Ho": the term is written and spoken all the time. And the passage of time and the continual exposure to collective hardships serve only to lend more weight to it. In more recent days the familiar countenance has assumed the pallid, incorporeal look of a holy picture. Until 1958 he was habitually portrayed flanked by the Russian and Chinese leaders, a man in his fifties, a man of action. Nowadays

---

* *Ibid.,* p. 402.

the ubiquitous photographs show an old man with a white beard, his features softened by the short-lived peace which followed the Geneva Conference, looking rather faraway, as though he were already taking a historical view of the struggle. This is indeed the "revered one," the figure who for half a century has been molding and directing the Vietnamese revolution and striving to achieve unity. For Vietnam he is a Lenin who has lived long enough to defeat the Nazis, a Gandhi who has deserted his spinning wheel to build factories and direct a war of resistance.

Why "Uncle"? One explanation is that no other form of address was available to colleagues such as Dong and Giap, who are twenty years his junior. *Ong* (Mister or grandfather) was too distant, *anh* (brother) reserved for people of similar age or rank, *dong chi* (comrade) confined to party members.

But this use of the word "uncle" must also be related to the particular climate of Vietnamese society and traced back to its roots in Confucianism. *Bac,* or "uncle," is what a man calls his father's elder brother, a member of the family who outshines even the father in dignity and prestige. The concept of old age is very important in traditional Vietnamese society. No hint of irony or disrespect has ever been directed at the old. The old man remains, as he has always been, the key figure in a social structure based on the soil, the village and the home—this home being centered on the ancestral altar. The revolution has scarcely affected such ideas.

Though it implies affection, the word *bac* implies respect to an even greater degree. Family hierarchy may no longer be observed quite so rigorously as in the past, but it remains a touchstone. Some sociologists, however, argue that the word "uncle" does not altogether convey what is meant in the particular case of Ho Chi Minh. According to them, a better translation would be "Father," in the sense in which Catholics apply the term to a priest. This would bring us close to an essential connotation of "*bac*," the use of which is likewise not confined to the family circle. It would be less than apt, however, to speak of "Reverend Father Ho Chi Minh."

In the minds of the Vietnamese, Ho is identified with the soil to which they all cling, in defiance of foreign intervention (seeing the Frenchman or American as intruder rather than aggressor)—the soil to which the old man with the sparse beard returned after an absence of thirty years, and which he wrested from the foe within the space of eight.

But in connection with the relationship between Ho and the Vietnamese people, there are two other words which crop up all the time: *nghia* and *hieu*.

The idea embodied in *nghia* is close to the idea embodied in "duty." It is an awareness shared by individual and group alike of what should be done. The *nghia* binding Ho and his people is the consciousness of a two-way obligation, of devotion on one side and loyalty and discipline on the other. But to this is added a second bond which is summed up in the word *hieu*, habitually translated as filial piety.

Uncle, nephew, nieces—the other architects of Socialism show little sign of fostering this type of relationship with their fellow citizens. Walter Ulbricht would not do so in a million years. Even genuine "popular leaders" like Gomulka or Tito do not go in for this kind of thing. In Peking, the "Thoughts of Mao Tse-tung" shine at such a height that they confer a sense of aloofness even on those who have the signal honor of conveying them to the bedazzled masses. One has to go as far afield as Cuba to find any real traces of kinsmanship between leader and led, a kinsmanship stemming from that leader's warmth and simplicity. But Castro is the *líder máximo,* not "Cousin Fidel."

In fact, no other leader in the world today is viewed by his followers as being both inventor and protector, source and guide, theory and practice, nation and revolution, yogi and commissar, good-natured uncle and great war leader.

It would, of course, be a mistake to overemphasize this point and indulge in saccharine sentiment—even though the President himself is fond of handing out sweets. His authority, like Mao's, *"issued from the muzzle of a rifle,"* and that rifle has fired more than one round. The fond uncle is quite capable of playing the heavy father when he wishes. In the north, his firm hand was felt by the anti-Communist nationalists (V.N.Q.D.D., Dai Viet) and the Catholics between September 1945 and July 1946. And in the south he dealt sternly with the Trotskyites and the Hoa Hao recalcitrants.

Again, in 1955 and 1956 the land reform campaign was applied so harshly that the diocese of Xa-Doai in his own poor, proud native province of Nghe Tinh, birthplace of the "Xo-Viets" of 1930, rose in rebellion once more; and this time they were rebelling, not against the grasping mandarins or the invaders from the north or the French colonialists, but against the administration headed by their savior. The repression which followed was extremely harsh, and in 1960 officials in Hanoi were forced to admit that a third of the people condemned as "feudalists" had been wrongfully convicted.*

A year later, the "Intellectuals' Revolt" was put down with a ferocity which brought suffering to men of the stature of Tran Duc Thao, whom Sartre held in high esteem and who in 1951 had turned his back on a great career as a philosopher in Paris in order to go and fight in Vietnam.

To what extent did Ho seek to apply the brakes, to moderate? In this type of regime, once the leader has established strong personal ties with the masses he is automatically exempt from any public criticism of the system. It is those about him, his advisers and executives, who have to

---

* William Kaye, "The Economy of North Vietnam," *China Quarterly* (Winter 1962), p. 85.

bear the blame. And this is especially true in the case of a man like Ho, whose background, personal charm, moral authority, shrewdness—and also, it must be admitted, his skill in the art of public relations—have invested him with a radiance beyond compare.

Another unusual aspect of Ho's popularity is the manner in which he continually seeks to channel it toward the party. Unlike most heads of state in the new nations, he is ceaselessly concerned that the Lao Dong and its cadres should share to the full in the prestige which his past history, fighting spirit and spellbinding personality have conferred on him personally. True, the party's propaganda machine is continually active on his behalf, forever devising articles, slogans, songs, birthday celebrations. But there are certainly no grounds for imputing deification.

One cannot refrain from pointing out that high among his assets has been the crude lack of intelligence shown by his foreign opponents in two wars. Would his fame burn so brightly if France's leaders in the years 1946 to 1954 had not piled blunder upon blunder? Would his authority still be so intact if American bombers did not reestablish his raison d'être day after day, confirming him in the role of national hero and father figure?

Power such as Ho's cannot be maintained simply by smiling, uttering witticisms and patting children on the head. Ho is the kingpin of a complex structure of authority which, extending upward from the regional *can bo* (cadre) and village council to the head of state, party secretary and army commander in chief, maintains North Vietnam in an advanced state of discipline, organization and preparedness.

But the part he plays in all this is imperceptible, or at any rate difficult to pinpoint. Even before American air raids made precautions unavoidable, he led a curiously nomadic life in and around Hanoi, as though he regretted the caves and huts which had sheltered him as rebel and resistance leader. He still entertains from time to time in what used to be the governor general's palace; it was here I saw him for the last time, late in 1961. But he much prefers to lodge in the gardener's cottage at the far end of the grounds. There he tends his flowers and tomatoes, poses for photographers (especially on his birthday, May 19) and receives a number of "friendly" journalists—that is, journalists from the Socialist camp. But this is only one of many haunts where Ho the indefatigable rests his weary body. A cotton tunic, a scarf, a pair of sandals, a stick, a portable typewriter are luggage enough for this old traveling salesman of revolution who trudged the world for so many years until at last he roused his people and built a state.

Some reports suggest that Ho's prestige and authority were somewhat dimished by 1964. But within two years the foreign threat had made his fatherly guidance as indispensable as ever.

An admirably vivid first-hand impression is given by J. Raffaelli, the Agence France Presse correspondent in Hanoi in 1966. Every September 2, the Republic of North Vietnam celebrates the anniversary of its independence. In 1966 the commemorative rally was made public at the last moment in the interests of greater security. Foreign diplomats and journalists were invited to attend but given only two days' notice. Raffaelli reports:

> Everyone in the hall seemed to jump for joy when Ho Chi Minh appeared, a frail-looking figure with his narrow, bright-yellow tunic, his *samaras* (sandals tied with straps) made from an automobile tire, his diaphanous skin and his cheerful face. President Ho Chi Minh was showing himself in public for the first time that year. Behind him were the "Big Five" of the regime: MM. Pham Van Dong (government), Vo Nguyen Giap (army), Le Duan (party), Truong Chinh (parliament) and Nguyen Duy Trinh (diplomatic service).

On the little platform with its five rows of seats, some thirty men—many of whom represented divisions fighting in the south or on a war footing in the north—settled down behind the leaders, among the flowers and the floor-level fans; less than forty people altogether. . . .

. . . The ceremony began in Russian style, with flowers being presented to the leaders by pioneers wearing red scarves; it ended in Vietnamese style, in an atmosphere like that of a family gathering. Employing exorcism, punctuated by three successive waves of undulating arms, the rally warded off the imperialist demons before intoning the battle hymn "We Shall Win."

M. Giap beamed; his dark uniform, with the general's insignia, was open at the neck; he clapped vigorously in time with the music. M. Dong walked to the edge of the orchestra pit, handed his bouquet to the conductor and said: "The whole world knows we shall win. So I think we can safely sing an encore."

Gradually the character of the meeting changed: from a political gathering, it turned into "Grandfather's Day." M. Ho Chi Minh smoothed down his white beard and addressed the audience, seeking and finding opportunities to make contact with them. "The front rows," he said, in an atmosphere of collective worship, "did not sing very loud. . . ."

The officials in charge of security looked at the time. The leaders vanished amid clapping and cheering, obviously sorry to go. Outside, it was dark. The shadowy figures headed back toward the city; already the mood of guerrilla warfare had returned. . . .*

Here we see Ho surrounded by his own people, the men whom he has been molding for the past forty years, from the Thanh Nien of his Canton days to Pac Bo and Tuyen Quang. The old leader may be better at getting through to the masses than at refashioning Marxism, less good at in-

* *Le Monde*, September 3, 1966.

venting doctrines than at popularizing them, but he must still be credited with an exceptional gift: that of maintaining harmony at the center of a controlling group faced with problems of every kind, of preserving a stability without precedent in the history of modern revolutions.

The governmental team which I saw in action early in 1946—at the time when it was negotiating with Jean Sainteny and Léon Pignon, on the eve of a war with France which was to last for over seven years—has survived almost intact to this day. When I returned to Hanoi at the end of 1961, the list of appointments which I presented to the information office was substantially the same as the one I had drawn up fifteen years earlier—apart from the names of Tran Huy Lieu, Minister of Propaganda in 1946 but since then in charge of historical research, and of Le Duan, formerly political commissar in the south and now Secretary of the party.

All these men have figured in the story. Two of them, Ho's favorite lieutenants—Pham Van Dong, who as Prime Minister now shoulders the complex machinery of state as he once shouldered the risky negotiations at Fontainebleau and Geneva; and Vo Nguyen Giap, creator and strategist of the People's Army—are in some respects the Chou En-lai and the Lin Piao of the Hanoi regime.

I have also noted the part played by Le Duan, Party Secretary for nearly ten years, apparachik man, one-time guerrilla fighter, the only personality at the top who was not fully groomed for office by Ho himself, and the contribution of Truong Chinh, doctrinarian, journalist, Le Duan's predecessor as controller of apparachik (he was General Secretary of the I.C.P. and later of the Lao Dong) and now chairman of the Standing Commitee of the National Assembly—which in theory makes him the third-ranking figure in the country (below the Vice-President, the elderly Ton Duc Thang, but above the Prime Minister).

Newer to senior posts are Nguyen Duy Trinh, former

head of planning and Minister of Foreign Affairs since spring 1965, and Pham Hung, deputy premier, previously head of guerrilla warfare in the south and Pham Van Dong's right-hand man.

But the other members of the politburo—Le Duc Tho, influential theorist, General Nguyen Chi Thanh, political commissar to the army, Le Thanh Nghi, head of planning and the man who negotiated the 1966 agreements with Moscow, and Hang Van Hoan, a member of the Vietminh delegation at Geneva who afterward became ambassador in various capitals—are all "seasoned Bolsheviks," as are Ung Van Khiem, who first became Minister of Foreign Affairs, then Minister of the Interior after active service in the south and his former colleagues in Nam Bo—Dr. Pham Ngoc Thach, Minister of Health and Pham Van Bach, President of the Supreme Court.

The same stability is evident in the careers of the fellow travelers: the Socialist, Hoang Minh Giam, at one time Minister of Foreign Affairs, now in charge of culture, and the "Democrat," Phan Anh, another member of the Vietminh delegation, now responsible for external trade. There is an old saying about not changing horses in midstream, and if Ho has not quoted it, I shall quote it for him, since it is thoroughly in keeping with his style and fits the situation. The Democratic Republic of Vietnam has had to cross a good many streams—and not a few rapids—during the past twenty years.

Among so stable and compact a team (though it is not totally united, as we shall see in connection with the Sino-Soviet dispute and its repercussions in Hanoi), where are the potential successors to Ho, with his magisterial powers of judgment, his inspirational gifts and his miraculous ability to act as mediator among the masses, doomed to never-ending war, austerity and a harsh, often brutal regime?

The normal machinery of power ought to operate in

favor of Le Duan, who as General Secretary of the party can claim to be in possession of the commanding heights. But the army has powerful candidates too, beginning with Giap and Nguyen Chi Thanh. And who would dream of overlooking Pham Van Dong, the man who has so ably served as Ho's understudy during the past forty years that today he seems indistinguishable from the state itself?

Yet can anyone really "succeed" Ho? He towers above the political scene, and he knows it. Earlier, I have mentioned his flight to France in the company of General Salan late in 1946. The aircraft made an overnight stop in Rangoon. At one point, Ho came into the general's room and unceremoniously installed himself under the mosquito netting. Salan asked whether he was not alarmed at the prospect of being away for some time and leaving the country in the hands of young hotheads like Giap and Truong Chinh. "What could they possibly do without me?" asked Ho. "It was I who made them. . . ."

Such, then, is this glittering, many-faceted figure, whose colorful and romantic brand of Communism is blended into a formula whose secret appeared to have vanished with Karl Radek and Victor Serge. A man like Ho is the result of countless experiences and ordeals without number: a pathetic childhood in abject surroundings; the harsh apprenticeship of growing up in a rural society of an underdeveloped country; the discovery of the wonderful, tragic and welcoming city of Paris in the years following the end of the First World War; the companionship of men who were at once the last of the "forty-eighters" and the first of the "Leninists"; a long period of exile; the chance to work side by side with the architects of the October Revolution; imprisonment; hunger; guerrilla warfare in the mountains; the rise to power; terror endured and inflicted; moments of triumph.

The man thus molded by action, guile and power has come to occupy a position without parallel. However ruthlessly the people of North Vietnam may be governed, it would be wrong not to indicate how fully Ho has managed to identify with his fellow countrymen, and what an unusual relationship he has established with them. He is forever addressing ordinary citizens in an easygoing or fatherly tone, forever distributing oranges or other tidbits to the children. This is partly play-acting—why deny it? The character he projects is too well rounded to be entirely spontaneous, and his large red handkerchief has often dabbed at dry eyes.

Here we have another of the more disconcerting aspects of Ho's nature: this mixture of play-acting, charm and urbanity adds up to a personality which seems more Chinese than Vietnamese. The people of Annam and Tonkin are as a rule more straightforward, more sentimental, less demonstrative, although the thin shell of traditional reserve is easily broken. Anyone who has ever met Vo Nguyen Giap or Pham Van Dong knows this—and here I have been careful to pick disciples of Ho, men who, like the President himself, have been molded by the disciplines of Marxism-Leninism; but of course they are younger.

Indeed, where does acting begin and end in the behavior of such a man? He is continually stage-managing himself, continually looking at situations with a producer's eye. During his "public-relations" visit to France, in 1946, he was invited to the Hotel de Ville. At first he declined all offers of food and drink, but eventually he changed his mind, picked out a fine-looking apple, put it in his pocket and, before the astonished gaze of the French President Vergnolles, walked out of the building; he then hurried down the steps and before the cheering mass of people presented the apple to a little girl. And yet, however "artistic" he may be, a producer invariably expresses his inner temperament. For all his artfulness, there is something warm, friendly and beguiling about the way Ho addresses his fellow citizens; it is difficult to convey this impression to anyone who has not heard him. I have already quoted several examples of his public manner. Here is another that is highly characteristic:

> You have reached the age of reason, my nephews.
> Your uncle is very pleased.
> This autumn I am sending you a nice letter
> and with it my love, dear nephews
> in provinces near and far. . . .
> . . . From the nearby hamlets to the distant villages,
> eating their fill and wearing warm clothes,
> our countrymen are making progress, forging ahead . . .
> . . . High up in the clouds floats
> the red flag of victory.
> You are joyful, my nephews.
> And I, your uncle, tell you with equal pride:
> our next autumn will be an even happier one!*

This may sound mawkish to Western ears—Red politics tied up in pink ribbon. But plainly this kind of thing does not sound either laughable or old-fashioned to Ho's immediate audience. One of his ex-ministers told me recently:

> That he is still in control is largely due to the fact that no other Vietnamese is capable of achieving a comparable synthesis of political authority and popular appeal; no one else could be on the one hand the uncompromising militant, and on the other the Vietnamese scholar, sensitive, learned and full of feeling. . . .

There is something very special, and probably irreplaceable, about the bonds that unite Ho and the Vietnamese people in a relationship so different from that existing between other leaders and their followers. The importance of

---

* Bernard Fall, *Le Viet Minh* (Paris: A. Colin), p. 37.

the family link has already been touched on; but there is is another vital aspect which needs to be stressed in any consideration of the spell which Ho casts—the persuasiveness of the man.

Power such as his is in many ways totalitarian and prompts reservations, even when it is harnessed to a heroic fight for a just cause. But one thing about Ho is beyond dispute: his passionate desire to persuade people, his thoroughly democratic urge to win acceptance for measures by argument rather than compulsion.

I saw him brave the crowd—a restive, suspicious, excitable crowd—in Hanoi on March 7, 1946 and talk it into accepting the agreements which he had just signed with France. He could have enforced this temporarily unpopular policy without consulting them, but he wanted them to share in his convictions; similarly, a few months later, he went out of his way to argue the soundness of his policy to the Vietnamese living in France, who were inclined to regard it as a sellout.

Perhaps it is this strong urge to persuade and involve the masses which has led him to stress popularization and simplification.

If ever developments in the war and American public opinion compelled Washington to believe that the Vietnamese aspirations were serious and steadfast (though this awareness need not entail eliminating either the military presence or the political pressures and bargaining powers of the United States and her allies or protégés), it would be the signal for Ho, frailer and more affable than ever, to call his people together and preach in favor of accepting an honorable peace. And as he stood on the platform beside his portrait, the party members and the ordinary men and women in the crowd would chant the phrase which for over twenty years has been more familiar than any other in the political life of Vietnam: *Ho chu tich muon nam,* "May President Ho live a thousand years!"

Ho Chi Minh—is the magic of this final *nom de guerre* of Nguyen That Thanh as powerful in the south for the Vietnamese who are living face to face with foreign intervention? Are the name and legend of this northerner (hailing from a province north of the seventeenth parallel, whose grimness and earnestness are far removed from the pattern of life in the south) effective weapons in Hué, Saigon and Cantho? Less effective probably, for reasons of accent, style, tradition and recent history too. The southerners have always regarded the northerners as vagrants on the lookout for work, land and administrative posts; this is one of the reasons why Ngo failed. Those in the south who were anxious to bring down the Diem regime came to the conclusion that the north was overcautious and far too slow in intervening. Even before that time, many were disappointed by Ho's acceptance of the provisional partitioning of the country in 1954 and by his failure to react sharply when the deadline for reunification in 1956 came and went without result. He seemed to be remarkably easygoing with Diem.

But such social and political differences in no way affect two basic realities: the general longing for unity among the Vietnamese people, and the fact that except for Ho Chi Minh no one from the Chinese border to Point Bai Bung (Cape Camua, at the southernmost tip of Vietnam) can claim the past record and present stature of a truly national figure.

Indeed, a whole school of literature has emerged in the south whose theme is the "return of the uncle" who, "after setting out from Saigon in the old days, has still not returned." Among the items in *Recollections of Ho Chi Minh* is a poem by a Saigon writer named Thanh Hai:

> *When evening comes I dream of your return, dear Uncle,*
> *On the glorious day of reunification.*
> *Triumphal arches will shelter your path.*

You will stand at the top of the City Hall steps.
A smile on your lips, your eyes shining like stars,
You will give us your advice.

Well, it may not be Mayakovsky but it's better than
Fadeyev. And the word "advice" is worth savoring: it fits in
so well with the "Uncle" theme.

In 1965, young Nguyen Van Troi was executed by firing
squad in Saigon for plotting to assassinate the United States
Secretary of Defense McNamara. According to an anony-
mous poet, he shouted just as the bullets struck him: "Long
live the revered President Ho!"

Here I should like to quote a witness who, I assume,
would be generally accepted as trustworthy. I asked a senior
American officer, who had spent two years as administrative
adviser in the Mekong delta conducting a thorough political
inquiry, how he thought the war would end. "It's quite
simple," he said. "What keeps the guerrillas fighting and
the peasants supporting them is the magic surrounding the
name of Ho Chi Minh. So long as our enemies have 'Uncle'
to turn to, they will hold their own. But Ho Chi Minh is an
old man. One of these days he'll die; and when he does, the
Vietcong's resistance will crumble for lack of inspiration."
That may well be—but we can imagine the Vietnamese
guerrillas continuing the fight, and singing "Old revolutionaries don't die!"

12

CLUES
TO
A
REVOLUTIONARY

"Is he *really* a Communist?" How often one has heard the question. Doubts have been raised not so much by any particular episode or episodes in Ho's political career as by his style of government and general behavior. Is it possible for a man to be a real Communist and yet remain so genial and whimsical, at times almost clownlike, amid the turmoils and complexities of total revolution?

Those who think in this way are too ready to overlook the fact that Ho was molded as a man and as a revolutionary in the days before Zhdanov, Ulbricht and Liu Shao-chi set the fatal seal of dullness on Marxism-Leninism, substituting didacticism for analysis, vindictiveness for purposeful anger. At the time when Ho studied the art of dynamiting capitalism, Lenin's speeches were garnished with fierce language and lively anecdote, Karl Radek's with wit and paradox, Vaillant-Couturier's with laughter. Colorfulness was as unlikely to be branded counterrevolutionary as poetry, bohemianism or freedom of discussion. The wooden faces and stodgy speeches came later, with the sweeping purges and the growth of the personality cult. When the Comintern first came into being, neither Khrushchev nor Castro nor Ho Chi Minh would have seemed in any way eccentric. The revolution had gone beyond its utopian stage without becoming regimented.

But in fact it is the record of his conduct as leader of the Vietnamese revolution, rather than his personal style, which has fostered reservations. Lenin of course would have understood most of his changes. But very few people share Lenin's familiarity with Marxist terms of reference; and many find Ho's behavior difficult to understand. Let us see if we can clarify the problem.

In her book, *Von Lenin zum Mao,* Ruth Fischer writes: "The thing that struck us most about him, in the midst of this abstract, monolithic International, was his ardent nationalism. . . ." She appears to share the view that for "Nguyen Ai Quoc" Marxism was primarily a means to an end, and International Communism a mere springboard to victory for his underlying patriotism. In May 1947 the Vietminh delegation in France put out a pamphlet entitled *President Ho Chi Minh,* completely glossing over his Communist background and seeking to present him as an out-and-out patriot.

Anybody who has had a chance to converse directly with Ho can well understand why doubts exist concerning his membership in the Communist club. For no one could make less use than he does of party jargon, that dog Latin of Marxism which is a barrier to those who do not speak it and which helped to give Communism such an ecclesiastical air in the thirties, forties and fifties.

It is not Marxist-Leninist phraseology that Ho uses in conversation but the idiosyncratic language of the League of Human Rights and of a kind of social-laicism which he picked up from his left-wing associates in the Paris of the twenties. I advanced this view to some Vietnamese friends, and they retorted, "When he is talking to us, his vocabulary seems to owe more to social-Confucianism. . . ."

We have seen how, on December 26, 1920, a slight man of thirty, who looked ten years younger, got up in the middle of the Socialist Congress at Tours and falteringly delivered himself of a few sentences which were hard to catch, difficult to fathom and not listened to with any great attention. However disturbing the questions were that he raised, they had not the slightest effect on the course of the debate. His words were a cry of pain, but they were too remote from the concerns of the day, too artless, too clumsy, to be understood by anyone but his fellow countrymen.

The young revolutionary from the colonies had been spellbound by *Imperialism, the Final Stage of Capitalism,* published in Petrograd three years earlier, and did not hesitate to borrow from Vladimir Ilyich's crudely didactic simplifications. A man whose compatriots had been employed as cheap labor during the war could not fail to warm to sentences like ". . . The 1914–18 war has been, on both sides, an imperialist war (in other words a war of conquest, plunder, brigandage), a war concerned with the dividing up of the world, with the distribution and redistribution of colonies and spheres of influence. . . ."

Apparently Ho had not studied the principal Leninist writings closely enough—especially the celebrated article on nationalities drafted by Stalin in 1913 under the direct inspiration of Lenin—to register the fact that in accord with the "Marxist principle of the secondary and subordi-

nate nature of the national question," Lenin's underlying
aim was to let the "worldwide revolutionary strategy" profit
from the "tactical contribution which could in certain circumstances and certain areas be furnished by struggles for
national liberation."*

Ho had probably declined to enter the maze of Socialist
self-contradictions on the subject, which ranged from
Marx's support for the struggle for Polish independence (on
the grounds that it undermined Czarist might, which was
then the chief obstacle to the progress of Socialism in
Europe) to the opposition to that same struggle voiced by
Rosa Luxemburg and afterward by Lenin (on the grounds
that the secession of Poland could only weaken the state
which held the best promise of Socialist revolution).

The young Vietnamese revolutionary was bound to realize how great was the gulf between these "national problems" and the "colonial problem" which he had experienced at first hand and was now rethinking in terms of
Marxism-Leninism. He did not need to be told of the difference in condition between the Slovaks and the Vietnamese,
between the people of the Cameroons and those of Galicia.
As he had bitterly noted, few European Socialists were then
aware of the form of relationship existing between the
industrialized nations and those races which had to endure
total hardship and deprivation. His denunciation of the
French Communist Party's indifference to overseas problems, at the July 1924 congress of the International, shows
that he had detected a type of collusion which was above
and beyond the class conflict.

Yet, however conscious he might be of certain gaps, he
was able to refer to a number of texts of unimpeachable
origin. For instance, there was Stalin's observation that "we
are in favor of the emancipation of the colonies, for it

* Annie Kriegel, "La Seconde Internationale devant les questions
nationales en Europe (1889–1914)" *Socialisme*, 76 (July 1966).

weakens imperialism,"* which was motivated of course by opportunism but was more applicable to the problems of colonial Vietnam than the textbook cases examined by the major theorists of Marxism.

If the orthodox Marxist texts were sometimes hard to relate to the Vietnamese context, Ho could always refer to Jaurès's famous saying: "Nations are the repositories of human culture." But all this was still jumbled together in his mind at the end of 1920, and his confusion showed in his public utterances.

His debut in professional politics was therefore a quiet one. Later, a legend was deliberately built up around the episode at Tours, which was exaggerated in private and public conversation by Marcel Cachin, Gaston Monmousseau and several others. But at the time he was just "an Indochinese," and his contribution to the debate made little or no impression on anybody except perhaps the intelligent and sensitive Paul Vaillant-Couturier. Ho might well be accused of "banality." And certainly the peasant from Annam was only a modest figure among this gathering of intellectuals, which included Longuet, Sembat, Faure and Blum. The impressive thing about Ho Chi Minh has never been brilliance of thought or expression. He had to school himself in the important art of communicating with an individual or a crowd. But his thought processes have always retained a certain artlessness. He is an admirably effective popularizer, but except in two or three telling expositions of revolutionary strategy he has seldom risen above the level of genial didacticism, enlivened by a highly personal sense of humor.

Before letting the experts have their say, we should note the principal traits of this singular personality that was

* *The Selected Works of Ho Chi Minh* (Hanoi: Foreign Languages Publishing House, 1962), IV, 84.

molded by half a century of fighting for the Marxist cause.

Acumen, dislike of violence, a quite exceptional gift for making contact with people, the culture of a self-taught man (fairly wide-ranging, but distinctly uneven), a sense of humor which draws alike on his background in Asian traditions and on Western influences, frugality, a natural austerity reinforced by will power, unsurpassable energy: these are the characteristics of the man as he faces the ordeals of public life.

I have already quoted many of his speeches—homilies to the old, exhortations to the young, appeals to the fighting men and words of homage to his countrymen, his "nephews." Examined with a cold appraising eye, they can look very dull indeed. At times they read like the work of a country priest or an unworldly schoolmaster. Is he quite serious? In Truong Chinh's life of the President, which has been referred to earlier, there is a section headed "Of Revolutionary Morality"; Ho is presented as a master of that particular brand of morality on the strength of remarks like "In order to become rich, every individual, every family, and indeed the entire people must intensify production and make economies." Is this old Guizot speaking, or a little "notable" in Hué, or a Chinese shopkeeper in Cholon? In fact it is a sound tactician talking the language of his subjects, piously using traditional words to express the modern and collective notion of productivity. The tone, the vocabulary, the style are altogether different from those employed by the other prime movers of the Marxist-Leninist revolution.

In his analysis of Ho's doctrine, to which I shall be returning, Truong Chinh writes: "He detests the parading of theory and dry, pedantic quotations from the classics of Marxism-Leninism." And in fact the President advances very little theory of any sort.

Uncle Ho's language is truly avuncular. Joseph Stalin, too, was capable of sounding like a schoolmaster. But did

Stalin use those expressions from early lessons in character
training which are part of Ho's stock in trade and the most
significant of which is "emulation"? In the three volumes of
The Selected Works of Ho Chi Minh the word appears
more than a hundred times. "Engage in emulation"—he
returns to the theme again and again, seeing emulation as a
commendable and friendly form of rivalry in the interests of
improved behavior. According to Truong Chinh, the President's motto is "Work transforms the world, emulation
transforms man." Materialism may have a smaller share in
this two-fold process than was allotted to it by Engels.

Does Ho's extraordinary career have an ideological basis,
or was he merely a brilliant manipulator, an outstandingly
gifted jack-of-all-trades? It is possible to trace, in broad outline, the ideological progress of the man and his revolutionary organization. It is also possible to provide a definition of his "doctrine," or at any rate to list the ingredients
which make up his ideological behavior. I shall quote from
friends and foes alike, and then I shall try to work out a
"middle-of-the-road" interpretation.

One of the enigmas surrounding his career can be expressed as follows: Why was his name not associated with
any of the conflicts which, from 1924 to 1939 led to the
downfall of most of the leaders of the Third International?

Most of the writers who have considered this question,
from Ruth Fischer to Bernard Fall, have been content to
answer that Ho was, and is, too much of an empiricist to
get involved in doctrinal disputes.

A more elaborate explanation of his exceptional position
within the Third International is offered in a pamphlet
(in French) entitled *National Movements and Class Struggles in Vietnam,* written by Anh-Van and Jacqueline Roussel and issued by the publishing house of the Fourth
International.

The Trotskyite authors base their reasoning on the
doctrine and themes enunciated by *Thanh Nien,* Ho's news-

paper in Canton, during the years 1925 to 1927. Quoting a passage from *The Communist International After Lenin* in which Leon Trotsky accused Stalin and his group of seeking, among other things, "ready-made revolutionary forces outside the proletariat" and of "exaggerating the role of the Peasant International at the expense of the Red Trade-Union International, Anh-Van and Jacqueline Roussel write:

> These lines help to shed light on the political character of Nguyen Ai Quoc, who has faithfully followed every twist and turn of the Communist International. In the first place, it must be remembered that he acquired his fundamental training as a leader during the years 1923 to 1925 . . . in the midst of the Peasant International, at the very moment when, as L. Trotsky emphasizes, revolutionary forces were being sought outside the proletariat. Consequently the character which Nguyen Ai Quoc conferred on the Thanh Nien Party from the outset is readily explained: he intended to make it a nationalist rallying point, Socialist in tendency. . . . He did not distinguish between the Indochinese proletariat and the national bourgeoisie. This conception of the revolution in Indochina was expressed in the program of the Thanh Nien; it was to be carried out in two phases—first, a national revolution securing the country's independence with a bourgeois-democratic regime, then a further stage (as yet remote), the proletarian revolution. . . .
>
> "All the same," people will object, "it did develop into a Communist Party in the end. Was there a break with the previous line?" Here again, Nguyen Ai Quoc and his fellow leaders followed the fluctuations of the Third International. . . . By 1930 the Communist International had abandoned its rightist course, though without learning from the experience, and plunged into a new leftist course, the famous and disastrous "third period" which ended tragically for the German proletariat with Hitler's assumption of power in 1933." (This was the time, in fact, when the Communists branded social-democracy as "social-fascism" and declined

to form a popular front. The outcome of their isolated stand against the Nazis does not need repeating.) In the colonial countries the third period took the form of relentless opposition to the nationalist bourgeoisie, whose "definitive betrayal" was denounced.

It was against this change of course that a stand was taken by the Indian Communist leader Roy, till then the Asians' spokesman inside the International. His brand of Communism, like Nguyen Ai Quoc's, was steeped in nationalist tendencies. So he refused to break with Moscow's own previous line of working in coalition with the "bourgeois parties," and this resulted in his expulsion from the movement. Ho, on the other hand, fell in line, though with obvious reluctance, because the national front doctrine was closely attuned to his temperament and also to the basic facts of the situation in Indochina, where the proletariat was still so insubstantial. This act of discipline, at a crucial moment, lent considerable weight to the future Ho Chi Minh in the councils of the Stalinist International.

It is important to discount the resentment which animates these two comrades of all the Trotskyite militants slain by the I.C.P. Having done so, however, we can accept several points in their analysis, amend others and carry it further, although a stronger emphasis should be placed on the purely Vietnamese motives behind Ho's strategy.

What must be emphasized above all else is the two-sidedness of his every move, making him the most nationalist as well as the most internationalist of the Communist leaders. He is the most nationalist, for none of the other leaders has achieved revolution in his country with less foreign aid and fewer foreign cadres; none of them, not even Mao or Tito or Castro, is so little in anyone's debt.

True, the uprisings he has launched and the wars he has led have been anchored to a Communist world and rooted in an international context. But in Vietnam there has been no sign of a Borodin, a Guevara, a Malraux or a MacLean.

The few representatives of the Third International, the O.S.S. and the Peking government who have in turn co-operated with Ho have played only a tiny role before and after Dien Bien Phu; and although the artillery from eastern Europe and the workers and trucks from China may have been—and still are—useful to Giap's strategy, they have served in a strictly Vietnamese framework and under Vietnamese colors. Passionate concern for his country animates Ho above all else, just as it animates Giap and most of the hard-core militants.

But unlike Giap, his most brilliant disciple, and his "nephews," Ho is an internationalist, because of the particular time and context in which he has been molded. In Paris in the twenties, a student worker by the name of Chou En-lai wrote: "Although we are Chinese, our attitude must be cosmopolitan."* And in Moscow, the revolution was still viewed in international terms, both in theory and in practice. This was the period when the Bulgarian Dimitrov was active in Germany; the Serb Vouiovich in France; the Frenchman Ducroux in Malaya. Ho's nationalism amazed people like Ruth Fischer; contact with these great "cosmopolitans" did not weaken it but added to it a broader dimension. Moreover, he retained from his Paris days that sense of solidarity with all colonial peoples which he expressed in Le Paria. In its pages, the Madagascans and Moroccans had been seen in exactly the same light as the Vietnamese, and Ho had needed no encouragement to look beyond colonialism and attack the racialist problem.

In short, this national Communism is rooted in a broadly based internationalism, and Ho has always felt involved in the debates of the Third International, even though his diffidence toward matters of doctrine has prevented him from playing as large a part in its discussions as his acknowledged

* C. Brandt, "Les Origines idéologiques des dirigeants du P. C. chinois," Le Mouvement social (Paris, July–September 1963).

status would allow. Indeed, he has engaged in a perpetual attempt to achieve a synthesis between the respective demands of proletarian internationalism and Vietnamese nationalism, long before he was obliged to steer a difficult course between Soviet pressures and Chinese incitements.

It is possible to argue, as Anh-Van and Jacqueline Roussel do, that his attitude dates back to the founding of the Thanh Nien in Canton. Socialist-style nationalism? The charge cannot be denied. A rightist policy of collaborating with the bourgeoisie? The facts speak for themselves (although, as we have seen, Ho had an out-and-out Communist "brigade" at his disposal which formed the nucleus of the organization). But if the Trotskyite authors, in the light of European or American examples (La Follette, the trade unions), are irked by the conservatism of the International's "second phase," they have fewer reasons for objecting to the use of this strategy in Asia, where the proletariat was until recently insignificant compared to the middle class and the peasantry. This can be seen clearly in the case of China, where the leftism of Li Li-san plunged Chinese Communism into the catastrophe of 1926 and 1927.

Besides, Ho did not confine himself to collaborating with the Vietnamese bourgeosie. While writing *Le Chemin de la révolution*, (The Road to Revolution), which followed a more strictly Marxist line, he was preparing the cadres for a revolution based on violence. Unquestionably, the "national front" strategy adopted by the Thanh Nien at the time was the strategy best suited to its character and aims. But it must also be acknowledged that such a strategy in no way conflicted with the decisions made in Moscow at the Fifth Congress (which, as we have seen, Ho attended in July 1924); in addition, it was carried out in the presence of a man who can hardly be accused of siding with the "rightists" in the Comintern—Mikhail Borodin.

Does this mean that we should accuse the Vietnamese of recanting or being blind followers because of their decision to align themselves with the leftist policies laid down by the Sixth Congress in 1928? Anh-Van and Jacqueline Roussel contrast the firmness of Roy, in refusing to abandon the "national front" strategy, with the docility of Ho Chi Minh. But it must be pointed out at once that the Indian leader was head of a far more powerful organization and thus enjoyed a much greater sense of personal authority. It should be remembered also that the Indochinese Communist Party was not founded until 1930.

Moreover its birth, which entailed a break with the "national front" strategy as applied to the Thanh Nien, was precipitated by the blundering initiatives of men other than Ho. It was only after several proto-parties had been created, amid much rivalry and confusion, that he was summoned from Siam to restore order and reestablish unity. In fact, at the time of the Sixth Congress in Moscow—and throughout the following year, when the International's leftist "third phase" was put into effect—Ho was very much in the background; whether by accident or design, he was training cadres in Siam. During this period, the man at the helm was (to all appearances, at least) Tran Phu, the first General Secretary of the party. Which makes it difficult to assert that Ho veered instantly from right to left. The truth is that in 1930 he slowly came around to a policy which was already in part contradicted by the facts.

There is little or no written evidence available that he regarded the creation of the Indochinese Communist Party as premature, but it seems likely that he did. Once it was founded, however, he had to seek a way to fit it into the "national front" strategy. Such a course was condoned by the Sixth Congress held in Moscow in 1935 which came out in favor of "antifascist Fronts." The International upheld his views against those of certain other I.C.P. leaders who, meeting in Macao while he was away, had sought—only a few weeks earlier—to cling to the "hard" line.

He was therefore free to apply the strategy of his choice.

But not with the instrument which he would have preferred to use. At Moscow's behest, the Vietnamese Communist Party very soon turned into the Indochinese Communist Party. At this period, the Comintern leaders mistrusted nationalism. The patriotism of Ho and his associates had to be blended into a broader entity: for ten years they had to keep their patriotic banners and slogans under cover and campaign on an essentially proletarian basis and in close cooperation from 1936 until 1940 with the French working class and antifascists.

At the Pac Bo conference in May 1941, held within safe reach of the Chinese border but on Vietnamese soil, Ho calculated that he was now at liberty to reunite the movement with the powerful current of nationalism. The result was the birth of the Vietminh, a "national liberation front" whose program, as we have seen, was revisionist and ardently nationalist. Four years later he went still further—much further—by disbanding the Indochinese Communist Party and setting up the Lien Viet, which was even more effective at propagating the revolutionary zest of the Vietminh.

Everything has been said that needs to be said about the dissolution of the I.C.P. And many close observers of the Vietnamese revolution—P. J. Honey, for instance—see it as no more than a tactical ruse. And indeed, in support of their theory they can quote Ho's comment in a political report dated February 1951: "One fact struck many people as barely comprehensible—the party proclaimed its dissolution. In fact it went underground. But it continued to direct the state and the people."*

Granted. But what he here represents as a mere change of register caused much agitation at the time among the Chinese Communists and their French comrades. A Communist party is no mere tactical instrument. To Marxist-Leninist militants it is a basic scientific fact, the concrete

* The Selected Works of Ho Chi Minh, II, 232.

manifestation of the will of the masses and their emancipation. "The Party" is not a party. It is the public projection of an idea which is considered flawless and the weapon whereby this idea can transform society. To disband it, even temporarily, and even in exchange for advice to join in the labors of "Marxist study groups" (which was offered by the I.C.P. leadership in 1945), was a step of unprecedented boldness; and it was generally regarded as such.

When Ho arrived in France in the summer of 1946, this was the first topic raised by his French comrades—and there was little warmth in the way they tackled him. He made much of the fact that if the I.C.P. had not resorted to camouflage it would have been smashed by the Kuomintang, whose troops were then occupying northern Vietnam. Neither the German nor the French Communists had responded in like manner to Nazi oppression.

Ho Chi Minh could not be accused of lacking courage or revolutionary fervor. But the strangeness of the step he took in 1945 is intensified by the fact that it was justified in different terms on different occasions. "We have done it," the Vietminh newspaper *The Republic* insisted at the time, "in order to insure the unity of the race."*—an odd way of putting it.

It seems to indicate that Ho saw the party as a means, a revolutionary instrument, rather than as an end. Never, perhaps, has his pragmatism shown more plainly or appeared more audacious.

At all events, after the official disbanding of the I.C.P. in late 1945, the Vietminh leadership advanced a long way on the path of the common front by founding the Lien Viet, in May 1946, and inviting all "patriots" to join. The opening of hostilities with France made it imperative that the political spectrum of the forces engaged against her be as broad as possible. But in 1950 the Communists won control

* Devillers, *Histoire du Vietnam.*

of China. Ho and his colleagues were restored to contact
with the outside world, namely the Socialist world. Suddenly
they had allies next-door. In consequence, they could afford
to show their true colors again. February 1951 saw the
foundation of the Lao Dong, the Workers' (or Labor) Party.

This did not altogether mean the resurrection of the
I.C.P. In theory the I.C.P. belonged to the Indochinese
context, but the Lao Dong was exclusively Vietnamese. In
fact, there were three stages to the operation. In 1930 the
emphasis was on internationalism: there was no specific
reference to Vietnam; it was the *Indochinese* Communist
Party. In 1941, on the other hand, nationalism prevailed
over ideology with the establishment of the Vietminh. In
1951 the Lao Dong took its doctrinal rigor from the I.C.P.
and its patriotism from the Vietminh, while at the same
time fitting into a less exclusive organization, the "patriotic
front." The new structure had two separate layers, and Ho
was free to draw on two distinct sets of relationships. The
old strategist had triumphed again.

As noted earlier, the work of political organization and
action figure more prominently in the career of Ho Chi
Minh than the elaboration of doctrine. Yet his masterly
helmsmanship is definitely based on a doctrine, a method
of interpreting and adapting Marxism-Leninism in the light
of the prevailing situation in Vietnam.

This doctrine has recently been defined by the most
orthodox Marxist among Ho's lieutenants, a man who cannot be accused of blind loyalty because in fact he champions
a line directly opposed to the one which the President is
generally regarded as having laid down.

Not that Truong Chinh's life of Ho, published in 1966,
departs from the tradition of venerating the leader (the
biography's title is revealing: *President Ho Chi Minh,
Revered Leader of the Vietnamese People*). Indeed, it seems

that the former General Secretary of the Lao Dong is so strongly Maoist in persuasion that he cannot help treating Ho with the same kind of veneration enjoyed by the Chairman in Peking. But beneath the hagiographic tone lies careful Marxist analysis. Phrase by phrase, Truong Chinh presents his clues to an understanding of Ho's career. These are the main points of this ideological summary:*

On the nature of the Vietnamese revolution:

> Applying Marxism-Leninism to the concrete situation in Vietnam, Ho Chi Minh saw at a very early stage that the Vietnamese revolution was a *bourgeois-democratic revolution of a completely new kind* . . . which, as it developed . . . was bound to lead to the Socialist revolution . . . *the national- democratic popular revolution* . . . carried out by the people, in other words by the working class, the peasantry, the petty bourgeoisie and the national bourgeoisie, under the leadership of the working class and on the basis of worker-peasant alliance. . . . This was a radical line founded upon the Marxist-Leninist theory of uninterrupted revolution. . . .

On whether priority should be accorded, in revolutionary strategy, to the changeover to Socialism in the industrialized nations or to the emancipation of colonies still in a rural condition:

The biographer quotes a statement contained in an article which Ho wrote in 1924, *The Russian Revolution and the Colonial Peoples:*

> Colonialism is a leech with two suckers, one of which sucks the metropolitan proletariat and the other that of the colonies. If we want to kill this monster, we must cut off both suckers at the same time. If only one is cut off, the other

---

* Truong Chinh, *President Ho Chi Minh, Revered Leader of the Vietnamese People,* p. 47.

will continue to suck the blood of the proletariat, the animal will continue to live, and the cut-off sucker will grow again.*

An excellent résumé of a revolutionary course of action primarily animated by a passionate desire for Vietnamese emancipation but enlightened by Ho's lengthy contacts with the French proletariat. It is this two-sidedness which makes him such a highly unusual practitioner of Marxism.

On methods of action:

President Ho was the first leader of the Vietnamese revolution to discern the fault in the methods—isolated assassinations, mutinies—employed by his predecessors, who relied on adventurous acts of individual heroism. He was convinced that if the revolution was to triumph, action must be taken to rouse the political consciousness of the masses, to organize them, to draw them into the struggle for commonplace demands. . . .

On the question of leadership and the exercise of revolutionary power:

We take the view that it is man who shapes history and we do not deny the part played by great men. . . . In our time, the heroes who want to lead the Vietnamese people must found a revolutionary party. . . . The virtuous and experienced leader must be a man forged by the revolutionary movement of the masses, whom the community entrusts with the mission of acting as helmsman at the head of the controlling organization of the party.

On the peasantry and the agrarian problem:

In our country, the national issue is fundamentally a peasant issue, and the agrarian problem is at the heart of the problem of democracy. . . .

* Bernard B. Fall (ed.), *Ho Chi Minh on Revolution: Selected Writings, 1920–66* (New York: Praeger, 1967), p. 33.

Our race is made up almost exclusively of peasants. It is thanks to the vigor of the peasantry that we have resisted victoriously. It is thanks to that same vigor that the resistance will win and the work of national reconstruction be carried out. . . . Here we have *the Marxist-Leninist line in an agricultural and colonial nation. Here we have the synthesis of Marxist-Leninist principles and the realities of the Vietnamese revolution.**

The distinction drawn between principles and realities is a fascinating one, conveying the whole spirit of Ho Chi Minh, even though the words are another's. And the observations concerning the peasantry faithfully echo those expressed by Ho at the Fifth Congress of the International in July 1924. The old Vietnamese strategist speaks with the same voice as the young pre-Maoist revolutionary.

Thus, through the prism of Truong Chinh's mind, there emerges a body of doctrine which is pieced together by actions rather than words. Nationalism and internationalism are openly interwoven, like letters on a coat of arms. The prominence of rural problems does not prevent an increasing emphasis on proletarianization. Much less inventive than Mao, Ho comes closer perhaps to the thinking of Lenin—a Lenin given the time and opportunity to look beyond the marginal "nationalities" of the great European empires and see the real "colonies"; to observe how "imperialism, the final stage of capitalism," subsequently became a fundamentally strategic phenomenon; to watch national conflicts reemerge from the clash of financial interests and the struggle for markets.

Ho's singularity as a Communist has shown clearly enough in his way of life, his manner, his speeches and writings and in initiatives such as the dissolution of the

---

* Truong Chinh, pp. 49–50.

I.C.P. Yet his ability to disband the party without ruining his standing in the international Communist movement and to carry the Vietnamese revolution safely through the successive ordeals of cooperating with the "nationalists," going to war with France and standing up to the United States indicates the extent of his authority over his immediate colleagues and over the cadres and masses. As we have seen, this authority does not always shrink from methods of the crudest coercion.

Is this to imply that Ho Chi Minh is just a "fringe" Communist, a mere nationalist cloaked in red? To accept such a view, one would have to shut one's eyes to the evidence he has given time and again of his readiness to accept the rulings of the International, as in 1954 when he agreed to conditions at the Geneva Conference which undoubtedly served the immediate interests of world Communism better than those of the Vietnamese nation. Reference to such acts should remove all doubts concerning Ho's deep-rooted and deliberate adherence to the Communist movement.

Although his fluctuations with regard to doctrine may be disconcerting, although he could hardly give less of an impression of being a theorist and although he would seem to be unconcerned with the theoretical aspect of his task (and indeed makes scant attempt to conceal the boredom or mistrust aroused in him by doctrinal discussions), it appears likely that this very realism, empiricism, opportunism even, has served him in good stead within the hierarchy of the Communist church, where prosecutions for heresy follow harder upon new paths of thought than upon unusual lines of action.

How can anyone doubt a man's total allegiance to a movement which has absorbed his energies for so many years and which, indeed, he has helped to shape? Ho is what one might call an "organic" Communist, as well as a pragmatic one. To an even greater degree than a member

of Western society, the Asian is molded by his experiences.*
The ordeals he has suffered, the dangers he has run, the
honors and successes he has reaped, the power he has
wielded—all these things bind the Vietnamese leader to the
international party which selected him, wrought him and
conferred stature on him and to the local party which he
himself has created, directed and led to victory.

* L'Asiatique est fait par ce qu'il fait.

13

HANOI:
PEKING
OR MOSCOW?

To a Vietnamese revolutionary endowed with a broad view of the world and aged thirty in 1920, the October Revolution is *the* revolution, Moscow is the home of Socialism and Lenin and his successors will always be the true exemplars. The same is not necessarily true of a Vietnamese born twenty years later—to him the struggles of Chinese Communism, and its eventual victory when he was forty years old, are closer, more eloquent and more meaningful to his own life as an Asian revolutionary.

Whatever conflict may exist in Hanoi is a conflict not of generations as such, but of a difference in historical periods of growth and maturation. It is worth bearing in mind, however, that all of them—whether they look for enlightenment to Moscow or Peking—"studied Lenin before they read Marx," to quote a reliable expert on Vietnamese affairs. In other words, both groups put practice before theory and see Communism as having incorporated the "national question," which was so alien to the author of *Das Kapital*.

The obvious and indeed insistent nationalism of Ho Chi Minh himself ("my sole aim is to see Vietnam free and independent") obviously weighs in favor of close relations with Moscow. Ho cannot implement in North Vietnam the Stalinist concept of "Socialism in one country only." Everything prompts him to resort to alliances and joint ventures. But China, as an immediate neighbor, is able to bring strong political and military pressures to bear. Moscow is a long way off, and distance is a wonderful aid to harmony between peoples of different nations, even Socialist ones. A favor from Russia does not entail such an onerous debt as a favor from China.

Quite apart from these Machiavellian considerations, Ho's preference for the Soviet Union is sustained by theory and sentiment alike. We cannot overestimate the impression which must have been made on this spirited young man, so ardently dedicated to the purpose of transforming the world, by the discovery of Moscow as it was in 1924, by the atmosphere of the Fifth Congress and the exchanges between Zinoviev, Bukharin and Trotsky. The articles he wrote at the time are filled with religious fervor, and the effects of his visit to the Mecca of Communism were rendered even more lasting when the presidium secured his allegiance by imposing the strongest ties of all—those of risks and responsibilities. His work as Borodin's deputy in Canton, then as the Comintern's representative in Southeast Asia, and finally as coordinator of all revolutionary activities in Indochina gave him an indestructible sense of solidarity.

There was a time when his loyalty might have weakened:

around 1934 Moscow seemed to be pinning its hopes on younger leaders, men like Le Hong Phong and Ha Huy Tap. But in 1935 his faith was revived by the Comintern's decision to encourage popular fronts, in collaboration with nationalist or revisionist movements. This was where wisdom lay, not in the proletarian leftism of the "third course" prescribed in 1928. His confidence in Moscow's discernment and judgment was fully restored.

Does this make Ho a Bukharinist, a rightist, a precursor of Khrushchevism? Ho should never be viewed in a theoretical light, but rather in the context of developing situations and problems to be solved. Some observers may feel that he has been inclined to deal more sternly with the leftists than with the moderates. It is true that the only major crisis in the short history of the Democratic Republic of North Vietnam was triggered in 1956 and 1957 by the temporary removal from office—or rather demotion—of Truong Chinh, the leftist leader, which was followed by the brief imprisonment of Nguyen Chi Thanh, his nearest associate. But it is also true that, although relations between Moscow and Hanoi were especially cordial during the first part of Nikita Khrushchev's term of office (1957–62), they afterward soured and were no more than indifferent by the time "Mr. K's" words and deeds began to lay him open from 1962 to 1964 to charges of "modern revisionism."

The fact remains that Ho has always shown great equanimity in discussing this brand of deviationism, even at times when Peking has denounced it in the fiercest terms. Even in September 1964, while answering questions about "revisionism within the Socialist camp," he was content to remark that "disputes of this kind among the revolutionary parties have always been settled satisfactorily" and that North Vietnam, for its part, adhered to the "revolutionary principles of the Moscow declarations of 1957 and 1960."*

* *Le Monde*, September 15, 1964.

Should Russia ever prove unduly neglectful of the essential interests of North Vietnam or of the fate of the guerrillas in the south, then he will turn to Peking. If it could be shown that the Red Guards held the key to Vietnam's salvation, he would even rally to the side of Lin Piao. But such an alliance would weigh heavily on him.

Concerning Ho's attitude to Peking, it would be a mistake to dwell on his personal memories of time spent in China; some of those memories are far from happy. It is more profitable to refer to the history of relations between the two countries. Two-thirds of Vietnam's national heroes won fame and glory doing battle with the Chinese (who in modern Hanoi, are referred to as Mongolians—often with justification). P. J. Honey* sees a similarity in Sino-Vietnamese relations and those which in time developed between the Russians and Poles or the English and the Irish. But that is to place a European pattern of relationships, in which religion played a large part, on the same footing as an Asian pattern incorporating economic exploitation, military control and a civilizing process.

In addition, when Ho turns his eyes toward Peking, he inevitably confronts the figure of Mao Tse-tung. It is by no means certain that the old suspicions have been allayed. He well knows how much he and Vo Nguyen Giap owe, as strategists, to the Chairman of the People's Republic. According to Truong Chinh, the most influential Maoist in Vietnam, "Comrade Mao Tse-tung's contributions to the theory of revolution in the colonies and semicolonies have been of considerable assistance to our party and to President Ho in working out the political line and policy for our country."†

But when Ho himself talks or writes about Mao he is more reserved, and sometimes sarcastic. In the political report dated February 1951 which is probably his most

---

* *Communism in North Vietnam*, p. 28.
† Truong Chinh, *op. cit.*, p. 221.

important piece of political analysis, because it gives the fullest expression thus far to the subtleties of his thinking, the Vietnamese leader writes: "Comrade Mao Tse-tung has skillfully synthesized the doctrine of Marx-Engels-Lenin-Stalin, applied it in the most judicious fashion to China's situation and led the Chinese revolution to total victory."* In other words Mao is a competent adaptor, and no more.

Not long ago a foreign visitor asked Ho whether he hadn't thought of publishing articles, or even books, "as Chairman Mao does." Ho winked at his guest and retorted, "If there is a subject Chairman Mao hasn't written about, tell me and I'll try to fill in the gap. . . ."

He knows that in formulating concepts and theories he is no match for the author of the *Red Book*. Does this inferiority disturb him? Clearly it does not. As he sees it, revolution is a thing that needs to be organized rather than written about. It was Mao himself who once said, "Power issues from the barrel of a rifle." His Vietnamese colleague gives his mind to the powder charge in preference to the shooting manual.

Moreover, Ho often holds distinctly aloof from Chinese initiatives. Hanoi may have fallen in step with Peking between 1954 and late 1956, but afterward a greater degree of reserve was shown—especially by the President himself. In an interview with the correspondent of United Press International in January 1959, he declared that his country "had no immediate intention of following the example of the People's Republic of China," which was then suffering the first aftereffects of the "Great Leap Forward." Ho went on to say that in the course of the year he hoped to see a relaxation in tension between East and West. The general tenor of his remarks placed him closer to Khrushchev than to Mao.

He was even more explicit with Danielle Hunebelle, special representative of Télévision Française, during an

* *The Selected Works of Ho Chi Minh*, p. 221.

interview given in July 1964. She asked whether North Vietnam's position of isolation did not make it inevitable that the country should become a satellite of China. He held up his hand. "Never!" he retorted crisply.

In addition to being a nationalist instinctively on his guard against any increase of Chinese influence in Vietnam and an empiricist always slightly suspicious of doctrinaire views, Ho is aware of the fact that his long career as a revolutionary began long before that of Mao, Chou En-lai or Lin Piao. Not one of them was a delegate at the Fifth Congress of the International in 1924. Chou was still only a young student worker when "Nguyen Ai Quoc"—who dismissed the group of young Chinese Communists as merely the "left wing of the Kuomintang"*—set out for Moscow as the representative of the French Communist Party. At that time, such a status and such a mission impressed the Chinese. Lin Piao was a mere youth then, and Mao a provincial ringleader.

Ho is too intelligent to regard seniority as a sound basis for revolutionary authority. But it must not be forgotten that he is the ruler of a small nation which for a long time was looked down on by the Chinese, who took such pride in their country's greatness and antiquity. To this extent, he is eager to make the most of the fact that no other leader can claim to be so deeply rooted in the history of the Socialist revolution in Asia.

Ho's ties with Moscow and coolness toward Peking are not shared by all members of the Lao Dong or even by all leaders of the party. Many Vietnamese feel only distantly involved in the Soviet revolution, but they are engrossed in the revolution the Chinese Communist Party is carrying out just over the border. Except in Mongolia, Russia carries

* *Le Paria,* August 7, 1925.

far less weight than China does among the countries of
Asia. And this general bias is intensified by the pull of
Chinese culture, which in one form or another is shared
by most Vietnamese, and by the similarity in the economic
and military problems that have confronted the two ruling
groups during the past twenty-five years.

In short, there is a powerful and active body of opinion
pressing for unreserved support of the Chinese line and for
increasing coordination of the efforts of the two revolutions.
The acknowledged leader of this group is Truong Chinh,
son of a Tonkinese mandarin and an intellectual whose
command of French culture is as great as his command of
Chinese. For a long time he was General Secretary of the
I.C.P.; then he became editor of *La République,* doctrinal
organ of the Vietminh, and afterward wrote *La Résistance
vaincra* (The Resistance Will Conquer) which became the
bible of the Vietnamese guerrillas. He was appointed General Secretary of the Lao Dong in 1951 but was removed
from office at the end of 1956, following the failure of his
over-hasty land reform measures. He remained a member
of the politburo, however, and two years later he was made
Chairman of the Standing Committee of the National Assembly, a rank which gives him precedence over the Prime
Minister.

The fact that he is head of the side of the party which is
referred to, for the sake of simplification, as "pro-Chinese"
does not make him Ho's opponent. It could be argued that
his short biography of the "revered President," published
in 1966 and from which I have already quoted several times,
was a deliberate attempt to conceal his hostility under rose
petals. But this does not appear to have been the case, although there may be a certain mischievousness in his decision to include certain quotations which make Ho appear
a rather clumsy practitioner of the art of expressing scientific Socialism. Ho must certainly be glad that the pro-
Chinese wing of the Lao Dong—and circumstances make

it inevitable that such a wing should exist—takes its lead from a man whom he knows well, whom he has trained, whose intellectual qualities (and loyalty too, most likely) he is familiar with and who, as we shall see later, is certainly no unquestioning supporter of the Maoist line.

Other supporters of this line advocating a prolonged local war within the framework of polemical coexistence are perhaps less well disposed toward the old leader. Notable among them are three more members of the politburo: Le Duc Tho,* formerly one of the resistance leaders in the south, a major political theorist and the author of virulent attacks on the "defeatists"; Nguyen Duy Trinh, Minister of Foreign Affairs, who was once in charge of purging the intellectuals; and Nguyen Chi Thanh, political commissar of the army, Giap's sole rival in military circles, a brilliant orator and previously head of resistance in the Hué area. Outside the politburo, there are four others holding prominent posts: Hoang Quoc Viet, leader of the trade unions, whose leftism dates back to the thirties and who is the only man still active in Vietnamese politics capable of matching Ho's long experience; Hoang Van Hoan, former ambassador to Peking, one of President Ho's companions in his underground days; and To Huu, talented poet and fearless censor as deputy minister of culture, whose conceptions anticipated those of the Red Guards.

A good many of the younger citizens of North Vietnam find the rate of Chinese revolutionary development very much to their liking. In the army the trained personnel tend to look across the border for inspiration. And the industrial elite dreams of Chinese successes in Manchuria. None of which makes it any easier for Ho to maintain the balance between Moscow and Peking.

On the other hand, a considerable number of Vietnamese remain deeply attached to the policy of friendship

* One of his articles published early in February 1966 seemed to portend a "cultural prerevolution" in Hanoi.

with the Soviet Union, and their admiration for the victories of Maoism is tinged by fear of Chinese dominance. This by no means negligible group is headed by General Giap, the only North Vietnamese whose fame and reputation can be compared with Ho's. His forceful personality and his imaginativeness put him in a class by himself, and there are good grounds for seeing him as the Trotsky of Vietnam, although such a title would be distinctly harmful to him in Hanoi.

However great his debt as a strategist to the men of the Long March—a debt which he frankly acknowledges—Vo Nguyen Giap would never be prepared to see his country subjected to Chinese control, as the people's democracies of eastern Europe were subjected to Russian control from 1945 to 1960. He is among those Asian revolutionaries who welcome the Soviet leaders in much the same way that Chou En-lai was welcomed by the people of Warsaw in October 1956 and by the people of Bucharest in 1966. In view of his notorious antipathy to Truong Chinh, it seems natural to regard Giap as the leader of a "national Communist" group which considers the possibility of Chinese "protection" a disaster that must be avoided at all costs. This may be conjecture, but there is no lack of words and attitudes to support it.

The second most prominent member of this group is the Prime Minister, Pham Van Dong. Like all faithful disciples, he tends to accentuate the attitudes of the master—in this case, Ho himself. And whereas the President is primarily concerned with keeping relations with Peking on an even keel, Dong allows himself a hint of bitterness toward the Chinese. But he is too self-controlled and too loyal to Ho to indulge in polemics.

Also of this persuasion are his close friend Pham Hung, the deputy premier, whom he brought in to the politburo to counterbalance the mounting influence at the time of Truong Chinh and the Minister of the Interior, Ung Van

Khiem, previously Minister of Foreign Affairs. And membership in the same group is ascribed, in addition, to the Vice-President, old Ton Duc Thang (who took part in the Black Sea mutinies in 1905, side by side with André Marty), and the economist Le Than Nghi.

There remains an enigma—the attitude of the Party Secretary, Le Duan. Because he was promoted to this key post in September 1960, during a phase when Soviet influence appeared to be growing, experienced observers like P. J. Honey have generally associated him with the views of Giap and Dong. (Honey further argues that Le Duan's allegiance to this group springs from his active dislike of Le Duc Tho, one of the leaders of the rival faction, during the past fifteen years; the motive seems somewhat artificial.)

In fact, Le Duan's approach to the crucial problem of South Vietnam would appear to ally him with the more radical group, for he has come out strongly in favor of the most revolutionary strategy and the firmest possible commitment. Yet, on other issues, such as the rate of collectivization or the need to preserve ideological neutrality between Moscow and Peking, he could be said to stand at the very center of the party and the administration and to be very close to the point of exact balance which Ho himself has taken up, despite his old tendencies and his natural bent toward moderation.

Thus the President, assisted by the most powerful member of the party, fulfills the role of arbiter between the pro-Russian and pro-Chinese elements. If his personal attitudes were to incline him too far in favor of Moscow, Le Duan would immediately tilt him back to dead center—which is indeed his rightful place, both as head of state and as a Vietnamese patriot. For it is by avoiding the infernal dialectical conflict between Moscow and Peking that the Vietnamese leaders can best preserve and enrich their fundamental attachment to the "Vietnamese way."

The intricate course which Ho and his colleagues have steered in their attempt to work out a "Vietnamese way" and maintain it—between Soviet "revisionism" on the one hand and Chinese "dogmatism" on the other, between temptations to maintain a relatively peaceful coexistence and incitements to engage in a "war of long duration"—can be divided into four reasonably distinct phases: 1954–57, the Chinese phase; 1957–61, the Soviet phase; 1961–64, charges of "Khrushchevism" and certain illusions of "peaceful coexistence"; 1965–67, return to dead center—less in the interests of achieving "neutrality" between Peking and Moscow than of healing the rift between the two Socialist camps.

After the Geneva Conference, it was only natural that the rulers of North Vietnam should turn to the Chinese for help. True, they had previously received more or less equal assistance from both camps, but they were mindful of the fact that it had taken Moscow five years to give them official recognition. Further, at the time of the negotiations in Geneva there were signs that Russia and China had decided to share the tasks confronting them, with Peking assuming a greater measure of responsibility in Asian matters. After all, there was no harm in Hanoi's making such a choice at a time when relations between the two great capitals of the Communist world looked serene—as serene as relations between allies can ever be. In consequence, while displaying the wariness inherent in their national pride, Ho and his team put their wartime connections with the Chinese People's Republic on a peaceful footing.

During this phase, "Sino-Vietnamese friendship associations" were set up throughout the country, a propaganda campaign was launched to encourage them, and Hanoi willingly followed Peking in speeding up the land reform program and imitating the general pattern of the regime of the "Hundred Flowers." But the underlying "leftism" of the first path of action proved as catastrophic as the "right-ist" opportunism of the second. The "Great Leap Forward" in the agrarian sphere led to an uprising by the peasants of Nghe An (Ho's native province), and the repression that followed probably cost tens of thousands of lives. Mean-while the "Hundred Flowers" induced so many illusions among intellectuals that the years from 1956 to 1957 saw a real challenge to authority on the part of the nation's writers. The liberal journal *Nhan-Van* (Humanities), edited by Phan Khoi (an elderly scholar of progressive outlook, a kind of Ho Chi Minh of literature) was banned. By early 1957, imitation of the Chinese line had plunged North Viet-nam into a grave, two-fold crisis. The bloody excesses com-mitted by the men responsible for carrying out the land reform policy nearly severed the links between the masses and their leaders.

This crisis was to have profound repercussions on the party. Ho secured Truong Chinh's resignation as General Secretary of the Lao Dong, and he himself took over his duties in an attempt to restore public confidence in the party, while General Giap was given the task of delivering in November 1956 the major speech of self-criticism which the situation demanded. This took the form of a stern indictment of the "serious and sustained errors" which had imperiled the very existence of the state. A few weeks earlier in Warsaw, Gomulka had spoken in scarcely harsher terms of the "NATO-ites." In short, the time had come for Hanoi to reset its sights. And in spite of the bad impression created even in Vietnam by the crushing of the Hungarian upris-ing, Ho and his colleagues did their best to establish closer relations with Moscow. The President traveled to eastern Europe toward the end of 1957 and in November attended the celebrations to mark the anniversary of the Russian revolution.

But the pro-Chinese faction—or at any rate the faction which for the past two years had been fostering the policy of alignment with Peking—was by no means resigned to defeat. While Ho was away, there seems to have been an attempt to seize power in Hanoi. According to P. J. Honey, Giap disappeared from public life for several weeks, and at the rally marking the anniversary of the October Revolution Nguyen Duy Trinh made a speech full of references to China but containing no mention of Russia.* However, nothing came of these developments; the situation returned to normal as soon as Ho arrived home from Europe.

The "pro-Soviet" trend began at the end of 1957, reached its height in 1959 and declined around 1962. The switch was caused by the poor results which Chinese methods yielded in Vietnam along with the disastrous consequences of the "Great Leap Forward" (1959–60) in China itself, but pro-Soviet feeling was progressively weakened by the series of setbacks sustained by Khrushchev—from the breakdown of the summit conference in 1960 to the Cuban crisis in 1962.

Throughout the pro-Russian period, Ho paraded the strength of his fellow feeling for the Soviet Union in speech after speech, paying homage to the "U.S.S.R., leader of the Socialist camp" and never mentioning the Chinese People's Republic. However, he was too skillful a strategist to go beyond a return to the balance which had been upset between 1954 and 1957 by Mao's overzealous supporters in Vietnam. And when relations between the Big Two of Communism grew strained to a point of crisis, he continually did his best to insure that North Vietnam's position was that of a halfway house.

In September 1960 the Lao Dong held its third congress in Hanoi. The welcome which the delegates gave to Mukhitdinov, the Russian representative, was conspicuously warmer than that extended to Peking's envoy, Li Fuchun. A strong pro-Soviet atmosphere prevailed through-

* P. J. Honey, "D.R.V. (North Vietnam) Leadership and Succession," *China Quarterly* (Winter 1962) p. 33.

out the conference.* It might be thought that the Chinese arguments would carry more weight once the emphasis was placed on the need to fight for the country's reunification, a need which would entail an early increase in Hanoi's support for the anti-Diemist guerrillas in South Vietnam. But the decision to provide such assistance can be explained entirely without reference to Mao Tse-tung—it was first and foremost a Vietnamese affair.

Ho was shocked, however, by the increasingly bitter relations between Moscow and Peking as revealed by the speeches of their respective envoys. Before the congress broke up, he laughingly took the pair by the hand, and before the incredulous diplomatic corps, bade the assembled delegates join in an "All Pull Together" type of refrain.

Two months later he was in Moscow for the congress of the eighty-one Communist parties. He campaigned staunchly in an attempt to avoid a breach between Moscow and Peking, went part of the way with Chou En-lai but still tried to act as arbiter. His words were listened to with respect. But his country was so poor and so faraway. He was unsuccessful in his bid to work out an acceptable compromise, either on this occasion or at the congress of the Communist Party of the Soviet Union the following year, when he refused to lend his signature to the official condemnation of the Albanian party.

Six weeks later I saw him in Hanoi. He adamantly refused to discuss the rift. In a neighboring building, a large exhibition was devoted to the People's Republic of Albania. What struck me most, however, was the fact that official portraits of the President were everywhere flanked by two other effigies, those of "Ko-Rut-Sop" and "Mao Trach

---

* P. J. Honey, "North-Vietnam Party Congress," *China Quarterly* (December 1960), p. 73.

Dong" (to give phonetically the Vietnamese versions of the foreigners' names). The pro-Soviet phase was already moving in the direction of the "third way." There was a perfectly simple reason for this; now that a real crisis was developing between Moscow and Peking, Hanoi had no choice but to draw closer to the Chinese—though without, of course, accepting their overlordship. The Vietnamese leaders might feel a greater or lesser degree of sympathy with the Soviet line, but they could not behave antagonistically toward Peking without jeopardizing their external security and internal balance. A clash with the Chinese Communist Party would aggravate to bursting point the tensions within the Lao Dong. Hence the need for a wary, subtle, conditional return to the Chinese line.

Now, therefore, began the "third phase," which was the gradual discovery of the "third way," the Vietnamese way. Initially, between 1962 and 1964, the task of reestablishing links with Peking proved somewhat injurious to the "pro-Soviet" group. Ho's star seemed to grow dim. Little was seen or heard of him; he stopped making speeches and giving interviews. Once again there were rumors that Giap had been or was about to be demoted. His rival, Nguyen Chi Thanh, was promoted to equal rank.

As a result, China's influence appeared predominant in the early days of 1964. To mark the end of the general meeting of the Lao Dong in January, a statement was published which could have come from Peking itself. Attacks were concentrated exclusively on "modern revisionism," while the "Titoist clique" was reviled in similar terms to those used by *L'Humanité* in 1949 and 1950. There was not a word about "dogmatism" or "leftist adventurism."

What made the statement even more remarkable was the fact that it was the work of Le Duan, the Party Secretary appointed during the 1960 Congress, at the height of the pro-Soviet phase. This key figure now appeared to be toeing the Chinese line, in collaboration with the group centered on Truong Chinh. Ideologically, the leadership presented a united front, whatever might have been thought of the innermost convictions of Ho or Dong.

By spring, however, there were signs of a return to the earlier, balanced policy. This same Le Duan was sent to Moscow to sound out the Soviet government's intentions if the Americans should carry out their threats to extend the war into North Vietnam; it was said at the time that he received every assurance that Hanoi could have desired. Meanwhile, a "special political conference" was held in the North Vietnamese capital during the month of May. This time the drafting of the summarizing statement was left to Ho himself. The wording was notable for the restraint and sense of proportion that have characterized his political career throughout the past twenty years. And the North Vietnamese militants were warned against leftist excesses as well as rightist opportunism.

There was a danger that escalation might upset the delicate balancing trick perfected by Ho and the men around him. Outbreaks of violence never benefit the prestige of supporters of peaceful coexistence. But he has survived more dramatic crises, especially in the period 1945 to 1954.

The year 1965 saw him fully restored to his earlier standing; at the height of the storm the masses and even the cadres felt the need for the old leader, with his moral authority and his composure. Who cared whether or not he was a revisionist? What did labels matter in times of real danger? The father of the nation was again acquiring complete ascendancy. Under his leadership the "Vietnamese way" was finding its real direction and equilibrium.

Ample evidence of the continual attempts made by Vietnamese policy to consolidate its intrinsic independence is to be found in official and semiofficial statements published in Hanoi. Take for example the September, 1966, issue of

Hoc Tap (Studies), the doctrinal organ of the Lao Dong. The editorial emphasizes the urgent need for creative activity by the party and observes in particular: "We must study the experiences of foreign countries. But we are against the idea of studying only those experiences, without making a deep examination of the experience of our own country. . . . Dogmatic tendencies must be overridden, as well as pragmatic ones. Some comrades responsible for theoretical studies have an inferiority complex; they are incapable of making a close study of the realities of our country."

In another article, dealing with the Moscow declaration of 1960 (which had met with a cool reception in Peking), Truong Chinh himself reasserts that "the clash between the Socialist camp and imperialism is the most fundamental clash of our time." (Which is not in accord with the strictest, or at any rate most up-to-date-minute Maoist doctrine!) Finally, an article by Tran Hieu amounts to a plea on behalf of democracy, against bureaucratic and authoritarian methods: "Contrary to the opinion of certain comrades, loyalty to the party does not exempt anyone from observing the law. . . . Side by side with supervision from top to bottom, we must develop supervision from bottom to top."

Allegiance to Moscow? Allegiance to Peking? To neither —the allegiance of government, party and masses is purely and simply to Hanoi. While in China the Red Guards burn ancient books within yards of Tien An Men Square, the librarians in Hanoi microfilm seventeenth-century manuscripts which cannot be taken from the city so that any guerrilla fighters wishing to do so may study their cultural heritage through the works of Nguyen Dun. In Hanoi the young people—far from taking their cue from the puritanical watchwords of the Chinese rulers—are quite capable of parading a quiet elegance and giving free rein to warmth and humor (the girls, unashamedly feminine, even let their hair trail loose).

Moscow? Peking? When he is asked what his war aims are, Uncle Ho retorts, "Nothing is more precious to the Vietnamese than independence and dignity."

14

UNCLE HO
AND UNCLE SAM

Misunderstanding, misappreciation, misperception (to repeat the general title employed by an American review in
a special issue on Vietnam)—these words keep cropping up
whenever anyone attempts to describe relations between
Hanoi and Washington. There is certainly a striking contrast between this total failure to communicate and the
infinite complexities of Franco-Vietnamese relations, held
together by hatred and complicity, by a sense of partnership
and rancorous enmity, by intermittent effective communications, by blows and shared ordeals. The ties between
Vietnam and France are somewhat like those of an old
married couple in a Strindberg drama.

Is it true that contact between the Americans and the
Vietnamese, between Uncle Ho and Uncle Sam, is impos-

sible? If it is, it was not always so. The United States and
her particular form of civilization are not altogether alien
to the astonishing figure who presides over the destinies of
North Vietnam. When Tito decided to cooperate with the
Americans, his personal knowledge of them was limited to
Ernest Hemingway, whom he may have glimpsed in Spain.
When Gomulka offers a friendly welcome to Richard Nixon
or Robert Kennedy, what does he know of American society? But in Ho's case, personal experience—coupled with
a close study of documents and skill in political analysis—
provides a bridge between the United States and the nation
that he has brought back to life.

Of course, he is much closer to Paris than to Washington.
His political career, his personal style and his particular
brand of humor all testify to this. And yet there are obvious
signs of intellectual and political links with the United
States; the most striking of them is in the opening words
of the proclamation of Vietnamese independence on September 2, 1945:

> All men are created equal. They are endowed by their
> Creator with certain unalienable rights; among these are
> life, liberty and the pursuit of happiness.

The lines with which this Vietnamese, this Asian, this
Marxist opens his historic pronouncement are derived, not
from the legendary writings of Mai Hac De or the works
of Lao-tzu, nor from the celebrated texts of the French or
Russian revolutions, but from the American Declaration
of Independence, to which he specifically refers.

Quite apart from the incongruity of a Marxist paying
homage to the Creator at such a solemn hour and before a
predominantly Buddhist audience, the choice of quotation
is surely remarkable and as disconcerting as it is significant
in view of Ho's familiarity with the literatures of Asia,
France and Russia. It was not as though there were a back-

ground of rapport between Vietnam and the land of Thomas Jefferson. With quite a few countries in the Third World, the United States has links as old as herself. But contacts with Vietnam were almost nonexistent, apart from an exchange of emissaries and messages in 1864 between President Lincoln and Emperor Tu Duc, sovereign lord of Hué, who was engaged in a relentless fight against Catholicism, which he saw as a mere agent of Western infiltration.

Subsequently, French colonization tended to monopolize cultural contacts as well as economic ties. Echoes of American ideology may have reached a very small section of the Vietnamese intelligentsia via nationalist elements in Japan and China. But it was not through these channels that Ho Chi Minh became acquainted with the United States, its society and its problems.

Little is known of his experiences on shore leave in New York and Boston in 1915 and 1916, while serving as mess boy aboard a French ship. But hints of his experiences are found in his writings, especially in some of the articles he contributed to *Le Paria* and *La Correspondence internationale*. In 1924, for instance, Numbers 59 and 74 of the official publication of the Third International contained two articles by "Nguyen Ai Quoc" (not all contributions are signed, so it is sometimes impossible to identify his work) concerning racial problems in the United States. One wonders whether Ho personally witnessed scenes such as he describes in the first of the articles which is devoted to lynching, and in the second which gives an impression of the Ku Klux Klan. The answer would seem to be no. The instances which he cites are generally drawn straight from American newspapers, published in such cities as New Orleans and Memphis. The tone of these articles is, as one might expect, violently polemical and designed to arouse indignation. But he scrupulously refrains from adopting racist attitudes and is quick to point out that some whites, notably Harriet Beecher Stowe and

John Brown, have been prepared to take the risk of siding with the blacks.

One result of his brief American experience was a deep absorption of Lincoln's speeches and writings. Even before the proclamation of independence in 1945, his works as a journalist and polemicist was faintly inspired by Lincoln's ideas. From 1918 onward, of course, his thinking was more closely allied to that of Rousseau and Jaurès, Marx and Lenin. But his mind retained a tendency to moralize in democratic terms, a particular form of puritanical egalitarianism, a distinctive brand of antiracist indignation, all reminiscent in tone of the clashes between the American abolitionists and the Confederates in the eighteen-sixties.

By 1915 or 1918 Ho had certainly started to read the British Fabians and some of Proudhon and Guesde. He was almost totally unacquainted with the writings of Marx, if not with those of Lenin and Kautsky. For a nonwhite who had suffered personal humiliation as a member of a colonized race and who had recently observed that things were equally bad for the native populations in and around African ports, it came as a dramatic revelation that Lincoln, a white stateman, should have taken the stand that he did. It is impossible to say where he first learned of the American president, but even a second-rate book or a superficial feature article can set the mind working along important new lines.

Ho appears to have seen Lincoln as the complete "antiracist," which—to his way of thinking in those days—implied absolute anticolonialism. It is somewhat surprising that his discovery of Marxism-Leninism did not sweep away his attachment to one of the great early proponents of emancipation for the oppressed peoples. But there is proof of his enduring loyalty in the declaration of September 2, 1945.

But long before this date he had given public expression to his affinity with progressive American ideology. Accord-

ing to the official historians in Hanoi, the event that marked
the true beginning of the revolutionary struggle in Vietnam was Ho's decision to lay an appeal before the Versailles
Peace Conference in January 1919. An appeal of this kind
can scarcely have been aimed at Clemenceau and Lloyd
George; in their eyes, as the Arabs soon found, victory was
not an occasion for liberal-minded policies. No, the Vietnamese appeal was unquestionably aimed at Woodrow Wilson, the author of the Fourteen Points. It may be that Ho
became disenchanted with American-style democracy because of the silence with which this successor to Jefferson
and Lincoln greeted his eight-clause program. Two years
later, following the added disappointments in his contacts
with the majority of French Socialists, Ho joined the ranks
of the Third International.

One of the best-informed specialists in the problems of
Asian revolution, Enrica Colotti-Pischel, has suggested to
me in a letter that Ho's "Lincolnism," which may have
been weakened by his long exposure to French revolutionary circles and by his Marxist-Leninist studies in Moscow
from 1923 to 1925 probably revived soon afterward during
his Canton period (1925–26), on the eve of the formation
of the Thanh Nien. It is not certain that the policy statements of this "Association of Revolutionary Young Comrades" are directly influenced by Lincoln. What is clear,
however, is that the Vietnamese leader was at this time an
admirer of the man who was still the great hero of the Chinese popular renaissance, Sun Yat-sen. And Mrs. Colotti-
Pischel goes on to emphasize that, in his *San Min Chu I*
(Three Principles of the People), the Chinese president
dwells at length on Abraham Lincoln. Here, then, is
another link between Ho and his beloved American—a
link strong enough to have withstood, at least until 1945,
the influence of Borodin, of Li Li-san and of such leftists
within the Vietnamese revolutionary movement as Ho
Tung Mau.

Even before the crucial period 1944 to 1945, the life and works of Ho Chi Minh were marked at long intervals by sudden flashes of interest—highly unusual for a man of his background—in the political traditions of American democracy, with its various vices and virtues.

For example, one of the poems which he wrote in jail in 1942 is entitled "A State Reception Is Being Organized for Willkie." (Wendell Willkie, Roosevelt's Republican rival in the 1940 presidential election, was sent on a mission to China in 1942.)

> *Both of us are friends of China,*
> *Both are going to Chungking,*
> *But you are given the seat of an honored guest,*
> *While I am a prisoner, thrown under the steps.**

It is odd that the Vietnamese leader should call attention to this journey by a foreign politician and furthermore that he should call him a friend of China. Would he have said as much, at the time, of a British public figure? Clearly, he still had a certain attachment to the United States.

But we are now approaching the period when Ho stepped from vague intellectual affinities to substantial political contacts. By September 1944 he was out of jail and back in his cave at Pac Bo, where he and Giap were planning to set up their "armed propaganda brigades." In Liuchow, as an associate of Chang Fa-kwei, he had already established contact with American agents, who probably subsidized him a little and may also have provided him with arms and ammunition.

In the autumn of 1944 Ho formed a number of personal ties with Americans. Engine trouble forced a United States Air Force pilot, Lieutenant Shaw, to bail out over a sector of Cao Bang Province which was already in

---

* Bernard B. Fall (ed.), *Ho Chi Minh on Revolution: Selected Writings, 1920–66* (New York: Praeger, 1967), p. 137.

Vietminh hands. He was picked up by partisans and taken to Pham Van Dong's command post at Nuoc Hai. Vy Anh relates how the future Prime Minister "secured [Shaw] an audience with Uncle Ho." (The use of the word "audience" is disarming when one thinks of the conditions in which Ho was living.) "[Shaw] was absolutely delighted. The good treatment he received and the welcome he got from Uncle Ho came as eyeopeners. He realized that all the bad things he had been told about the Vietminh, prior to his capture, were nothing but slander. . . ." Even allowing for propaganda, the story is a significant one. In the atmosphere of 1944, there was every reason why an American should have been won over to the kind of men and the type of policy which confronted Lieutenant Shaw.

Subsequently, contacts were stepped up, and it was the Americans who made the first move. What led them to do so? This strange relationship between Ho and the United States, which endured throughout 1945, seems incomprehensible until one recalls the nature of American policy in southern Asia at the end of the war. That policy can be summed up in one word: anticolonialism. And it had a single objective—to stop the French from moving back into Indochina.* To the ideological convictions of Roosevelt were added memories of how the French colony, after coming under Axis control in July 1940, had served as a springboard for Japanese strategy during the next three years.†

Washington was anxious to recruit allies in the area, chiefly in the hope of subduing Japanese resistance but also as a preliminary to establishing a new order in Indochina— one based on a policy either of international protection or of cession of the entire territory to China (which, by the

---

* In his *Histoire d'une paix manquée* (p. 95), Jean Sainteny quotes a telegram found among the papers left behind in Hanoi by officers of the O.S.S.: "In no circumstances must the French get inside Indochina."

† At Columbia University in 1944, Professor Nathaniel Peiffer ran a course on Indochina for officers of the United States Navy who had been detailed to "liberate" the country.

same process, would also have recovered possession of Hong Kong). The Americans' first concern was to broaden and consolidate their intelligence networks. Their need to do so became all the more pressing after the Japanese coup on March 9, 1945, had completely dispossessed the French and purged those elements which might have helped the Allied cause—the Gordon, Bocquet and de Langlade networks. At this point the United States provided clear proof of her hostility to any form of French presence in Indochina. Strict orders came from Washington that no air support was to be given to the French military columns retreating northward in a desperate bid to escape the Japanese. Yet the administrations in Washington and Chungking were officially allies of the French government. Bernard Fall quotes the opinion of General Claire Chennault, creator of the "Flying Tigers" and at that time commander of the Fourteenth Air Force in southern China. In his *Memoirs* the general said he was disgusted at the idea of leaving the French to get slaughtered in the jungle.

It was against this background that United States representatives in southern China linked up with Ho Chi Minh, two of whose objectives—the defeat of Japan and the abolition of the French colonial system—fitted in perfectly with the strategy laid down in Washington.

The first organization to establish regular contact with the Vietminh was the O.S.S. (Office of Strategic Services), forerunner of the present-day C.I.A. (Central Intelligence Agency). This paramilitary structure was headed by General William Donovan who, on his way to China in August 1945, had a long talk with Jean Sainteny, leader of the French mission which had specific instructions to restore France's position in northern Indochina. Their exchange of views, however cordial it may have appeared in retrospect to Sainteny, does not seem to have modified Donovan's attitude. He had no qualms about standing by Washington's instructions to evict the French, and these orders were carried out with alacrity by his subordinates, Colonel Paul Helliwell (the man who had the most direct dealings with Ho and Giap throughout this period), Major Robert Buckley, Lieutenant Phelan and George Sheldon who was later appointed United States vice-consul in Saigon.

In an interview on a program on Ho Chi Minh televised on January 20, 1966, Helliwell told of his meetings with Ho in southern China ("a charming character, with a tremendous sense of humor"), but he maintained that O.S.S. assistance to the Vietminh had been negligible and that it was furnished on the clear understanding that it should not be used against the French.

So far as the O.S.S. was concerned, this was true. It supplied the Vietminh with revolvers, a few light arms and some money, but very little else. However, another American organization, the United States Combat Section (Southern Command), attached to the armies of the Kuomintang but acting on direct orders from General Wedemeyer, American commander in Chungking, fulfilled a role, which although less striking psychologically, was in fact more effective.

Under the command of General Gallagher, this organization established networks in Tonkin by the early days of August 1945. One of General Gallagher's deputies, Major Archimedes Patti, played an extremely active part during the period from early August to late October 1945; within those weeks the Vietminh came to power, the republic was proclaimed, and a good deal of revolutionary and anti-French propaganda was broadcast. It would be misleading to claim that the whole future of Vietnam would have been different but for the efforts of Gallagher, Patti, Captain Farris and a few others; yet one may doubt whether without them the Vietminh would have emerged so strongly and so quickly or whether the confidence of the new leaders would have been so complete.

At that time, inscriptions in the English language were

displayed in every part of Hanoi. Here was a Vietnamese city, until recently a French colonial capital, occupied by Chinese troops and controlled by a party whose first allegiance was to Moscow. And yet the most conspicuous slogans ("Vietnam for the Vietnamese!" "Independence or Death!") were written in English, rather than in French or Chinese or Russian.

There was a striking difference in the attitudes adopted by the representatives of the United States on the one hand and by the British on the other. Indeed, the events in Hanoi were enacted against the background of a keen struggle for influence between the American and British G.H.Q.s in Asia—Lord Mountbatten's in Kandy, Ceylon, and General Wedemeyer's in Chungking. Washington's idea of replacing the French colonial presence either by an international authority or by the protective wing of Chiang Kai-shek was systematically opposed by Churchill and his Labour Party successors. The British saw quite clearly that the overthrow of French rule in Indochina would create a precedent that would undermine their own position in the area. The correspondence between Roosevelt and Churchill, and the attitude of Eden and Bevin at international conferences in the closing stages of the war and the early postwar period, are clear indications of the view taken in London.

South of the seventeenth parallel, General Gracey and his Indian Army Gurkhas facilitated the return of the French forces—a step which prompted the Vietminh to "declare war on the British Empire" on September 15, 1945. Meanwhile, in the north, Trevor Wilson (the Consul General) and Commander Simpson Jones were far more sympathetic in their dealings with Sainteny and the French than were Gallagher and Patti.

Equally, the latter were accorded privileged treatment by Ho and the other Vietminh leaders. By the end of August, a "Vietnam-America friendship association" had been formed. Even though Washington had not recognized the new republic, it was under its auspices that a rally was organized in Hanoi at the beginning of October. Several of the Vietnamese leaders took part—Vo Nguyen Giap, ex-Emperor Bao Dai (now Citizen Vinh Thuy) and Ta Quang Buu, Political Commissar to the army standing side by side with General Gallagher and Major Patti. Bernard Fall gives the following details of this strange political event: "Gallagher made a speech in which he promised the Vietnamese that their students, if sent to America, would get a warm welcome from the coeds; and he concluded his speech, broadcast by the Vietminh Radio in Hanoi, with a short song."*

It is hard to re-create the psychological climate of that time and place and assess the true value of the good will which the founders of the Democratic Republic were displaying toward their American allies. To some, it may appear a calculating charade, a clever strategem designed to promote a mood of confidence among the people and induce them to believe that—although she might be overrun by Chinese hordes, cut off from the rest of the world and confronted by the might of France—young Vietnam had powerful allies.

I am certain there was more to it than that for Ho himself. It would be wrong to make too much of those opening lines of the proclamation of independence. Yet a revolutionary patriot like Ho Chi Minh would scarcely have quoted the words of the Philadelphia Convention at that most solemn of moments unless he felt a strong historical affinity with the rebels of 1776.

The honeymoon was soon over. By late autumn of 1945, Gallagher and Patti were already less prominent in Hanoi, where due note had been taken of the statement issued on October 25 by John Carter Vincent, chief of the Chinese

* Bernard Fall, "La Politique U.S., au Vietnam," *Politique étrangère*, Paris, July, 1955.

Affairs Division of the State Department: "The United States will respect French sovereignty in Indochina." The Roosevelt era was at an end.

The reversal of American diplomacy which this statement foreshadowed was immediately felt in Hanoi. Illusions were destroyed. Other American voices, however, remained loyal to the spirit of Roosevelt and to a brand of anticolonialism bold enough not to fear association with the "Reds" of the Democratic Republic. A group of writers, sociologists and journalists did their best to preserve a climate of fellow feeling with Ho and his compatriots. Harold Isaacs,* for instance, endeavored courageously to champion Vietnam as Owen Lattimore had championed the Chinese revolution, though his efforts created less of a stir and entailed less distressing consequences for himself. His articles in newspapers and in *Harper's* magazine and *Newsweek* are as notable for their sympathy with the Vietnamese people as for their antiFrench feeling. (No one can have been more disconcerted than Isaacs by the rapprochement between Hanoi and Paris since 1963 or by the persistence with which liberal intellectuals in Vietnam have maintained their links with France.)

Good relations between the United States and the Vietnamese revolutionaries survived a year or two longer. As late as 1948, the Vietnam-America Friendship Association held a banquet in New York, organized by the same Major Robert Buckley who, as we have seen, was active with the O.S.S. toward the end of 1945.* But already America's policy was being rocked by the demands of her antiCommunist strategy, by the pressures of a pro-Bao Daist lobby led by William Bullitt, former ambassador to Paris and by the warnings and castigations of the French govern-

* *Now at the Center for International Studies at the Massachusetts Institute of Technology.*—Ed.

* Hilaire de Berrier, "How We Helped Ho Chi Minh," *The Freeman*, April 19, 1954.

ment. At the end of 1949, impelled chiefly by the need to preserve France's loyalty within the framework of the Atlantic Pact, Secretary of State Dean Acheson persuaded President Truman to turn his back even more fully on the Rooseveltian tradition in Indochina by backing the French war effort there. Mao's victory in China and the outbreak of the Korean War set the seal on this new trend in 1950.

From then on, Paris and Washington were vilified equally by the Vietminh, especially in the speeches, messages and interviews of President Ho. In July 1950 he told Leo Figuères:* ". . . The [American] intervention is intrinsically aggressive and undemocratic, and there is truly nothing beautiful (*my*) about it." (*My*, used in original text, is a Vietnamese word, one of whose meanings is "beautiful"; it also means "American.")

In January 1953 he went further, denouncing the "French colonialists" in a message to his people but insisting that the French were merely acting "on the orders and with the assistance of their masters, the American interventionists . . . who have domesticated them." And among the Americans he singled out for special blame "a gang of senators, spies, generals, businessmen, bankers and even a bishop."† Things had certainly changed since September 1945.

Soon the interventionists turned into imperialists, and the abettors into warmongers. Indeed, France, the Vietminh's declared enemy in the field, tended after a time to take second place. When the Geneva Conference opened, for example, Ho declared that his government's aim was now to "foil the policy of the American imperialists." A few days before the armistice was concluded and therefore at a time when the Vietminh army was still fighting the French, he published a political report in which he said, "American imperialism is the main enemy of the peoples of the entire

* *Selected Works of Ho Chi Minh,* II, 190.
† *Ibid.,* p. 299.

world."* The situation had come full circle even before the "French" war was over.

It would be tedious to dwell on the bitter observations made about the United States, after the establishment of the Diem regime, by this one-time disciple of Lincoln and keen admirer of Woodrow Wilson and Franklin Roosevelt. Of more interest is the fact that occasionally, even at a time when his country is being pounded by American Air Force bombers, he is still capable of recalling his firsthand knowledge of the qualities and ideals of the American people.

On May 21, 1964 he sent to the American magazine *Minority of One* "a fervent appeal to our American friends." And even after the bombing of North Vietnamese harbor installations on August 5, 1964, he declared that he was "certain of the support of the peace-loving peoples of the whole world, including the people of the United States."†

In November and December he gave interviews in quick succession to two British journalists, James Cameron and Felix Greene. He assured them that Hanoi's hostility to American policy would abate the moment Washington made up its mind to stop the war. "We would roll out the red carpet for them," he added laughingly.‡ (Can anyone imagine Joseph Stalin making such a remark about the Germans in 1942?)

A visit to Washington after a visit to Hanoi, or a talk with an American embassy spokesman—after a talk with one or other of the Vietnamese diplomats in Paris or Prague—fills one with the depressing feeling that the thought barrier and language barrier are insuperable and that the cultural differences can never be reconciled. With the Japanese, the Americans share links forged by a hundred years of diplomatic contact and cooperation in technical research and industrial effort. With the Chinese, they can refer, with

* *Ibid.*, p. 464.
† *Le Monde*, August 10, 1964.
‡ Associated Press, December 20, 1965.

varying degrees of satisfaction, to the missionary past, to Pearl Buck and to a host of specialist scholars (sociologists, linguists and historians) living on the campuses at Berkeley, Columbia and Harvard.

But with the Vietnamese, they have hardly anything in common except the great ghost of Abraham Lincoln hidden in the consciousness of the old man who has been carrying on the fight against them for the past fifteen years. That ghost has been almost banished by Dean Rusk's political stupidity and General Westmoreland's bombers; but the incessant wrangling between Lenin's heirs and Sun Yat-sen's may yet serve to raise it.

15

THE
FINAL
BATTLE

"Today it is a case of the grasshopper pitted against the elephant. But tomorrow the elephant will have its guts ripped out. . . ."

Like Khrushchev, Ho Chi Minh has a taste for truculent proverbs. But he makes more skillful and deliberate use of them. He quoted this one in 1951, during the war against the French. He has had occasion to repeat it since. The elephant has grown even bigger. So has the grasshopper.

It might be said that, from Ho's standpoint, there has never been any break in the war. In the previous chapter I alluded to his denuciations of American intervention as long ago as 1950 and to his statement that by 1953 the main enemy was the United States because the French expeditionary force had become Washington's tool. And during the Geneva Conference he contrasted the peace-seeking efforts of Mendès-France and his Cabinet with the hostile initiatives of the American government.

Indeed, for him—as for many analysts of the situation— the "qualitative" change in the struggle did not occur *after* Geneva, as a result of the simple substitution of American for French aggressor, but in 1950 when the colonial expedition directed from Paris turned into a Franco-American anti-Communist crusade carried on side by side with the Korean War.

Dulles's aloof attitude toward the Geneva negotiations, the signing of the Manila pact (which brought SEATO, or the Southeast Asia Treaty Organization, into being), the attempt to make South Vietnam a show window of capitalism and anti-Communism—none of these things can have encouraged Ho and his colleagues to put their faith in the settlement reached on July 21, 1954. But reference to his statements between 1954 and 1956, prior to the open violation of the agreements (that is the refusal to hold elections as a preliminary to peaceful reunification), reveals that, to his credit, he spoke like a man who anticipated that the agreements would be adhered to in the main if not *in toto*.

It was in the confident hope of early self-determination for the South Vietnamese that he declared after the Geneva Conference:

Our compatriots in the south were the first to wage the war of resistance. They possess a high political consciousness. I am confident that they will place national interests above local interests, permanent interests above temporary interests and join their efforts with the entire people in strengthening peace, achieving unity, independence and democracy all over the country. The party, government, and I always follow the

efforts of our people and we are sure that our compatriots
will be victorious.*

Some might argue that Ho's statement is mere verbiage,
a hollow piece of propaganda. Yet if he had simply wanted
to pass himself off as an angel-faced pacifist, he could have
emphasized North Vietnam's loyal observance of the agreements by castigating all the other parties and organizations
concerned. Nine months later he was asked by Christopher
Mayhew, in an interview for the B.B.C., whether he was
satisfied with the work being done by the International
Control Commission;† he replied that he was. By way of
contrast, at that very time Diem's police were shamelessly
participating in the sacking and burning of the commission's premises in Saigon.

   True, the Hanoi government had maintained in the south
about one-fifteenth of the eighty thousand or hundred
thousand fighting men who, under the terms of the Geneva
agreements, were supposed to be regrouped north of the
demilitarized zone. But who could expect the Communists
to behave impeccably, when already the most intricate
maneuvers were being mounted against them, pending such
time as a counterattack became possible?

   In the course of 1955, Ho and his colleagues took note of
the following developments: first, on and after February 15
Paris effectively transferred its responsibilities to Washington, in clear violation of the spirit—and indeed the letter—
of the peace terms, which forbade the introduction of new
materials or foreign personnel into either zone; second,
South Vietnam became fully drawn into the orbit of American strategy, contrary to the neutralist spirit of the Geneva
agreements; third, now that he had triumphed over the

---

* Bernard B. Fall (ed.), *Ho Chi Minh on Revolution: Selected Writings,*
1920–66 (New York: Praeger, 1967), p. 272.
   † Made up of delegates from India (chairman), Poland and Canada.

dissident Bao Daist sects, Diem was master of the southern zone and it looked as if he would remain so.

It seemed equally plain that the Saigon regime—busily boycotting the International Control Commission, showing contempt for the 1954 agreements (but for which it would certainly not have survived the fall of Dien Bien Phu by more than a few weeks) and denouncing "violations of human rights" in the north—was quite determined not to stand by the clauses dealing with reunification. And Dulles was giving unreserved support to the Diemist line. Ho did his best to counter these trends by sending Pham Van Dong to New Delhi with instructions to lay the case for a united Vietnam before Nehru and world opinion. The Indian prime minister spoke out strongly in favor of implementing the agreements, but Saigon took little notice.

In April 1956, Paris further aggravated the situation by withdrawing its troops three months before the date (July 20) laid down for reunification. As sole signatory, with the Vietminh, of the main text of the Geneva agreements, France was the only power unreservedly bound by them; which in turn made her their guarantor. It is hard to imagine that what little was left of France's forces in South Vietnam by early 1956 could have compelled Diem to agree to an electoral confrontation with the north which was wholly against his wishes. But by removing even this token pressure, the French government was leaving him free to postpone the referendum *sine die*. And so he got away with it, to his own intense satisfaction and the alarm of a good many experienced observers—Americans among them. It seemed unlikely that such a trick could be played on the victors of Dien Bien Phu without the most serious repercussions.

In July 1956, Ho had no choice but to explain to his people why the promised elections were not being held. He foretold a "long, harsh and involved struggle." No one could accuse him of being unduly pessimistic, especially as neither

Moscow nor even Peking (despite two violent editorials in the *People's Daily*) showed any sign of wishing to compromise themselves in the interests of upholding Hanoi's rights. Bulganin and Khrushchev were more concerned with upholding Colonel Nasser's rights at that time.

By January 1957, the North Vietnamese National Assembly had to admit that the "struggle for unification" would have to be preceded by the "consolidation" in the north of Socialism, which, as we have seen, had just passed through a grim crisis resulting from the failure of the land reform policy which culminated in long sessions of self-criticism in November 1956. It was then that Ho returned to the helm as party secretary. The Democratic Republic of Vietnam had never needed "Uncle" so badly, with his tactical genius and his matchless ability to speak to the masses in homely, straightforward terms. There was a lot of painful explaining to be done.

But it took more than this to discourage Hanoi, which patiently resumed its campaign for unity, stepping up the number of presidential visits (the most important being Ho's trip to New Delhi in February 1958) and diplomatic notes. Among the continual flow of exhortations to Saigon, all rejected out of hand, a few are of particular interest. In March and May 1958, Hanoi submitted proposals for the "reestablishment of commercial exchanges." This would obviously have entailed an easing of the regulations governing the movements of individuals. In view of the fact that far more people were trying to move from north to south than from south to north, one can only be amazed at Diem's refusal. He must indeed have felt vulnerable if he felt he had to rule out an experiment which was plainly in the interests of South Vietnam. Such sustained and senseless obstinacy could have only one result: a hardening of the Hanoi line. On May 14, 1959, the fifteenth meeting of the Central Committee of the Lao Dong voted in favor of fighting "jointly and severally" for the country's liberation. The phrase "jointly and severally" meant that the fight had begun in the south, that the active opponents of the Diemist dictatorship were now resorting to arms. As early as 1958, in fact, Gerald C. Hickey reported in his excellent *Village in Vietnam* (published by Yale University Press) that an organization known to the peasants as the "Liberation Front" was recruiting men and inciting them to rebellion. And in a report compiled for the Chicago symposium of February 1967, Harold Hinton of George Washington University stated that the anti-Diemist revolution had begun in 1957.

Not until September 1960, two or three years after these developments and sixteen months after the decision of the Central Committee, did the third congress of the Lao Dong indicate, in its final motion, Hanoi's avowed support for the guerrillas in the south. And indeed, even official spokesmen in Saigon and Washington admitted that only a negligible number of guerrillas had infiltrated from the north during the previous year—three hundred, according to official figures.*

The decision to tread warily earned the Hanoi government a good deal of criticism. Some of it came from the more aggressive elements within the Lao Dong, men like Hoang Quoc Viet, Le Duc Tho and Nguyen Chi Thanh; some from southerners regrouped in the north under the 1954 agreements and eager to help their kin in Nam Bo; some from these kin themselves, weary of looking northward for help.

But—and Ho is the last person who needs to be reminded of this—nothing is more costly to a revolutionary leader than wariness, precisely because nothing is of greater value to revolution. The man who bides his time is the man always mindful of the "favorable moment." All the indica-

---

* Press conference of Tran Van Do, South Vietnamese Minister of Foreign Affairs.

tions are that Ho deliberately restrained a general impulse which was dangerous on two counts: it would provide the Americans with a motive for attacking North Vietnam, which was underprotected, and it would deplete the defences of that portion of Vietnamese soil which was already under Socialist rule.*It may well have been this attitude which cost him the relative eclipse that he suffered between 1961 and 1964.

Yet it would be quite wrong to see Ho as a man anxious to block revolutionary initiatives. He may once again have exerted influence, as in April 1945, February 1946 and June 1954, in favor of minimizing risks, but in September 1960 he had a hand in the appointment of a new party secretary, Le Duan, champion of the guerrillas in the south. Ho allows the dialectical process to take its course, and he plays his part in it. A part which may yet change.

In his large office in Government House, Hanoi, the Prime Minister, Pham Van Dong, was explaining to me how France, which still had great influence among intellectual circles in the south, could help in the quest for a political settlement. He said, "We enjoy the confidence of the masses, you enjoy the confidence of the bourgeoisie. If we could get together in the task of clearing the way for a representative government in the south. . . ." It was a November day in 1961. As usual, Dong was speaking on Ho's behalf. He was even speaking in the President's tone and manner.

The door opened just a few inches, and Ho came into the room. As on that other occasion fifteen years earlier, the sound of his footsteps was soft as rustling silk. He smiled and signaled that we were to remain seated. "The Prime Minister is better at explaining our policy than I am. I'm

* Philippe Devillers, "The Struggle For Unification," *China Quarterly*, March 1962.

just looking in as a friend, to chat about old times. How's Paris?" He laughed freely and lit a fresh cigarette with the one he had been smoking. (Oh yes, he said, he still smoked American cigarettes—and no one could accuse him of stealing them.)

He had altered. His eyes had lost a little of the brilliance which used to strike one so forcibly, and his face was no longer ascetically thin. His hair had turned white, of course, and this made his beard look less sparse. The body covered by the sand-colored tunic was as frail as ever; but his cheeks had filled out and taken on a pinkness which gave him a somewhat artificial air. There was still a strong hint of mischief in his expression, however, and his dry laugh supplied the finishing touch—he looked and sounded like some old scholar whose wisdom had led him to discover the virtues of poverty. He has a wonderful way of not taking himself seriously, and this, perhaps, is the quintessence of the art of teaching people which he learned, half a century ago, at a time when he was also learning how to blast capitalist society out of existence.

A remark an elderly mandarin had made to Paul Mus during the war against the French came to mind: "Bao Dai is plump, Ho Chi Minh angular. In time of crisis, the angular man is the one to trust." Today Ho is plumper than he was. But history is not compounded of the wisdom of mandarins. And although the President may have lost some of his physical angularity, his characteristic sharpness is preserved in the shape of the party he founded.

At the time of my visit, he and the Prime Minister had known for more than five years that the regime which the Americans were supporting in Saigon had not the slightest intention of holding a referendum as a preliminary to peaceful reunification. Yet while I was with them they talked of nothing but the need to negotiate and to come to terms with a properly constituted government in the south for the purpose of achieving gradual reunification. And all this was in line with a whole series of communications which Dong had addressed to Saigon. A few months later, in the summer of 1962, Hanoi once again took the initiative and suggested to Diem that talks be started as a means of establishing human relations, if nothing more, until such time as reunification became practicable. But it was another wasted effort.

The only answer to these feelers from Hanoi was the hounding of Communists in the south and the total segregation of the north, a north whose economy had been recast under French colonial rule to complement in the industrial sphere the economy of the south, which was meant to provide food for the whole of Vietnam. Now that Saigon was in possession of the rice bowl, the north was able to survive only at the cost of drastic rationing. The ruling circles in Saigon and Washington, which had declined to fight the Vietminh while it was dangerous to do so, and which had afterward acted in seeming contempt of the Geneva agreements, were in fact the only people to derive any real benefit from the said agreements, repudiating those clauses which inconvenienced them but making full use of any that would make it easier for them to starve North Vietnam.

From Washington, charges of "imperialism" began to be leveled against Hanoi. (A century ago, the newspapers in London and Paris were full of similar charges against the "Yankee" northerners, accusing them of belligerence against the luckless southern Confederates.) The result was an ever-increasing number of casualties among the American "experts" sent to Vietnam in the hope of putting an end to the "aggression." And eventually Diem paid with his life for being an unsuccessful, awkward and unduly independent ally of the United States. A few weeks earlier Ho had told a visiting Indian diplomat, "Diem may be a patriot too, in his way."

The death of Diem and, almost simultaneously, of President Kennedy made things easier, as it turned out, for those

who favored an intensification of the war and who wished
to see the fight against Vietnamese Communists elevated to
the level of a massive punitive expedition. It was early in
1964 that Washington's war aims took on a more definite
shape: American intervention in Vietnam was to provide an
enduring example, a permanent lesson to all underdeveloped countries which might presume to question the
validity of a regional power structure guaranteed by the
United States. Vietnamese peasants were to die in ever-
increasing numbers for the greater peace of mind of the
Brazilian bourgeoisie, the Moroccan royalists and the ruling
clique in Manila.

It is easy to say that Ho and his team should have governed and developed their meager territory with greater
care, moderation and regard for fundamental freedoms.
But given the way they were cheated of the promises of
unification held out at Geneva and were ostracized, condemned to permanent want and hardship; given the way
their friends were treated in the south—hunted, imprisoned, transported, shot; given the way the Americans
continually built up their forces in plain violation of the
1954 agreements, which prohibited any further form of
foreign intervention—given all this, could anyone reasonably expect Ho not to commit North Vietnam to the
struggle?

By the beginning of 1964, some three or four thousand
combatants from the north had joined forces with the
hundred and twenty thousand or so guerrillas then serving
with the National Liberation Front. Confronting them
were the half-million men fighting under General Khanh
(soon afterward removed from office by his protectors) and
their fifty thousand American "advisers." Was there still a
chance of limiting the conflict, or even stopping it? President Johnson was said to be anxious to put an end to the

fighting, if reelected in November. During the months that followed, Ho, having emerged once more as effective leader of his country, was approached at frequent intervals.

At the end of May 1964 he was asked in an interview for French television whether it might not be possible for General de Gaulle to act as referee. "Referee?" said Ho. "We're not football teams!" But he let it be known through various channels that de Gaulle's suggestions, which included American disengagement and neutralization of Southeast Asia, "deserved careful analysis." And he reacted favorably to various attempts made soon afterward by U Thant and others to gain acceptance for the idea of a negotiated settlement—this, despite the start of escalation represented by the two incidents in the Gulf of Tonkin on August 2 and 4.

The United Nations Secretary General's first attempt came after a round of visits to Paris, Cairo and Moscow in August 1964. On his return he saw Johnson and Dean Rusk in Washington. He emphasized that negotiations would have to be preceded by private and semiofficial contacts; their replies were in no way discouraging. Early in September he sent a message to Ho, via Moscow, asking whether the idea of such exchanges was acceptable to him. Ho answered that he was willing to send an emissary to talk things over with a representative of the American government. U Thant passed on this reply to Adlai Stevenson, who was then United States Ambassador to the United Nations, but Washington made no attempt to follow it up.

In January 1965, the Secretary General asked Stevenson what the American reaction was. To his surprise, he was told that Washington had requested Canada to sound out the position in Hanoi and had implied that Ho Chi Minh had no real desire to negotiate. U Thant pointed out politely that if Ho wanted the talks to be strictly private, he would hardly react well to the introduction of a third party. Moreover, he had learned that the Canadian emissaries in Hanoi had spoken directly with the Vietnamese president.

On his own initiative, Stevenson asked the Secretary General how such talks could be achieved. U Thant suggested they might best be opened through the ambassadors in Rangoon. Stevenson subsequently asked him, on January 16, whether Burma would consent to this scheme. Within forty-eight hours U Thant delivered a favorable reply, which Stevenson transmitted to Washington. Ten days later, the American government rejected the plan on the grounds that it might bring about the fall of the Saigon government. (At this point one is inclined to ask: Do we call that a government?)

At the beginning of February 1965, the "Indochinese Peoples' Conference"* opened in Phnom Penh in Cambodia; it had been organized by Prince Norodom Sihanouk. One member of the North Vietnamese delegation, Hoang Quoc Viet (who does not, as has been said before, have the reputation of being among the moderates in Hanoi), observed in answer to a question by a foreign journalist, "Negotiate with Washington? Why not?" Immediately after this episode came the first air attacks on the north. These had been decided on as far back as September, or so at least I gathered from talks with a responsible American spokesman. The purpose of the attacks was to "encourage" the "authorities" in Saigon; a few months later, nobody could recall who those "authorities" had been.

Thus, February 7, 1965, marked the beginning of escalation in the full sense of the word. In the eyes of some, escalation was not so much a policy of systematic reprisal, or a strategy designed to bring North Vietnam to her knees (did anyone seriously think the victors of Dien Bien Phu

---

* Cambodia and North Vietnam were represented by their governments, Laos by the Pathet Lao, South Vietnam by the N.L.F. and various neutralist groups.

could be brought to their knees?) but a scheme to give the American government bargaining power. Previously, the United States had held precious few trump cards; now she could offer to halt the bombing in return for the withdrawal of North Vietnamese units. It would seem that Hanoi played into the enemy's hands by making the cessation of bombing an essential preliminary to negotiations.

At this point, an unanswerable question arises. Washington's decision to escalate the war by pummeling a nation which had no real air force to defend it was of a cowardice startlingly uncharacteristic of the American people. The whole world recognized the total inequality of the weapons which the two sides had at their disposal. Why, in these circumstances, did Ho and his ministers persist in denying North Vietnam's military intervention below the seventeenth parallel? America's new strategy so flagrantly violated the fundamental articles of the Geneva agreements that there was every justification for Hanoi's intervention. Moreover, regular units from the north* had been positively identified in the fighting zone as long ago as 1962. Their strength must have been about sixty thousand men by the end of 1967—the main effect of American bombing raids having been to promote this high level of infiltration within the space of three years. The argument that Hanoi may want to avoid giving the Americans any excuse for their actions does not carry much force, for did the Americans wait for such excuses before striking? Truthfulness in this and other matters could only benefit the standing of Ho and the people behind him.

In April 1965, within a few hours of each other, the two sides (not, of course, the N.L.F. and the Saigon government)

* These may be groups originating in the south that were transferred to the north in 1954.

laid their cards on the table. On the seventh of the month President Johnson, speaking at the Johns Hopkins University in Baltimore, insisted that Washington is ready to "negotiate unconditionally." On the eighth, Prime Minister Pham Van Dong announced Hanoi's conditions for talks. These were the famous "Four Points": independence, non-intervention, reunification and a political settlement in the south in accordance with the program of the N.L.F.

The initial reaction of Washington was to ignore the "Four Points." After a few weeks, the authorities consented to analyze them. Llewellyn Thompson, former and future ambassador to Moscow and an acknowledged expert in Soviet affairs, ruled that Pham Van Dong's statement was of no significance. After her Canadian and French allies had suggested that a pause in the bombing might induce Hanoi to take a softer line, the United States suspended the raids for four days in the second half of May. Whereupon, acting on behalf of President Ho, the North Vietnamese envoy in Paris, Mai Van Bo, called at the Quai d'Orsay and explained that the "Four Points" should be regarded as general principles; provided they were accepted as such, talks could be started. But before Washington had time to gauge the full significance of this move, the bombing was resumed. A little more of Ho's trust crumbled away.

Nor can that trust have been bolstered when, in the following June and July, the war was escalated still further by the massive landings of United States marines at Danang, at a time when the South Vietnamese army showed signs of an early collapse. Washington had staved off a second Dien Bien Phu. But the question arose whether escalation was not a natural and unavoidable consequence of waging war in Vietnam.

On August 14, in reply to a questionnaire addressed to him by Philippe Devillers, author of a major history of the background of the first Indochinese war, Ho indicated that the following was essential:

. . . that the United States government should furnish tangible evidence that it accepts the four-point stand of the government of the Democratic Republic of Vietnam which tallies with the key clauses, political and military, of the 1954 Geneva agreements on Vietnam; that it should immediately end air attacks on the territory of the Democratic Republic of Vietnam; that it should immediately end the war of aggression against the southern part of our country; that it should withdraw all its troops, together with all American arms. That is the pattern of peace with honor. There is no other way.*

Few political commentators at the time singled out the real point of interest in this statement: that the word "immediately" was attached only to the demanded cessation of air raids in the north and of the "war of aggression" in the south, and not to the withdrawal of American forces. In other words, what North Vietnam was calling for was the end of bombing and a "de-escalation" of the war, rather than the immediate departure of the American units. The failure of American observers to pay sufficient attention to this point lent a more or less sensational character to the statements of the Hungarian minister, Janos Peter, who insisted in October, on returning from a visit to Hanoi, that no mention of such a precondition had been made by any of the North Vietnamese officials to whom he had spoken. And it intensified people's reactions to reports of the mission to North Vietnam undertaken in November by Professor Giorgio La Pira, former mayor of Florence, a man more likely to "get through" to Ho than anyone else in the non-Communist world. (One is on equally good ground in calling the president a Marxist La Pira, or the professor a Christian Ho Chi Minh.)
Predictably enough, the meeting between these two masterly exponents of clearheaded evangelism resulted in a

* *Le Monde*, August 15, 1965.

mutual "revelation." On November 11 Ho declared that he
was "ready to go anywhere to meet anyone" in the interests
of peace.* La Pira reported this statement to his friend
Amintore Fanfani, Italian Minister of Foreign Affairs, who
was at that time President of the United Nations General
Assembly. Fanfani sent President Johnson a letter, stating
that Ho and Dong were of the view that talks would be possible following:

> (a) A cease-fire on land, sea and in the air over the whole
> territory of Vietnam (North and South), this cease-fire to
> apply to all war operations and to include a ban on the dis-
> embarkation of any further American troops;
> (b) A declaration indicating that the Geneva agreements
> of 1954 were accepted as a basis for negotiation, such a dec-
> laration to comprise the four points which they had drawn
> up and which represented in fact a clarification of the
> Geneva text, but which could be summed up in a single
> point—application of the Geneva agreements.

Fanfani added that La Pira had been reminded, in the
course of talks, that Hanoi was ready to start negotiations
without insisting on the previous withdrawal of American
forces.

But Dean Rusk refused to see anything notable in this.
He had, he said, his own "antennae"—and these antennae
informed him that Ho Chi Minh was opposed to peace. He
made sure that Fanfani's report was given a thorough airing;
and once the details became public, they were naturally
denied by Hanoi. Ho was decidedly getting to know, if not
the Americans, at least the men who governed them in 1965.

A few days later, in an interview with the English journalist Felix Greene, he talked of the authorities in Washington
with obvious bitterness:

---

* In a letter he kindly sent me, Professor La Pira wrote, "Ho Chi Minh
is a man with an open mind; [he is] open to peace at home, in Asia, and
I would go so far as to say in the world."

They say we want this war to go on. How can they say such
a thing? You have seen the country. You have seen the sufferings which the raids have inflicted on our people. How
can anyone want this dreadful war to continue? They leave
us with no alternative but to fight on. We shall never give
up our independence.

Greene quoted an old Chinese proverb to the effect that it
is always best to leave a door open so that the enemy can
make his escape.

"I know, I know," said Ho, "it's the old question of allowing
America to save face. . . . But you know, the door *is* open.
They can leave at any time. . . . Once they have made up
their minds, we shall do everything we can to help them.
we'll even roll out the red carpet for them."*

Meanwhile Washington, yielding to the entreaties of
several friendly governments and of the Vatican, announced
a second pause in the bombing, to begin on December 25.
This time, it was hinted, the pause would be long enough
for contacts to be established or information exchanged.
Everyone knew that the gesture was not without material
cause (there seemed to be a surprising shortage of bombs)
or ulterior motive. But it captured people's attention and
raised their hopes. Everyone waited for a verbal reaction
from Ho. It did not come until the end of January and did
not live up to the expectations of those who recalled his
earlier diplomatic initiatives.

His statement denounced the misleading nature of the
halt in the bombing. (In fact, both sides reinforced their
positions during the truce. Significant information about
American activities in this sphere was given by James
Reston in the *New York Times*.) Furthermore he insisted
that if the Americans wanted to negotiate, they must do so

* *Associated Press,* December 20, 1965.

with the N.L.F., "the only body truly representative of the South Vietnamese people." Far from leaving the door ajar, Ho was adding a bolt. The "Four Points" had brought the Americans up against the "program" of the N.L.F., but that program was reasonably vague. Now, by calling attention to the Front and its exclusive representation of South Vietnamese interests, Hanoi was making it that much harder for Washington to accept the conditions for a negotiated settlement.

It seems strange that Ho did not exploit the situation, if only to the extent of calling Washington's bluff. For some observers, the most tempting explanation is to be found in the visit he is said to have paid Mao in Peking between late November and early December 1965. It is suggested that although Mao failed to involve his guest in the "anti-revisionist" crusade, he talked him into toughening his line against the Americans. This is only a theory and not a very satisfying one. The Chinese People's Republic has no "right of veto" in Vietnam. Mao cannot decree war or peace for Hanoi. It is the Vietnamese who are fighting, not the Chinese, and the Peking government publicly admits that "the matter must be decided by the Vietnamese comrades." Not that they conceal the fact, when given the chance to speak on the subject, that they do not "advise" negotiation. If, disregarding this "advice," Ho decided to change tack and seek a political settlement, he would still have to persuade the leadership of the National Liberation Front in South Vietnam. It is here, perhaps, that the real problem lies.

One could speculate endlessly about the degree of genuine independence that the N.L.F. enjoys in relation to the Hanoi government. It came into being of its own accord, before securing first the theoretical backing, then the assistance and finally the direct intervention and perhaps rather heavy-handed protection of North Vietnam. Tactically autonomous, strategically controlled—that, possibly,

is as good a description as any. At all events, the Front is
distinctively southern in its reactions, its make-up and its
aspirations—even though the last is incorporated into the
Vietnamese national context.

What needs to be remembered in this respect—for the
Vietnamese are filled with a sense of contemporary history
and are passionately mindful of its lessons—is that if Hanoi
has had some reason to distrust its Western adversary since
1954, southern suspicions are kept alive by precedents even
more bitter, numerous and specific. The agreement between
France and the Vietminh in 1946 was concluded partly at
the expense of the guerrillas in the south. Ho had fought
hard to secure a referendum which would allow the people
of the south to link up with the Democratic Republic; but
they had remained under the strict control of the French
army. After the signing of the Geneva agreements, they
again found themselves the losers as the result of a referendum that failed to materialize. And when the more rebel-
lious among them took up arms, they had to wait many
months before the north came to their aid. So there is a
particular southern prejudice which tends to block progress
toward the political, as distinct from the military, stage in
the dispute.* This prejudice came into play at the end of
1965, when hopes of diplomatic contact were at last beginning to take shape—in spite of Rusk, who could not hide
the truth forever from the American people. It would certainly appear that the leaders of the N.L.F., sensing the
possibility of direct negotiations between Hanoi and Washington, insisted that Ho should be thoroughly explicit
about their position. Hence, in all likelihood, his curt and
negative statement at the end of January 1966. In Washington, and still more in Saigon, that statement brought delight

---

* In January 1967 a member of the Central Committee of the N.L.F.
informed me that even if Hanoi regarded the halting of air attacks on
North Vietnam as an adequate preliminary to talks, this would not satisfy
the N.L.F. if it had not asked for and agreed to it.

to the clique that had been waiting for an excuse to resume and intensify the air attacks: by January 31, North Vietnam was once again learning how to endure constant bombing. However, this certainly did not mark the end of diplomatic activity. Washington might be waging war, but the United States had allies. Perhaps something could be achieved through them?

On January 24 Ho sent a letter to General de Gaulle. After recalling how the war had stemmed from a violation of the 1954 agreements by Washington and Saigon, he requested that France should "assume fully her obligations in respect of the Geneva agreements," and that the general should "employ his prestige to help stop in time any further treacherous meddling by America in Vietnam and Indochina."*

The general did not care for the implication, however politely worded, that his country had not stood by its word. But he successfully mastered his feelings and replied, on February 8 that, in France's view, peace must be reestablished

> . . . by the return to the implementation of the Geneva agreements, the independence of Vietnam to be guaranteed on the one hand by the absence of intervention, in any shape or form, on the part of any outside power, and on the other by a policy of strict neutrality on the part of the Vietnamese authorities. . . . We rule out the possibility of any military solution and are opposed to the prolongation, let alone extension, of the fighting on the pretext of securing such a solution. . . .

De Gaulle concluded with the assurance that France was anxious to exert any influence that would help bring the conflict to an early conclusion and that she wished to play an active part as soon as there was a likelihood of a settle-

* *Le Monde,* February 1, 1966.

ment; to this end, she was prepared to maintain any contacts with the Hanoi government that might serve a useful
purpose.

This exchange by no means marked the end of the
"French episode." A high-ranking visitor presented himself
in Hanoi—Jean Sainteny had arrived on his fourth mission
to North Vietnam, following a visit to Peking where, despite his well-known friendship for the Vietnamese and his
closeness to General de Gaulle, he had been conspicuously
cold-shouldered by the Chinese authorities. On July 7, 1966
he was greeted by President Ho for the first time since their
rift, ten years earlier, over the Hungarian refugees.

Ho employed his standard procedure, appearing on the
spur of the moment in the office where Sainteny was con-
versing with Pham Van Dong and Nguyen Duy Trinh, the
Minister of Foreign Affairs. He flung his arms around the
visitor and reminded him in hearty tones of the good old
days in Deauville and Biarritz. "Come and see me tomorrow," he added with a wink, "there will be just the two of
us. . . ." Then he withdrew, leaving his two colleagues
in a state of astonishment—in North Vietnam the diplomatic tête-à-tête is hardly ever used.

The pair subsequently met for two private talks. Ho did
not put forward any new suggestions, however. When
Sainteny tried to point out that the sufferings of the Vietnamese people amply justified any attempt that their
leaders might make to get talks started, he was told that no
Vietnamese, least of all Ho himself, could possibly compromise "over the question of independence and honor."
As Ho saw it, the vast American build-up all the way from
Danang to Camranh could only mean that the Americans
were determined to establish permanent bases. Men for
whom poverty is the natural condition, men who have to
count every penny, cannot imagine anyone spending thousands of millions of dollars on temporary bases.

At the end of Sainteny's visit, a further exchange of cor-

respondence between de Gaulle and Ho Chi Minh was published. To the letter of recommendation which his guest
had brought with him, Ho replied:

> M. Sainteny is and will always be welcome in our country
> as an old friend. We have talked with M. Sainteny about the
> issue which concerns us most. We have told him that, in the
> face of American aggression, our people are determined to
> fight, whatever the sacrifices, until final victory is achieved.
> We are thankful that France, as signatory of the 1954 Geneva
> agreements on Vietnam, is striving to play an active part in
> reestablishing peace in this area on the basis of the proper
> implementation of those agreements.

There was nothing particularly new about all this. But
Sainteny's visit had at least served to confirm (a) that Hanoi
was genuinely anxious for France's help in keeping a door
open to the western world and (b) that the notorious insistence on evacuation as a preliminary to talks was a complete
illusion; if the Americans indicated they were willing to
withdraw at some point, the wheels of diplomacy might
begin to turn. Hence the idea which de Gaulle set forth in
Phnom Penh six weeks later, after discussions with Sainteny
—evacuation by a given date.

In the meantime, another peace initiative had ended in
disappointment for its promoters. In June the Canadian
diplomat Chester Ronning, a seasoned expert on Asia,
where he had spent his entire professional career, was dispatched to Hanoi by Prime Minister Lester Pearson, a man
who has striven from the outset to put an end to the war.
(Canada's status as member of the International Control
Commission gives her a position in Hanoi, enabling her to
maintain contact with officials and survey the general feeling there.)

But Ronning was not given an interview with Ho, and
it was adamantly pointed out to him that there could be
no question of talks unless air attacks on the north were

ended permanently and unconditionally. Was this the re-
buff mentioned at the time by the American press (including the *New York Times,* whose correspondent in Hong
Kong was then the able Seymour Topping, who happens to
be Chester Ronning's son-in-law)? By making the cessation
of bombing an essential preliminary to negotiations, Ho was
inviting an initiative on the part of Washington, which
might take Hanoi at its word and end the raids. But in fact
President Johnson did exactly the opposite, by sanctioning
the raid on the Hanoi and Haiphong fuel depots on June
29. There could be no better way of encouraging the North
Vietnamese authorities to reject misions like Ronning's.

For Ho and his countrymen, the summer of 1966 was a
time of psychological escalation. The prevailing mood was
one of intransigence and heroism, and as always the tone
was set by the President himself. On July 17, he issued what
might be described as a call to semimobilization, though
to all intents and purposes the country had been living on
that footing for a long time. From then on, the policy of
"resisting aggression" was summed up by the Hanoi press
and radio in terms drawn from Ho's broadcast. Displaying
courage, shooting down an American aircraft, breaking a
production record, opening a jungle school—these were so
many ways of responding to President Ho's appeal of July
17.

This mood of patriotic excitement, the inevitable result
of the increasing number of civilian casualties caused by
the United States Air Force, nearly led to tragic excesses, in
the shape of reprisals against American prisoners. At first,
captives were exhibited before predictably angry crowds;
then there was talk of a war crimes trial. American public
opinion, uncertain until then, flared up at what was seen
as a monstrous insult to Uncle Sam. There was strong feeling in favor of escalation and a great deal of argument over
what form it could best take. On July 24, in reply to a cable
from C.B.S. Television inquiring how far advanced his

plans were for prosecuting captured airmen, Ho announced that the proceedings had been postponed. Everyone breathed again. Once more he had applied the brakes at the right moment. Vietnam would have been the principal loser if the warmongering of Rusk, Cabot Lodge and their kind was intensified by jingoistic attitudes among the American people.

Unquestionably Hanoi's decision was rooted in self-interest. But the fact that it was taken so soon after the raids on Hanoi and Haiphong at the end of June was a "remarkable indication that all possibilities of halting escalation have not been exhausted."* Here, surely, was a "gesture" of the kind Dean Rusk had been demanding for so long as evidence that Hanoi was in earnest about wanting talks. A few weeks later, I put the question to various leading members of the American administration. I was assured that Ho's change of course had been dictated by fear of Washington's reactions and of adverse world opinion.

But if this is to be the attitude, what can Ho possibly do that will not be branded as weakness by his opponents? Such an interpretation of his restraint leaves only one course open to him: intransigence, the patience of a fanatic, faith in the final victory.

What could he do in February 1967 when, following suggestions by the N.L.F. that the temporary truce should be extended, Washington resumed the bombing after only four days, during which time both sides, as usual, improved their positions?

What can he do today, as he confronts adversaries who would rather dishonor their flag in one of the most unequal, dastardly and futile wars in history than acknowledge their mistake and effect that radical shift in diplomacy which would open the way to massive cooperation with the

* *Le Monde,* July 26, 1966.

"wealthy" Socialist world, pending positive coexistence with China and a Third World which is still in the throes of evolution? All he can do is hold out, leaving the door slightly open by agreeing to truces at Easter, Christmas, and the Vietnamese New Year; hold out while maintaining channels of communication via U Thant, the Vatican, Warsaw, Paris; hold out, pending such time as the American people's realism and sense of justice sweep away the dishonest, the incompetent, the hysterical, the Dean Rusks, the Curtis LeMays, the Walt Rostows; hold out, until Soviet-supplied missiles inflict such heavy losses on the United States Air Force that even the Pentagon's computers begin to show signs of emotion.

Such is the nature of the final battle in which Ho is engaged. History has turned this subtle, intricate man, this confirmed bider of time and braver of winds into a rock—the rock of Hanoi, pounded by the might of machinery and money. Should he have taken a different path and let Vietnam be divided forever, condemning the north to starvation and his kinsmen in the south to slaughter?

However firm his intentions and actions, there are certain questions which he cannot fail to ask himself. Is there not a danger that the war, if allowed to drag on and on, will give rise to a Sino-American conflict which could easily engulf Vietnam and destroy her as an entity? Or else to a Chinese intervention of the type seen in Korea? The Vietnamese Socialists may express the highest regard for the great revolution across the border, but such an intervention is not altogether in line with the Vietnamese patriotism which Ho symbolizes and sustains.

And this is not to speak of the sufferings endured by his people. In Ho's mind, quite plainly, there can be no question of cheerfully sacrificing them to the scientific needs of history. This man who has always shown a warm love for children must feel something more than anger at forms of

aggression which, according to figures compiled by a group
of responsible American Catholics,* have already condemned nearly a million young Vietnamese to death or
disablement.

Even when the subject is viewed against its revolutionary
background, no one should deplore the fact that Ho is not
the kind of leader who regards the agony of an entire race
as a negligible factor in political analysis. And it is surely
absurd to level charges of opportunism against a man who
has spent half a century fighting for his country. The day
the Americans demonstrate—by ending the bombing once
and for all, by recognizing the N.L.F. as a political and
military fact, by de-escalating the war, and by giving a clear
indication that they intend to evacuate their forces—that
they really want to make peace in Vietnam, he and his colleagues will surely make some hopeful gesture; they were
eager enough to explore the chance of a political solution
in 1946 and 1954.

When this happens, it is to be hoped that the veteran
of the Tours Congress, Dien Bien Phu and long years of
unyielding resistance will be spared certain "lessons of
revolution."

In September 1966, while on a visit to Washington, I
had a conversation with one of the most intelligent politicians I have met, a man thoroughly informed about Asia
and its problems, especially those concerning Indochina.
By instinct, as well as by the nature of his duties, he was in
favor of working out compromise solutions. We were talking about Ho, and, so far as I could see, our views were
almost identical. Suddenly this cultured and sensitive individual began to bristle with a sense of power, the colossal
power of the United States. "I admire Mr. Ho Chi Minh as

* The Pepper Report, summarized in *Le Monde*, December 23, 1966.

much as you do," he said. "He's an engaging, even a fascinating figure. But he is not going to achieve his lifelong
dream of uniting all Vietnam under his control. We have
decided not to allow it. We will not let South Vietnam fall
into his hands. I'm sorry, for *his* sake, but that will never
be."

Who knows? Uncle Ho is an old man now, and tired after
so many years of fighting for the revolutionary cause. But
even if Cung, alias Nguyen Tat Thanh, alias Ba, alias
Nguyen Ai Quoc, alias Vuong, alias Line, alias Ho Chi
Minh does not live to see Vietnam reunified and independent, all the way from the China border to Point Bai Bung,
others—deputies he has molded for no other purpose than
to fulfill the dream and who have fought hard themselves
—will live to see it for him.

CHRONOLOGY

1926	Organizes the revolutionary organization Thanh Nien
1928	Goes to live in Siam and pays visits to Moscow and Western Europe
1930	Founds the Indochinese Communist Party (originally named Vietnamese Communist Party)
1931	Arrested in Hong Kong
1933	Goes to live in Russia
1935	Participates in Seventh Congress of the International
1936	Popular Front Government in France allows Indochinese Communist Party to function legally and openly
1939	I.C.P. goes underground again
1941	Vietminh founded at Pac Bo (North Vietnam)
1942	Nguyen Ai Quoc adopts the name Ho Chi Minh; Ho is arrested in China
1943	Agitation starts in North Vietnam
1944	Agreement reached with nationalists at Liuchow
1945	Japanese overthrow French colonial regime; Japanese capitulate after Hiroshima; Vietminh form a provisional government; Ho Chi Minh proclaims independence; I.C.P. disbanded
1946	Ho visits Paris during negotiations with France; hostilities begin following violation of agreements
1950	French defeats at Lang Son and Cao Bang; newborn Chinese People's Republic recognizes Hanoi government
1951	Lao Dong, successor of the I.C.P., is founded
1953	Ho announces readiness to negotiate with France
1954	Dien Bien Phu; end of hostilities, following Geneva Conference; Vietnam divided into two "temporary" zones, pending referendum to be held in 1956; Ho returns to Hanoi
1956	Saigon refuses to hold referendum that was promised as a preliminary to reunification; failure of land reform program in North Vietnam
1957	Ho reorganizes Lao Dong

1958   In South Vietnam, guerrillas organize resistance to Diem regime

1959   Lao Dong decides in favor of helping guerrillas in south

1960   Ho is chairman at Third Congress of Lao Dong; Le Duan appointed Party Secretary; Ho attends conference of eighty-one Communist parties in Moscow; "Liberation Front" set up in South Vietnam

1962   American intervention assumes direct and military form

1963   Assassination of Ngo Dinh Diem and destruction of his regime

1964   Lyndon B. Johnson elected; U Thant's diplomatic initiatives accepted by Hanoi but rejected by Washington

1965   Attacks on North Vietnam by U.S. Air Force; massive landings of U.S. forces in the South

1966   Sainteny and Ronning carry out diplomatic missions in Hanoi; Ho insists talks with the U.S. must be preceded by cessation of bombing and recognition of National Liberation Front

1967   Heavy fighting along 17th parallel and near Laos border (Congthien, Dakto, Khesan)

1968   Tet uprising in the South on May 19, Ho's seventy-eighth birthday

INDEX

ABOUT THE AUTHOR

JEAN LACOUTURE, a resident of Paris, was born in Bordeaux in 1921. He attended the Jesuit Collège de Trivoli à Bordeaux, the Faculté des Lettres de Bordeaux, Faculté de Droit de Paris and Ecole des Sciences Politiques de Paris. He now teaches at the Institut d'Etudes Politiques in Paris.

The author of articles for *The New York Times Magazine*, *The New York Review of Books*, *Ramparts* and *The New Republic*, M. Lacouture has also written several books, among them *Vietnam Between Two Truces* and *De Gaulle*. A correspondent for the influential French daily *Le Monde*, M. Lacouture has covered politics in Algeria, Morocco, Egypt, Indochina and the Middle East.

In 1966 M. Lacouture was a research fellow at Harvard.